Blood Feud

Blood Feud

The Red Sox, The Yankees and the Struggle of Good vs. Evil

Bill Nowlin and Jim Prime

Rounder Books

ROUNDER

Cambridge, Massachusetts

Published by Rounder Books

an imprint of:
Rounder Records Corp.
One Camp Street
Cambridge, MA 02140

ISBN: 1-57940-111-2

Cover design by Steven Jurgensmeyer and Brad San Martin
Interior design and typesetting by Swordsmith Productions

Nowlin, Bill, 1945- and Prime, Jim, 1948-
Blood Feud: The Red Sox, the Yankees, and the Struggle of Good versus Evil

1. Boston Red Sox (Baseball team). 2. New York Yankees (Baseball team) I T.

First Edition
2004118132
796.357
ISBN: 1-57940-111-2

9 8 7 6 5 4 3 2 1

Printed in Canada

The authors sincerely deplore violence in sport and hope that nothing we have written will be construed as encouraging or condoning violence in baseball.

No animals and/or Yankee ballplayers were harmed in the making of this book.

To all the Red Sox players from teams
past who strived for a World Series title and fell short
of their goal, and for all the Red Sox fans who
stuck with their team through thick and thin.

And for Glenna, Catherine, and Jeffrey with whom
I was blessed to finally share the joy of a
Red Sox World Series victory.

—Jim Prime

To Emmet, who's 13 and has been waiting
all his life for the Red Sox to win the World Series.

—Bill Nowlin

Contents

Acknowledgments

The authors would like to thank the following people for their help in developing this book:

Dick Adams, Evelyn Begley, Jahaan Blake, Frank Bokoff, James Bomba, Laurie Cabot, Ethan Cohen, Roy Cohen, Bill Deane, Charlie Devens, Will Forest, Paul Giorgio, Dave Godowsky, Chip and Laura Goode, Doris Kearns Goodwin, Jeff Greenberg, Leigh Grossman, Jonathan Jacobs, Richard Johnson, Steve Jurgensmeyer, David Kruh, Bill Lee, Bill Lee (the other one), Diana Lee, Steve Lomasney, Garret MacCurtain, Dorian Massella, Vinny Natale, Rod Nelson, Steve Netsky, Don Novello, Emmet Nowlin, Doug Pappas, Angela Parker, Robert B. Parker, Clay Pasternack, Johnny Pesky, Mark Pogact, Elizabeth Rush, Brad San Martin, Father Guido Sarducci, Phil Sienko, Frank Solensky, George Steinbrenner, Cecilia Tan, Stew Thornley, Luis Tiant, Kevin Vahey, Bill Wilder, Karen Wilder, and the entire 2004 Boston Red Sox team.

Desrever esruc eht / la malédiction est brisée

Blood Feud

Foreword

The Garden of Good and Evil

by Bill "Spaceman" Lee

"Back in the '50s and '60s, we as players took the rivalry very seriously. We hated them. We didn't want to talk to them. It was as simple as that. Pure hatred." —Jerry Casale

"I was always a Red Sox fan. I hated the Yankees from the day I came out of my mother's womb." —Jimmy Piersall

"It will never be the same as it was in the '70s. Back then it was real hatred. Fisk hated Munson. Munson hated Fisk. And everybody hated Bill Lee." —Don Zimmer

I spent a decade (1969-1978) in the garden of Good and Evil that is the Red Sox-Yankees feud. As a diehard Yankee hater, and former Yankee killer, I even helped to germinate the seeds of the feud by spreading some fertilizer of my own.

At the sunny end of the garden are the Red Sox, innocent, naked, free of shame—and Good; at the other end lurks the malevolent and Evil serpent known as the New York Yankees. Babe Ruth was the first to be tempt-ed by the serpent to try the Big Apple. Most of the Red Sox pitching staff followed. And the Red Sox were left with barely a fig leaf to protect them, while the Yankees have been armed with a weed-whacker ever since.

Rod Dedeaux, my college coach, once said to me: "Tiger (he never knew rookies' names), cut yer head off, and let your body do the work!" To the chagrin of several general managers, managers and ex-wives, I have fol-lowed that sage advice all my life. I have spilled my guts and blood on the field of play for the Red Sox faithful in many parks, including Yankee Stadium. I left my medial-epachondi, my chromio-cavicular, in the dirt of home plate during a brawl with the Yankees.

My blood and all Red Sox blood is "O" positive—the universal fluid. The Yankees blood is "AB" negative or, as Mel Brooks says, "Abbey Normal." It is specific, and contaminating the health of the entire planet. Red Sox blood is generalized, and healthy for any recipient, whoever needs it—including Yankee fans who want to cross over. Attention, fans of the Evil Empire: this is a one-time offer for a transfusion of Boston's best.

Why do I hate the Yankees so much? As Shakespeare said, "Let me count the ways."

1. Opening Day, early seventies, cut to Yankee Stadium . . . packed house. Bottom of the sixth inning, bases loaded, in comes a young left-handed Red Sox pitcher, straight out of USC. Whack! Smoked in the chest with an empty pint of bourbon (cheap bour-bon to boot), first pitch to the batter, ground ball, double play, out of the inning. Next three innings were a cake-walk, all in relief of my roomie, Gary Peters, another Yankee killer. I now see that empty flask as an adrenalin motivator, and my baptism to the feud.

2. A warm Thursday evening in May 1976, first meeting of the year between the American League champion Red Sox and the also-ran New York Yankees. It was our first contest since Moret and I shut them out—in a doubleheader in Shea Stadium of all places. Bill Virdon, the manager, was fired after that shellacking, and that was how the infamous Billy Martin was brought onto the scene. So I was partially responsible for that, too. You could cut the air with a knife. With a 1-0 lead in the eighth, one spark would create

an explosion, and when Piniella steam-rolled Fisk at the plate, and Fisk held onto the ball, all hell broke loose. The Yankees were out of that dugout in a heartbeat, Nettles tossed me to the ground, and my fastball was history (whatever fastball I had, that is).

3. My comeback, premature as it was, came a mere six weeks after my injury. I tried to toe the hill against the Yankees at Fenway. Prior to the game, Billy Martin put two dead mackerel in a paper bag and had them delivered to me by a clubhouse boy, along with a note: "Put this in your purse, you Californian faggot." Let it be known, dear reader: Billy Martin was born in Oakland, California. I lost that game on a three-run homer to Nettles when my arm ran out of gas in the fifth.

4. Cut to '78, which I will refer to as "midnight in the garden of Good and Evil." It was Good, in that I rehabbed well, with the help of comedian Dick Gregory's food formula, the new Cybex machines, and hallucinogenic drugs; it was Bad because evil Don Zimmer, Haywood Sullivan, and Buddy Leroux, in their infernal wisdom, got rid of our good luck charm, Bernie Carbo. Zimmer would later gain fame as a Neo-Nazi sergeant sitting at the right hand of Joe Torre, and for scratching his ass in a hemorrhoid commercial. My last day in a Red Sox uniform was spent watching Bucky %°#x Dent. Is there anything else to be said?

You can see that I am more than qualified to comment on the blood feud between these two teams. I shed my blood in this fight and tried my best to combat the evil.

Which brings us to the present (notwithstanding the small wrench Aaron Boone threw into the time continuum in 2003). Why now—2004— for the reversal of fortune? Why? For one thing we now have "live" owners, not the "dead" Yawkey trust. These guys have real "O" positive oxygenated blood running through their veins. And, oh yeah, Big Money. Why did they win? Just look at Curt Schilling's ankle. 'Nuf said.

—BILL LEE
Calgary, Alberta

Introduction
The Wholly Red Sox Bible

In the Big Inning, God created the Red Sox and the Yankees . . .

The genesis of this book lies in our love of baseball and our fascination with the relationship that exists between its two most colorful teams. We set out to create a fair and balanced look at the Red Sox-Yankees "rivalry." But somewhere along the way, we gave up our role as creationists and allowed the book to evolve into a different sort of animal.

Originally, we were going to serve up platitude-laden pabulum on the relative strengths and weaknesses of the two teams, always painfully careful to delineate the rich tradition of the competition and the deep and mutual respect that exists between the two great franchises. And then we sat down to write. It wasn't long before we knew how the authors of the Bible must have felt. At some point they too must have realized that there is no way to give Good and Evil equal time and still sleep the sleep of the just.

It turns out that neither author of this book wanted to represent the Yankees point of view. In fact, neither of us could bring ourselves to write enough complimentary things about Steinbrenner's team to fill the back of a matchbox, let alone half a book (the morning after the Red Sox lost to the

4

Yankees in the 2003 ALCS, Jim Prime, one of this book's authors, conducted a previously-scheduled radio interview from the ledge outside Room 745 of the Prince Edward Hotel in Charlottetown, Prince Edward Island; the host of the radio show eventually talked him down). It was a revelation. Besides, we rationalized, that balanced, politically correct perspective on the Red Sox-Yankees phenomenon has been given, and there are several books on the market that take the "high road." It is a road paved with good intentions. These books speak of the "rivalry" in politically correct and antiseptic terms. We came to the realization that, for us at least, such an approach would ultimately be phony, and even hypocritical.

In fact, unless you were born in Idaho, or are currently sitting on the fence in downtown Purgatory, there is no balance to this rivalry. And that's another thing. Who's kidding whom? This is no rivalry. A rivalry is what happens between Pillsbury Bake-off contestants, or maybe Heinz and Campbell's or Hertz and Avis. Or between tourist bureaus in Maine and Massachusetts arguing who has the best fall foliage. No, this is no rivalry. This is a %$&°# feud. This is a duel to the finish, a knock 'em down, drag 'em out, survival-of-the-fittest cage match full of animosity, hatred, jealousy, pettiness and rancor. (God, that felt good!)

This is the unvarnished story of two teams that are scant miles apart geographically but light years apart philosophically. It is about Red Sox Nation and The Evil Empire. It is—not to put too fine a point on it—about Good vs. Evil.

Damn Yankees was a play about a guy who made a deal with the devil to ensure that his team—the Washington Senators (ha!)—finally beat the Yankees. That notion is almost blasphemous. Devilish deals are done *by* the Yankees and not *to* them.

As young baseball fans, and certainly over the intervening years, these writers occasionally pondered whether God was a Yankees fan, maybe even whether He hated the Boston Red Sox. How else could mere mortals explain the Yankees' miraculous success story and the Biblical proportions of the Red Sox' ineptitude? Year after year the Bosox suffered baseball's version of famine, plague and pestilence while the Yankees were perennial visitors to that Garden of Eden known as the World Series. By the 1960s our suspicion had hardened into deep conviction—a conviction that only very recently we have rejected.

We now believe. God may have switched teams for a while, but He is now a Red Sox fan. He watches them, He roots for them, and He even occasionally intercedes on their behalf—not on the field of course. He doesn't cause a Red Sox player to jump higher (what Manny Ramirez did to rob the Yankees' Miguel Cairo of a home run at Yankee Stadium last year was entirely above board). That kind of divine intercession would be wrong, and God is, above all else, fair. Once in a while a Red Sox player may do something that appears miraculous, but it is not a true miracle by God's high standards. And He would never strike a Yankee dead or anything like that. The most He would contribute would be to ask the umpires to confer on a call in order to get it right. In the past, He didn't even intervene to do that. He allowed mortals to make mistakes that robbed us year after year. So, as you can see, our lapse of faith was understandable, and hopefully forgivable.

Nevertheless, it was His fondest wish to have His Red Sox win the World Series. He also wants world peace, universal health care, the end of reality TV, a solution to those vexing problems in the Middle East, and nuclear nonproliferation. And maybe a little more respect for His environment and the natural world He gave us. Until the fall of 2004, all of these objectives seemed equally unlikely to be achieved.

God bends over backward to be neutral, but we now know that He's pulling for the Sox. Somewhere up there in those Sky Boxes in the clouds, he's sitting with Cy Young and Jimmie Foxx and Joe Cronin and Ted Williams and other saintly, celestial Sox and He's watching the innings play out. Once in awhile He even visits Fenway, sitting near the Red Sox dugout in a seat once occupied by superfan Lib Dooley. He pretty much keeps quiet, just orders a single Fenway Frank and a large Coke and observes. You can tell it's Him because He never participates in the wave and He covers His ears during some of the ruder chants. He is uncomfortable with the presence of Wally and other graven images (although ironically, He always got a perverse kick out of the New Jersey Devils mascot). His favorite player is David Ortiz, although His Son appreciates Johnny Damon in the same way that Jimmy Stewart used to grudgingly admire the work of Rich Little.

How do we know all this? Faith mostly. We follow those timeless words written on T-shirts. No, not "Yankees Suck", or even "WWJDD?" (What Would Johnny Damon Do?). We're talking about "Keep the Faith." After all, God also let His chosen people wander in the wilderness for forty years before sending Moses to lead them out of their misery. He sent us Ted to do the same for His Red Sox (although He later sent us Jerry Moses as a sort of ironic joke). Ted was well on his way until he hit a slump in the 1946 World Series. This time He sent Big Papi, giving Him a .500 average in such good works.

The truth is that God waited for Ted to arrive and get comfortable with the new surroundings before intervening to bring a World Series title to Boston. Because God loves Ted—in spite of some of the things that Ted occasionally said about him. Why does God like Ted so much? Well, for one thing, they are both right-handers who bat left, although He can throw a lightning bolt with either hand with decent accuracy.

As a life guide the Bible is pretty hard to beat, but it does drone on sometimes and you have to wade through a lot of begetting and other stuff to get to the point. And what's with all those verses? It really messes up the continuity and most of it doesn't rhyme nearly as well as "Casey at the Bat." The problem is that mortals wrote the Bible. Baseball, on the other hand, is God's ongoing parable.

Baseball, being a microcosm of life, offers a unique opportunity to both entertain and educate. This book is an attempt to use baseball, and more particularly, two specific teams in baseball, to impart the moral lessons of the ages to those whose attention span runs to nine innings or less. The Red Sox–Yankees rivalry exists at so many levels and has so many sub-categories that like *Seinfeld* or *The Simpsons* it teaches virtually all of life's lessons. Ted vs. Joe. Carlton vs. Thurman. Bill Lee vs. Billy Martin, Babe Ruth vs., well, Babe Ruth. Hellish Yankee Stadium vs. heavenly Fenway Park.

To countless fans, baseball is virtually a religion anyway and if the Grand Old Game can teach some of the verities, it may serve to alleviate the guilt associated with skipping church in order to attend a double header or of videotaping Passover services to catch the game live on TV.

This, then, is our own foray into the nature of Good and Evil. It is not meant to be in any way sacrilegious. Our suspicion that God may be a Yankees fan was admittedly in our darkest time of doubt and we have since tried to suppress this kind of thinking, mostly unsuccessfully, we admit, until 2004. No, God is a Red Sox fan. We're sure of it now. He was just testing us—and doing His usual fine job if we may say so. He has instilled us with the patience of Job (or Kevin Youkilis) and the wisdom of Solomon (or Theo Epstein), and the persistence of Moses (or Curt Schilling). We can handle anything now. Bucky Dent was a trial, Bill Buckner was a trouble, and Aaron Boone was a tribulation. They were the locusts and sores and boils that helped make us better people. Grady Little was our sackcloth; and a tired Pedro our ashes.

At the risk of alienating a rather large section of the northeastern United States and parts of Florida, our basic contention is that while the Red Sox are the incarnation of GOOD, the Yankees are the embodiment of EVIL. Boston is akin to Paradise and New York is so bad it makes Sodom and Gomorrah look about as wicked as Minneapolis-St.Paul. Again, not to put too fine a point on it: they have Beelzebub behind the plate, Lucifer in left, Mephistopheles in center, Old Nick at third, the Prince of Darkness at short, and Satan on the mound. They are accursed, demoniacal, diabolical, fiendish, infernal, malevolent, malignant, and wicked. Not only are they damn Yankees, they are damned Yankees.

They have struck a deal with the devil and up until very recently they have been reaping the benefits. The exact details of the deal are unknown but are said to involve Babe Ruth, Harry Frazee, and lots of money, which is where the expression "money is the Ruth of all evil" originated. The Red Sox and Yankees have fought tooth and nail since the early part of the 20th century, ever since Ruth was tempted by a serpent named Harry Frazee to help himself to the Big Apple and all the sin and debauchery that it represented. The Bambino was cast out of the Garden of Eden known as Fenway to occupy the nether world of New York. Thus Ruth became the first fallen Red Sox player when he was banished by Frazee, crossed the river Styx, and entered New York. (There was a long line of others. When the irrepressible Luis Tiant went from the losing Sox to the winning Yankees and was immediately featured in an Oscar Meyer commercial, he uttered the unforgettable tag line: "It's great to finally be with a wiener.")

Since then, the Yankees are guilty of having repeatedly committed all of the Seven Deadly Sins. Here are just a few examples.

Gluttony:	Let's face it, Babe Ruth really let himself go after leaving Boston.
Pride:	Who hasn't heard of the "Pride of the Yankees"?
Envy:	Why else would George Steinbrenner try to covet his neighbor's assets? El Tiante, Roger, Wade, A-Rod, etc.?
Lust:	Lusting for power is just part of it. Ever hear of

	Fritz Peterson and Mike Kekich? You could look it up, as Casey Stengel used to say. In addition, Yogi often referred to the "immoral Babe Ruth."
Anger/Wrath:	Did you see A-Rod after Varitek gave him a glove massage? Zimmer's face when he charged Pedro? Billy Martin when he ripped Reggie for not hustling? Steinbrenner after a loss to the Sox?
Greed:	This is too easy. Look at the payroll.
Sloth:	Face it: Babe Ruth really, really let himself go after leaving Boston.

This book is an attempt to teach some moral lessons about Good and Evil, using the Red Sox as a symbol of good and the Yankees as the essence of evil.

"Hating the Yankees is as American as pizza pie and cheating on your income tax." —Mike Royko

There have been countless great "rivalries" in the history of sport. The Montreal Canadiens and Toronto Maple Leafs once epitomized the zenith for the Zamboni set. The Boston Celtics and Los Angeles Lakers have fought bitter battles for basketball supremacy. The Dodgers and Giants confrontations began furiously on the east coast and continue at a more laid-back pace on the west; Harvard and Yale fight civilized but intense football battles in the calm, ivy-coated midst of academia, likewise Oxford and Cambridge have gentlemanly rowing rows. The very mention of Ali and Frazier conjures memories of poetic summitry in the sweet science.

But they were mere disagreements when compared to the all-out war that is Red Sox-Yankees. Ask former Red Sox southpaw Bill Lee if Graig Nettles was a friendly rival. In 1976, the two hooked up in a slugfest that left Lee on the sidelines for an extended period. Lee was on the mound for visiting Boston, with Lou Piniella and Nettles on base. Otto Velez singled and the always-volatile Piniella put his head down and charged home. Carlton Fisk was between him and the plate. Dwight Evans made a great throw to the plate but Piniella was determined to score. He collided with Fisk and the two came up swinging as both benches cleared. Lee and Velez paired off as Mickey Rivers attacked the vulnerable Spaceman from behind. Nettles joined in the mugging, tossing Lee to the turf.

The Spaceman won't be having his attacker over for tea and scones anytime soon. When he learned that Nettles had penned a book called *Balls*, Lee's comment was "He missed it by a couple inches, it should have been called *Asshole*." But at least now—more than thirty years after their brawl in Yankee Stadium—they have come to appreciate the confrontation as good hard competition, right? Wrong.

Steve Politi, writing in the *Staten Island Advance* as recently as October of 2004, reports that the two are still at odds. "Yeah, I keep a photo of Nettles in my back pocket, as a reminder," Lee told Politi. "I keep it face down on the right cheek of my (butt). The smell and the view from there are not so good for him."

Meanwhile the former Yankees third baseman was equally unforgiving: "We all got along pretty well. The only people that didn't get along are myself and Bill Lee."

The two antagonists were reunited recently at a Red Sox-Yankees banquet in New Jersey and Lee claims that Nettles admitted to trying to intentionally get him out of the game, a claim that Nettles now denies. "We had had an earlier fight," Nettles told Politi, "and Lee accused us of fighting like Times Square hookers, scratching with our nails and hitting with our purses. Well, I wanted to make sure we got some punches in to show him how tough the Times Square hookers were in those days."

"It was good to see him, since he's withering away," Lee said. "He spoke about it, and he said he was doing it intentionally to keep me out of the game. I didn't mind anything in the heat of the battle as long as it wasn't premeditated. The statute of limitations may be up legally, but not morally."

Those who elevate the feud between the Red Sox and the Yankees to Athens versus Sparta are just kidding themselves. The Red Sox and Yankees are the Hatfields and McCoys, the Montagues and Capulets, of the baseball diamond. To put it back in moral terms, the Cain and Abel of baseball.

This book is an attempt to present a very slanted view of the feud, a feud that entered a different phase and reached a unique climax in October of 2004. We will hear from players, owners, writers, and fans. We will hear heated rhetoric and slanderous commentary from various sources.

The sale of Babe Ruth to the Yankees in 1920 is generally acknowledged as the beginning of the Red Sox-Yankees feud. Prior to the fat man's departure, the Red Sox had been baseball's dynastic power, winning three World Series in four years. After Ruth donned the pinstripes, the New Yorkers were all but invincible, capturing six pennants and three World Series in the next eight years. At the ripe old age of 26, the Babe had already hit more homers than any player in major league history. But in actual fact the feud started much earlier than that. In 1904 the pennant race between the then Boston Americans and New York Highlanders came down to the next-to-last day of the season when the Boston nine won on a wild pitch by New York pitcher Happy Jack Chesbro.

The two teams seem destined to share a common history, and fate has repeatedly thrown them together in dramatic fashion. Fittingly, the first team to play the Sox at spanking new Fenway Park in 1912 was New York. The first visitors to sparkling new Yankee Stadium in 1923 were the Red Sox. Lou Gehrig hit his first homer against Boston; Ruth hit his first against New York. Ted Williams' introduction to major league pitching came at Yankee Stadium; he hit a double off former Red Sox pitcher Red Ruffing. Maris hit his 61st homer off of Red Sox pitcher Tracy Stallard. The Yankees had the first shot at signing both Ted Williams and Long Islander Carl Yastrzemski and failed to do so.

How deep does the rivalry run? Well, it's considerably thicker than blood according to Dom DiMaggio, who once robbed brother Joe of an RBI crown with not one but two all-out, full extension catches. "I was battling [Hank] Greenberg for the RBI crown the last two weeks of the season," Joe recalled years later. "The first two times I come to bat against the Red Sox the bags were loaded, and Greenberg's only leading me by three. I hit these terrific shots about 450 feet and Dom goes up and makes the catch on both occasions. So I get no RBIs out of it. When he was coming in from the field we crossed paths and he gave me a little smile. Later on that night we had dinner and he said to me, 'You know, Joe, I couldn't have gone another inch for those balls.' "

In some ways the Red Sox and Yankees are like two disgruntled neighbors, trying to outdo one another. The Yankees adopt a Californian named DiMaggio, the Red Sox bring in another Golden State kid called Williams; the Yankees get Munson, the Red Sox answer with Fisk. Boggs and Mattingly, Pedro and Roger. Nomar and Jeter. Varitek and Posada. The Red Sox have a high-strung player named Piersall, the Yankees pit him against another high-strung player in Billy Martin. The Sox purchase Lefty Grove;

the Yankees answer with Lefty Gomez. Both neighbors' houses are stately and grand: one with a short porch to the right and one with a short porch to the left. Both families are well-heeled and welcome lots of summer visitors. Both families are at times dysfunctional. The homeowners are frequently shouting invectives across the feuding fence that separates them.

They may be fierce opponents and at times even hated enemies, but if the Red Sox-Yankees rivalry were based purely on parity and the struggle for excellence on the field, it would not be much of a contest. The baseball gods have sided with the Yankees over the past eight decades. The Yankees have won 36 pennants and 26 World Series. Up until the 2004 season, the Sox had managed just four pennants and not a single World Series championship over those same eighty-some years.

In 1949 the Red Sox lost the AL pennant to the Yankees on the final day of the season. In 1978, they lost the pennant to the Yankees in a one-game playoff at Fenway. Despite this lopsided record, the feud remained red hot. Any incident between the two teams—any seeming slight—is served up in generous portions by the Boston media to an insatiable public. The New York newspapers and talk radio stations have become more vigilant in recent years as well, and the Yankees' public has increasingly been keeping a wary eye on the team to the north (and we don't mean the Jays.)

Seemingly, the very fact of losing feeds the growing appetite in Beantown. Where voracious Gotham fans feast regularly on victories but are never satisfied, the Boston fans, to whom losing was once abhorrent, often seem to thrive on near famine, subsisting on just enough gruel to come back each year like Oliver, pleading for "More, please." The Red Sox fan appears, like Sisyphus, almost superior by virtue of the long-suffering nobility of the vanquished.

The feud takes on a greater significance than simply the successes and failures of two -baseball teams; it is symbolic of two great cities. New York: sophisticated, huge, rude, and cocky. Boston: cultured, refined, intellectual, and maybe a tad arrogant. Even more broadly, the two teams represent opposing paradigms that reflect the split American personality. Americans love to be associated with winners (Yankees) and they also love the underdog (Red Sox). If those two things seem irreconcilable to you, welcome to the family feud, because in many ways it is just that, and as any tuners-in to the Jerry Springer show can attest, those are the worst kind.

But the feud goes beyond the personalities. It is Fenway vs. Yankee Stadium. New England vs. New York. Broadway vs. Back Bay. Baked beans vs. bagels. The *Globe* vs. the *Times* (it's a sign of the times that both are now owned by the New York Times Company) and the *Herald* vs. the *Daily News* and the *New York Post*. The Charles vs. the Hudson. But it is also commercialism vs. academia, large vs. small, tradition vs. modernity.

At times the rivalry has gotten well out of hand. After a battle royal in New York between the two teams, Bill Lee referred to the Yankees as Brown Shirts and Nazis. In 1974, Don Zimmer, then a third base coach for the Red Sox, was forced to don a batting helmet in New York to protect himself from debris that was thrown his way (one is tempted to say that the Yankees fans lobbed grenades at the Red Sox and the Red Sox pulled the pins and threw them back). Years later, when Zimmer became the Yankees' bench coach, it was only fitting that he was presented with a real army helmet, complete with Yankees insignia.

In 1950 an incident occurred that could have been much more serious. Phil Rizzuto, the slick-fielding Yankees shortstop, needed only one more hit to reach the coveted 200 level. The final three games of the season were slated for Fenway and a Red Sox fan sent a letter threatening that Rizzuto would be shot if he played. Casey Stengel, ever the pragmatist, had a reasonable solution. He had Billy Martin wear Rizzuto's uniform because the future Yankees manager was "more expendable." "Billy didn't stand still all day," recalls Rizzuto.

This book is not an attempt to further inflame these passions, as if they needed any such help—but to report them for what they are: the greatest blood feud in American sport. We will report, in short, with all the balance and fairness of Fox News or Al Jazeera.

Americans are a complex lot. They love winners but they root for underdogs. They appreciate perfection but relate much better to imperfection. The feud reflects a dichotomy that exists across America, which perhaps explains why these two teams draw such large crowds on the road. They represent divergent views of America. Views of Good vs. Evil and how each of us defines those terms.

That is why the Boston Red Sox, love them or merely like them a lot, are America's Team. The Yankees are, on the other hand, New York's Team, or at least one of the New York teams, the teams others love to hate. A New York baseball team played in the World Series in every season from 1949-

58. In six of those 10 years, a New York team played a New York team. Such blessings have showered down on the New Yorkers, and especially the Yankees since the Roaring Twenties, despite a couple of stretches where their fields lay fallow. Has Heaven now started to smile on the Red Sox once more? God only knows.

Chapter 1
The 2004 American League Championship Series, Games 1, 2, & 3

"There are some who are last who shall be first, and there are some first who shall be last." —Luke 13:30

"So the last shall be first, and the first last: for many be called, but few chosen." —Matthew 20:16

"Nice guys finish last." —Leo Durocher

"I could never play in New York. The first time I ever came into a game there, I got into the bullpen car and they told me to lock the doors." —Mike Flanagan, former Orioles pitcher

If God likes to test His people's faith, He outdid Himself with His Red Sox flock in Games 1, 2 and 3.

For the seventh year in a row, the Yankees finished ahead of Boston in the standings. In fact the Red Sox have finished second to the Yankees in the AL East pennant race so often, they are nauseous from the exhaust fumes. In 1998, it was Yankees in first place and the Red Sox in second place. Cleveland beat Boston three games to one in the ALDS. In 1999, it was the Yankees in first place and the Sox in second. Boston beat the Indians three games to two in the ALDS, but New York won four games to Boston's one in the ALCS. In 2000, the Yankees placed first and the Sox were second again. This time, both the Mariners and the Indians had better records, so the Red Sox were denied the Wild Card. In 2001, the Yankees finished in first and the Sox in second. Again, no wild card. In 2002, Yankees first, Red Sox second. No wild card. Then, of course, in 2003, the Yankees finished first and the Red Sox finished second, but Boston won the Wild Card and beat Oakland to earn the right to face New York in the ALCS. That series went to seven games, and Boston was beaten in the bottom of the eleventh inning.

Always the bridesmaid, never the bride. Second fiddle. Second banana. Close but no cigar. Call it what you want, it was a very discouraging pattern for Red Sox fans. Many fans thought the Sox were going to beat the Yankees in 2003, and many still bear the emotional scars seared into their psyche when manager Grady Little asked Pedro to go back out on the mound and pitch another inning, after Pedro had apparently turned over the lead to a very capable Boston bullpen.

In 2004, the Yankees finished first yet again and the Red Sox were in their accustomed second place. Seven years in a row now, but this time Red Sox fans were even more confident than they'd been the year before. They'd beaten the Yankees head-to-head 11 of the 19 times they'd battled in the regular season. The Yankees' pitching staff seemed vulnerable as never before. Momentum appeared to be on Boston's side, coming off a strong second-half recovery after nearly three months in the doldrums, playing .500 ball. One can never underestimate the Yankees, however. They'd now made the post-season 10 years in a row, and it had become their own little fiefdom.

Most Sox fans feared Anaheim more than the Yankees, and for good reason; the Angels, featuring the mighty bats of Guerrero and Glaus, did seem to present more of an obstacle to Boston hopes. Get past them, and bring on the Yankees! That was the macho mind-set. Some realists feared facing New York, not wanting to tempt fate yet again. Maybe we could more easily beat Minneapolis, they argued, but the prevailing sentiment was that the preferred way to the World Series was through the Yankees—for more reasons than one.

As things transpired, Boston swept the Angels in three straight games (there is some considerable irony in the Sox beating a team called the Angels in order to battle the forces of the Evil Empire, given the premise of this book) and was ready to take on the Yankees, who had beaten out the Twins.

As the American League Championship Series between the defending AL champion Yankees and the Boston Red Sox got underway, many observers, including those professional observers in Las Vegas, featured the Red Sox as favorites. It was a role in which they had little or no previous experience, even though they looked to match up well against their ancient and honorable rivals.

It was pretty hard to convince diehard, snakebit Sox fans that they held any kind of real advantage, however. There was some Boston bravado in the "bring on the Yankees" cries, but deeper down we all knew it would be very difficult to deny the cynicism that 86 years of heartbreak and disappointment had so deeply engrained in the New England psyche. The all-too-fresh memories of 2003 were still vividly etched in the minds of Red Sox fans. The nervous tics had scarcely begun to subside, and mentions of Grady Little's name could only now sometimes be served up without a sedative chaser. Were the Red Sox ready to take another swipe at those inseparable companions: Fate and Yankees Supremacy? Any talk of "advantage" or "favorites" was greeted with trepidation—even scorn—by knowledgeable (and nervous) Red Sox fans.

The hype began early, if indeed it ever stopped over the seemingly endless off-season of second-guessing, hand wringing, and blame passing. A meaningless spring training game between the two teams in Fort Myers brought national attention, tickets were scalped at ridiculous prices, and commemorative badges were struck to mark the occasion. The exhibition game attracted everyone from Wayne Gretsky to Stephen King, and the media scrutinized every move of Nomar Garciaparra, Derek Jeter and Alex Rodriguez. Did Nomar spend too much time fraternizing with Derek and A-Rod? Was he deliberately snubbing Sox owner John Henry? What about Schilling and Foulke, the two new pitchers in whom the Red Sox were putting so much faith? Were they a wise investment by young GM Theo Epstein?

And what about A-Rod? Would his presence lift the Yankees to new heights? Did the Red Sox' failure to secure him signal another disastrous season? There had been off-season sniping between Steinbrenner and Red Sox co-owner Larry Lucchino. One thing was certain: these two teams honestly did not like each other.

The Red Sox were set to go head-to-head with the Yankees 19 times in the 2004 regular season, providing enough frequency—and certainly enough fuel—to coax an already inflammatory feud into a conflagration. The Boston brass had been active in the off-season, trying to load up and to create a team with more depth. A total of 10 players on the Red Sox roster had not been on the squad that faced the Yanks in 2003. Their knowledge of the feud was therefore limited to what they'd seen on ESPN or in the pages of *Sports Illustrated*. They were about to get a baptism by fire because, once again, the Yankees' offense was loaded. Once again, their team had a mix of veterans and newcomers who constituted a "Who's Who" of baseball. Jeter, A-Rod, Sheffield, Posada, Olerud, Lofton, Matsui, Bernie Williams, Giambi. It was almost enough to make one lose heart even before the first pitch was thrown.

But still . . . there seemed to be an Achilles heel this time around. (It turned out that heel would be a very significant word this season: heel as in Nomar's ailing foot, heel as in Schilling's bloody ankle; heel as in the popular perception of A-Rod when he went to NY instead of Boston.) Gone were New York's pitching stalwarts "Rocket" Roger Clemens, Andy Pettitte, and David Wells. The Yankees brass replaced them with Kevin Brown, Jon Lieber, and Javier Vazquez—but can such key cogs be so easily replaced in such a finely-tuned machine? The Yankees and all of baseball were about to find out. Meanwhile, the Boston Red Sox boasted the fearsome foursome of Wakefield, Schilling, Pedro, and Lowe, with Bronson Arroyo seemingly about to blossom into a reliable fifth starter. It was to be a season of heels and heroes, histrionics and heroics, comebacks and collapses, culminating in one of the most exciting chapters in baseball history.

This is what most of America outside Minnesota and Anaheim wanted. The two archrivals: the David and Goliath of baseball. This time it would be a blood feud!

Game One—The (Im)perfect Game

This was the Mike Mussina show, featuring the man Yankees fans call Moose. Never was a moniker less appropriate for the man wearing it. The poised and stylish Yankees ace was at the top of his form, while Curt Schilling, the man who had been brought to Boston for this very moment, was ineffective. It was a bit of a battering.

Boston had beaten Mussina twice in the 2003 ALCS, both in Game One and then again in Game Four. He also lost a game in the ALDS, though he'd won Game Three of the 2003 World Series. He was 1-1 against the Red Sox in 2004, with a 3.50 ERA in 19 innings of work. The Twins beat him in a close 2-0 game in the 2004 ALDS. He'd lost four of his last five playoff starts. The Sox felt they had a shot, especially with Schilling on the mound. Schilling was 6-1 in post-season play.

Yankees ace closer Mariano Rivera lost two close friends in a tragic accident at his home in Panama, and he traveled there for the funeral. It was unclear if he would return in time for Game One of the ALCS, or what condition he would be in. Television cameras captured his return to Yankee Stadium, broadcast to viewers early in the game.

Mussina rose to the occasion, though, and shut down one Sox player after another. He was, in fact, perfect through six and one-third innings, retiring every one of the first 19 batters from Boston. Schilling, in the meantime, was shelled. He gave up two runs in the bottom of the first, and four more in the third. He was pitching in pain. "I just couldn't reach back," he said. "If we'd sent anybody else out there but me tonight, we would have won the game." Maybe not on this night, against this Yankees ace. In any event, the Yankees had a 6-0 lead and Mussina appeared unhittable.

The hopes and dreams of Red Sox Nation had been riding on Schilling's tendonitis-hampered right ankle. Before the game he had expressed a desire to render 56,000 New Yorkers silent. They were anything but. After surrendering six earned runs in three innings of work, Schilling left to derisive jeers from the capacity crowd of decidedly noisy fans. For the benefit of any Red Sox players with possible hearing impairments, the fans obligingly offered up some easily decipherable sign language, proving that not all Bronx cheers have to be audible to be effective. It now looked as if Schilling might be finished for the rest of the post-season, leaving Red Sox hopes all but dashed.

When the Red Sox offense finally got kick-started, it was already 8-0

Yankees. The Sox scored five times in the top of the seventh, though, and
it began to look like the Sox could salvage some semblance of respectabili-
ty. Mark Bellhorn ruined Mussina's perfecto with a long double to left-center field. Ortiz then singled to move Bellhorn to third and cue the comeback. Millar doubled, scoring Bellhorn and Ortiz. Nixon singled Millar
home and Jason Varitek homered to bring the score to 8-5.

Despite the flawless start, Mussina had weakened quickly and was
charged with four earned runs in 6⅔ innings.

Maybe Yogi thought it was over before it was over. He had thrown out
the first pitch but, after the seventh inning, Yogi left the building.

After holding the Yankees scoreless in the bottom of the seventh, the
rejuvenated Red Sox struck again in the top of the eighth, plating two more
runs on an Ortiz triple which hit the left-center-field wall at the 399-foot
marker, missing a home run by less than a foot. Now it was a ballgame! The
score was 8-7 and the Sox were breathing down New York's neck. But the
Yankees quickly answered the threat with a pair of insurance runs in the
bottom of the eighth. 10-7, Yankees. The Sox didn't go down easily. With
two on and the tying run at the plate in the top of the ninth, in the person
of 2003 batting champion Bill Mueller, Mariano Rivera closed the door on
any hopes of a Red Sox miracle comeback. New York's reliever extraordi-
naire stepped off a plane and into the breach, and wrote another poignant
chapter in his great career.

Several Yankees players share credit for the win. Hideki Matsui, a.k.a.
Godzilla, ran amok at the plate and tied an ALCS record with five RBIs,
sparking the New York offense. Boston partisans were somewhat appeased
by the comeback that had brought them within a run of the Yankees.
Players always look for glimmers of hope and ways to restore team-esteem.
David Ortiz found reason for optimism in the way that Boston had battled
back in Game One. "I like it, man. I like it. They've got their ace on the
mound, throwing a perfect game in the seventh inning. We're down 8-0
with, like, seven outs to go, and they had to use all their pitchers to keep us
from coming back. I like it. They know we keep coming back . . . they know
we never give up." The Sox could also take heart in the fact that they'd
scored seven runs or more in each of their four 2004 playoff games. But try
as they did to put a good face on it, it was an ugly game and there were a
lot of long faces in Red Sox Nation. When it was all over, the Yankees had
defeated the Red Sox 10-7 to take a 1-0 lead in the ALCS. And it didn't look

like Curt Schilling would be able to pitch again in the post-season.

Final score: Yankees 10, Red Sox 7

Game Two—Who's Your Daddy?

For the second time in two days, the words of a Red Sox starter came back to haunt him as the Yankees, behind the inspired pitching of Jon Lieber, dropped Pedro Martinez and the Boston Red Sox 3-1. On September 24, late in the regular season, Pedro suffered a 6-4 loss at the hands of the Yankees and uttered an ill-advised comment that would come back to haunt him: "What can I say? I just tip my cap and call the Yankees my daddy." That remark was born of frustration and grudging respect, but it reflected a certain reality. Lifetime, Pedro is 10-10 against the Yankees, despite a good 3.24 ERA. Against the rest of baseball, he's 172-66.

Yankees fans were gleeful. The Stadium was packed with "Who's Your Daddy?" signs, and the chants rained down on Pedro's head all night long. After the Sox were set down 1-2-3 in the top of the first, Pedro took the mound. He'd had some first-inning rockiness all year long, but this time escaped, with minimal damage. Jeter walked on four straight pitches, then stole second. Moments later, a Pedro pitch drilled A-Rod. Sheffield singled to center, scoring Jeter from second, but then Pedro buckled down and struck out Matsui and Williams, and got Posada to ground out.

Jon Lieber kept the Sox batters off-balance and allowed just two hits through the first seven innings. Pedro blanked the Yanks for the next four frames, and after 5½, it was New York 1, Boston 0. Veteran hitter (but new Yankee) John Olerud struck a two-run homer off Martinez in the sixth for all the run support New York would need. Pedro had struck out seven, but he'd walked four and two of the baserunners he'd walked had scored. The erstwhile Boston ace finished out the sixth, but he'd been worked for 113 pitches and Sox skipper Terry Francona called on Mike Timlin to take over in the seventh, with the Yankees on top, 3-0.

The Red Sox managed their lone run in the top of the eighth when Nixon singled, driving Lieber to the showers. Jason Varitek, whose bat had been dead in New York for most of the regular season, doubled against reliever Tom "Flash" Gordon. Nixon then scored on a ground out by Orlando Cabrera. Bill Mueller recorded the second out before Gordon gave way to the inevitable Mariano Rivera. Rivera, a perfect six-for-six in post-season save chances against the Bosox, promptly struck out the slumping Johnny Damon to end the threat. In the ninth, the Red Sox failed to cash in Manny Ramirez' one-out double as Rivera fanned Ortiz and Millar to end the game and put the Yankees up two games to none. Final score, 3-1 for New York. It was Rivera's 32nd post-season save, an astonishing pitching statistic.

First, Mussina and now Lieber; the Yankees pitching staff had posted back-to-back first-rate outings. Talk about quality starts: in his first six innings, Moose hadn't let a man reach base. In his first six, Lieber had allowed just a single to Cabrera, and walked one. This was a Sox team that had led the major leagues in runs (949, and no other team even reached 900), on-base percentage (.360), slugging (.472), extra base hits (620), total bases (2,702), and batting average (.282).

Meanwhile, Red Sox pitching ranked third in A.L. ERA, but led the league by holding opponents to a .252 average, and had 12 shutouts to their credit. Both Boston aces had now come up short in the League Championship Series, however—and it was revealed that Schilling's condition was not mere tendonitis, but rather a dislocated tendon which had come loose. It would require surgery to reattach it. Expected recovery time was three months. It now seemed all but certain his season was over.

It seemed to some that the Red Sox season was over, too. Game Three became a "must win"—no team had ever gone down three games and come back to win a best-of-seven series.

"We know we're in a hole," said Johnny Damon, 0-for-8 so far in the Series. Five of those outs were strikeouts. "But even idiots know how to dig themselves out of a hole." It would prove to be a Big Dig. Jason Varitek pointed out the obvious: the Sox could have scored some runs for Pedro and given him a chance.

The return to Boston represented a small light at the end of this vast tunnel they had excavated for themselves. Sox fans were staring into the abyss. Mike Barnicle wrote in his column, "I never thought I'd think this but maybe my Uncle Gerry was the lucky one. He was killed at Midway in June 1942 and didn't have to live through 1946, 1978 and this October when once again, baseball has me on a suicide watch list."

Grasping at straws, some began to think of a "reverse '86." In the 1986 World Series against the Mets, the Sox had won both Games One and Two in New York, then come back and lost the next two at home. If the Sox could win Games Three and Four, the ALCS would be even again. But with Schilling seemingly lost, their fortunes depended on the arms of Bronson Arroyo, Tim Wakefield, and Derek Lowe. And Lowe hadn't even been slated to start in the ALCS, after the shaky season he'd had. For Arroyo, it would be only the second start he'd had in the post-season. He was due to face the veteran Kevin Brown. Even though Brown had nearly kayoed himself, breaking a hand while duking it out with a clubhouse wall just weeks beforehand, he'd come around and, well, he had experience. And the Yankees, did they have Destiny on their side, or what?

The Yankees even crowed a little. Responding to the notion that this Yankees team was weak on pitching, manager Joe Torre basked in back-to-back gems from Mussina and Lieber, saying, "We've been hearing that since spring training. Everybody said we had a great lineup and no pitching. We won a hundred games with no pitching." They were feeling confident. They certainly had History on their side.

Final score: Yankees 3, Red Sox 1

"Thoughts of my first confession surfaced—when I had to tell the priest that I wished harm to others, namely, that when I said my prayers at night, I wished that various New York Yankees would fall down their stoops, cutting their knees, spraining their ankles, or even breaking their legs." —Doris Kearns Goodwin

Game Three—The Lowest of the Low

Game Three was set for Friday night, but was rained out, giving all concerned another day's rest. Hopes were high that the Red Sox could benefit from a little home field advantage, maybe a little home cooking, and maybe just getting away from Yankee Stadium where, after all, their season had come to a crashing halt the year before. No such luck.

It was the homecoming from Hell. It was a thrashing, a drubbing, a blowout, a pummeling, a trouncing, and a slaughter. Roget does not have enough pages in his thesaurus to adequately describe the parameters of the defeat. It was hardly worthy of being called a baseball game and certainly not worthy of the rivalry between these two great teams. If, by definition, a rival is required to be a peer, the two teams were not rivals this night. It was a losing margin that the New England Patriots, let alone the Red Sox, would have found embarrassing. 19-8! All that was missing was the 1, as in 1918, yet another stark reminder of the futility of being a Red Sox fan. Is this how it was all to end? Was this the reward for all the work that went into assembling a team that could actually go toe-to-toe with the ultimate foe?

The most optimistic spin that even the most diehard Red Sox fan could give this game was that the Yankees may have tired themselves out running the bases.

It's tempting to call the game batting practice for the Yankees but that would be almost too kind. Red Sox pitchers proved completely helpless against this newest manifestation of Murderer's Row. Bronson Arroyo, the young pitcher with so much promise, started the game and allowed six hits and six runs in two innings of work. He was replaced by former Yankee and major disappointment Ramiro Mendoza (one run and one hit in one inning), and Curtis Leskanic (three hits and three runs in one third of an inning). With the score now at 10-6 in the fourth inning, Terry Francona had a tough decision to

LCS records set in Game Three
Most runs by a team, 19
Most extra-base hits by a team, 13
Most runs by a player, 5 (both Hideki Matsui and Alex Rodriguez)
Most runs, both teams, 27
Most hits, both teams, 37
Most extra-base hits, both teams, 20
Longest nine-inning game, 4:20
Most humiliating defeat in recent memory in a non-clinch game: priceless.

make. Tim Wakefield, the classy knuckleballer and longest-term Red Sox player was scheduled to start the next day, but Francona needed someone to chew up some innings in a game that would soon be out of reach. Wakefield approached Francona as he was conferring with pitching coach Dave Wallace. "What do you need me to do?" he asked. Wakefield was a warrior; he sacrificed his chance to start, swallowed some pride, and pitched 3⅓ agonizing innings. He gave up five more hits and five more runs but Red Sox fans, among the most informed in baseball, knew and appreciated his sacrifice. So did every one of his teammates.

There were no Cy Young clones in the Yankees pitching ranks either. Starter Kevin Brown was driven from the mound after two lackluster innings in which he gave up four runs on five hits. Forgotten after the innings that followed is that the Sox actually held a 4-3 lead, ever so briefly, until New York scored three more runs in the top of the third. Javier Vazquez didn't fare any better than Brown, allowing another four runs and seven hits in his 4⅓ inning stint. Fittingly, it was enough to earn him the win in this pitchers' nightmare. After 6⅓ innings, it was Yankees 17, Red Sox 6. When the crowd rose for the seventh-inning stretch, a good portion of those who hadn't already abandoned ship decided that a simple stretch wasn't enough exercise to relieve the tensions of this game, and walked briskly for the exits. Some people had paid $1000 or more for a pair of prime seats, but it was already closing in on midnight and, if you were a Red Sox fan, well, who wanted to see this?

The Yankees established a new ALCS record for runs (19), and tied the mark for hits (22). The offensive heroics included two homers by Matsui and one each by A-Rod and Sheffield. Rodriguez, Sheffield, Matsui, and Bernie Williams were a combined 16-for-22, with 15 RBIs. The *Hartford Courant's* Jeff Jacobs wrote about all the records that had been set. "The most runs, most doubles, just about the most of everything in LCS history. Instead of recapping the records, major league baseball would have made it easier on itself had it simply handed out a list of records not broken."

Final score: Yankees 19, Red Sox 8

The Yankees had administered a crushing, demoralizing 19-8 thrashing in front of what remained of a thoroughly disheartened Fenway Park crowd and what remained of an equally deflated TV audience that extended throughout Red Sox Nation, from Nova Scotia to Nantucket and well beyond. Over the three games, the Yankees had a team batting average of .377, while the Red Sox pitching staff were embarrassed by an ERA of 11.52. The Red Sox were teetering on the brink of a humiliating Series sweep. By the time the final out was recorded, Fenway Park was all but empty. Those disillusioned fans that remained showered their former heroes with vitriol that would almost have made Yankee Stadium look welcoming. The latest battle in the ancient blood feud between the two venerable American League franchises from New York and Boston seemed destined to end with a whimper and not a wallop.

The talk shows in Boston were alive with invective, venom, finger pointing, and defeatism. There were calls for Terry Francona's head on a platter. He was being called another Grady Little, a name tantamount to Benedict Arnold in its infamy throughout these benighted colonies. In New

York, radio stations and tabloids were crowing loud and long about yet another Boston choke . . . like the one in 2003, the one in 1986, the one in 1978 . . . and on and on. The only Sox fans heard from, though, were those who still had enough energy left.

Most fans were beaten down, subdued. There was no chance now. Again and again, we were reminded that no team, ever, had come back from a 0-3 deficit to win the final four games. For the second year in a row, it looked like the Yankees would whip the Red Sox and go on to represent the American League in the World Series, but this time without even a respectable challenge by the Sox.

And so Game Four of the 2004 American League Championship Series was poised like a rusty guillotine above the bowed necks of Red Sox Nation. With the New York Yankees leading the ALCS three games to none—the last game a disheartening, embarrassing, soul-destroying slaughter in front of their own fans at Fenway Park—the only thing remaining was the final, fateful blow. At least the end would be quick.

It wasn't as if the Red Sox had not lost before, but they had always managed to make it excruciatingly close, to come within five outs—or even one strike—of victory. This time was embarrassing. Humiliating. This time it was nothing but a rout. Could anything conceivably be worse for a Sox fan? We're used to defeat, but this was shameful. 19-8. A sinking feeling that could sink no lower. Boston had bottomed out. We were reminded time and time again that no team had ever come back from such depths. We were condemned to another long winter, and another spring and summer of "19-18" taunts and T-shirts. The next season would find us all bewildered, groping to find any semblance of self-respect as Sox fans. At least there was some healing over the months after 2003's Game Seven. If the 2004 Sox were swept by the Evil Empire, the wound was going to sting and fester and might never heal. If it scarred over at all, the scars were going to run deep.

How did it all come to this? Let's step back and review a little of the history between these two teams, before resuming the story of the 2004 American League pennant race.

Chapter 2
The Blessing and the Curse
of the Bambino

"Blessed* shall you be in the city, and blessed shall you be in the field." —Deuteronomy 28:3

"Cursed** shall you be in the city, and cursed shall you be in the field." —Deuteronomy 28:16

"Dig him up and I'll drill him in the ass." —Pedro Martinez

He certainly was a blessing* in one city (New York) and on one baseball field (Yankee Stadium); and his curse**, real or imagined, has afflicted the other city (Boston), and the other baseball field (Fenway Park) for over eight decades.

The "curse of the Bambino" is a phrase known nationwide by baseball fans, and throughout New England by virtually everyone with a pulse. The notion of a curse visited upon the Red Sox by Babe Ruth may have first been put before a suggestible public in an October 1986 article by George Vecsey of The *New York Times*. In fairness to Vecsey, no one could have foreseen the orgy of curse-related activity that followed. History shows us that Boston won the first World Series in 1903, and then won again in 1912, 1915, 1916, and 1918. One of Boston's biggest stars for the latter two wins was George Herman Ruth—the Babe. He'd excelled both on the mound and at the plate. Though the Red Sox hadn't fared well in the 1919 pennant race, Ruth had a breakout offensive season with a then-astonishing 29 home runs, more than double the total of any previous American Leaguer.

After the 1919 season, however, Boston Red Sox owner Harry Frazee sold the Babe to the New York Yankees and the Red Sox didn't win another World Series for 86 years. The Sox initially suffered a dozen years that were about as bad as any team has ever endured, repeatedly coming in last in the standings. When wealthy Tom Yawkey purchased the team, they bought their way into contention, but never quite got over the hump—or the Curse. Not only did they never win a World Series during the nearly six decades of Yawkey family ownership, they suffered defeat after agonizing defeat, seemingly always in the ninth inning or even beyond.

In 1946, 1948, 1949, 1967, 1972, 1975, 1978, 1986, and 2003, the Red Sox were eliminated in sudden-death competition. Virtually every loss has its own assigned goat—whether the label was deserved or not.

Let's take a look at some of the post-1918 seasons in which the Sox fell short. We'll begin with the Babe. He'd led both leagues in home runs in 1918 and 1919, as he began the transition from pitcher to every day player. The most at-bats he'd had before 1918 was 136, but in 1918 he got 317, a total that increased to 432 in 1919. As a Red Sox batsman, he led the league in 1919 in homers, RBIs, runs scored, on-base percentage, and slugging—and even in fielding percentage! This made him a hot commodity, and the New York Yankees took advantage, purchasing him from the Red Sox. We won't go into the whys and wherefores here.

Boston seemed to have a dynasty in the making, but after Ruth left the Red Sox, it was a long, long time before they even contended once again. Even with Ruth, they'd already suffered a sixth-place finish in 1919. As a Ruth-less team, things only got worse. Where they'd finished 20½ games out of first place in 1919, in 1920 they were 25½ games back. Meanwhile, the new and improved Yankees finished just three games behind the league-leading Indians.

In the years that followed, the Red Sox went from bad to worse, from hapless to helpless to hopeless.

1921	Yankees first place, Red Sox fifth place (23½ games behind)
1922	Yankees first place, Red Sox last place (33 games behind)
1923	Yankees first place, Red Sox last place (37 games behind)
1924	Yankees second place, Red Sox next-to-last place (25 games behind)
1925	Yankees seventh place, Red Sox last place (49½ games behind)
1926	Yankees first place, Red Sox last place (44½ games behind)
1927	Yankees first place, Red Sox last place (59 games behind)
1928	Yankees first place, Red Sox last place (43½ games behind)
1929	Yankees second place, Red Sox last place (48 games behind)
1930	Yankees third place, Red Sox last place (50 games behind)
1931	Yankees second place, Red Sox sixth place (45 games behind)
1932	Yankees first place, Red Sox last place (64 games behind)
1933	Yankees second place, Red Sox next-to-last place (34½ games behind)

For Red Sox fans, this was, to say the least, a disturbing pattern.

Tom Yawkey bought the franchise in 1933 and began pouring money into the team, funding a major renovation for Fenway Park as well. The team gradually became more competitive.

Nonetheless, the years up to and including World War II saw the Yankees with 14 pennants. Ten times the New Yorkers won the World Championship. The Red Sox had zero and zero, for a grand total of zero.

Immediately after the war, Boston became even more competitive, and actually won the pennant in the first post-war campaign. Whenever it looked like they were poised to win it all, however, something always seemed to go wrong. As Johnny Pesky put it, "We thought there was a black cat on the squad or something."

The Yankees truly seemed to be God's favored team. They won 26 World Championships after signing Babe Ruth; the Red Sox won none through 2003. In a given year, the Sox might come out on top and make the World Series (mind you, this only happened four more times in the twentieth century), but even then something always went awry. They were like the guy in the TV advertisement who never seems to be able to seal the deal. Meanwhile, the Yankees won out as often as DiTech.com.

1946—The Cat and the Hat, the Mad Dash, and did Pesky hold the ball?

Every team got their stars back after World War II, but the Red Sox had an entire constellation returning. The team won its first five games, and just kept rolling. After the May 10 game, they were 21-3. They clinched early and finished the season with a 104-50 record. In hindsight, maybe they clinched *too* soon, and got a little rusty waiting for the World Series to begin.

The National League champion St. Louis Cardinals were a strong club, led by future Hall-of-Famer Stan Musial. Finishing the season tied with the Dodgers, the Cardinals won the first two games in a "best-of-three" play-off—while the idle Red Sox continued to kill time and wait. The 1946 American League MVP, Ted Williams, was hit on the arm and seriously injured while trying to keep in shape. He ended up having a disastrous Series.

When the Series finally got underway, the Sox and St. Louis traded wins, alternately winning and losing until it came to Game Seven on October 15. It was Boston's turn to win; and most observers expected them to do so. The final game mirrored the seesaw nature of the Series. Boston scored once in the first inning, and St. Louis matched that in the bottom of the second. Then the Cardinals took a 3-1 lead, scoring twice in the fifth. When Boston batted in the top of the eighth, they tied it up, 3-3. Two pinch-hitters, Russell and Metkovich, singled and doubled, respectively, putting Boston men on second and third with nobody out. Cardinals manager Eddie Dyer turned to his ace Harry Brecheen, who'd thrown a complete game 4-1 win just two days earlier. Harry "The Cat" got the next two batters, but Dominic DiMaggio doubled to drive in both Sox runners. Unfortunately, "the little professor" pulled a muscle while taking second base and had to be replaced by Leon Culberson. Culberson took his position in centerfield, and Red Sox players made mental notes that the replacement would be distinctly weaker on defense. Ted Williams came to the plate with a chance to drive in Boston's go-ahead run but the newly returned war hero popped up instead.

With the score tied, the Cardinals came up to bat in the bottom of the eighth and Sox skipper Joe Cronin called on Bob Klinger in relief. Enos Slaughter singled to lead off for St. Louis. He stayed put on first, though, as the Sox got the first out, and then the second. Had Cronin brought in lefty Earl Johnson to face Harry "The Hat" Walker (he'd hit .237 in the regular season, but was hitting .375 at this point in the Series), Slaughter would have had to stick a little closer to first base. Dyer might even have pinch-hit for Walker. Cronin stuck with Klinger, and when Harry "The Hat" Walker lined a pitch to left-center, Slaughter was off and running before the pitch left Klinger's hand—and he just kept on going. It was called Slaughter's "mad dash."

On what was scored a double, but was really a routine single, Culberson fielded the ball and tossed it in an arc to Sox shortstop Johnny Pesky on the edge of the outfield grass. Everyone in Sportsman's Park assumed Slaughter would pull up at third, and that Marty Marion would be up with runners at first and third. Except that Slaughter kept running, motoring around third base, streaking for the plate. By the time Pesky wheeled to throw, it was already too late. Did Pesky "hold the ball"? All the participants agree that Pesky had no shot at nailing Slaughter. Had the fleet DiMaggio been in the outfield, many observers thought he might have even caught the ball. But that discussion would have to wait for the hot-stove league. The Cardinals took a 4-3 lead. Cronin brought in Earl Johnson, who got the final out.

In the ninth, the Red Sox had a golden opportunity. Rudy York singled to lead off the ninth. Bobby Doerr followed with another single. With runners at first and second, Pinky Higgins bunted a little too hard and right at third baseman Kurowski, who threw to second base—rather than first—forcing Doerr. Pinch-runner Paul Campbell took third. First and third, still just one out, but Roy Partee fouled out to Musial at first base and it came down to the final out. Tom McBride batted for Johnson, and grounded the ball to the second baseman. The glacially slow Higgins was out, but not by much. Three times in the Series, the Sox had held the early edge in runs, but three times the Cardinals had tied it back up. Boston had held the lead in the first inning of this Game Seven as well, but couldn't bring home the bacon. Wait till next year, said Red Sox fans, confident that they now had an excellent contending team.

1948—Galehouse turned ghostly white

Still smarting from their defeat in the '46 Series, the Sox geared up to return and make amends. When virtually every pitcher on the staff was stricken with a sore arm in 1947, the year was lost, but in 1948 they finished the season in first place, with 96 wins against 58 losses. The only problem was: the Cleveland Indians were there too, with the very same record. With four games to play, the Sox had been two games behind the Indians, but Boston swept all four and Cleveland was on the short end of two of them. The dead heat tie required a single-game playoff and the venue was Fenway Park.

Even though rookie Gene Bearden had pitched a shutout just two days before, Cleveland manager Lou Boudreau called on him once again. Bearden was hot. He'd won three games in the previous eight days, with back-to-back shutouts on September 28 and October 2. He'd also won six games in a row since September 10 and had the lowest earned run average in the American League. Still, he was being asked to pitch on one day's rest. Most people figured Boston manager Joe McCarthy would choose Mel Parnell to start for the Red Sox. He had the best ERA on the Red Sox and had had three days off.

"I was disappointed that I didn't pitch that ballgame," says Parnell today. "My family had me in bed at nine o'clock the night before because I'd be pitching in the biggest game of my career the next day. I went to the ballpark expecting to be the starting pitcher. Joe McCarthy puts his hand on my shoulder and I turned around and McCarthy says, 'Mel, I've changed my mind, I'm going with the right-hander because the wind is blowing out strong to left field and the elements are against the left-hander today.' But hell, I've pitched many ballgames when the wind was blowing out and it didn't make any difference. He second-guessed himself to go with Denny Galehouse."

Ellis Kinder was another possible option for McCarthy; he too was rested and ready. But the legendary manager opted to rest the hopes of the team on Galehouse. In fairness, Galehouse was experienced, and he'd pitched extremely well against the Indians earlier in the year, throwing more than eight innings of relief and allowing but two hits. But apparently the Red Sox manager had forgotten the game on August 26, when Galehouse was driven from the mound by the Indians in a 9-0 rout that catapulted the Tribe into first place. Maybe he also forgot that Galehouse's last start was way back on September 18 or that he'd been knocked out in the fourth during that game. Or that, according to an interview of Galehouse by Glenn Stout, he'd spent a full six innings (!) warming up in the bullpen the day before, as Boston played the Yankees in a "must-win" game. "When McCarthy told him he was pitching that day," recalls Parnell, "Galehouse turned ghostly white because it was such a shock to him, and I think the ballclub was a bit disillusioned as well. Really it was my ballgame to pitch."

Cleveland player-manager Boudreau hit a solo homer in the first inning but Boston answered with a run of their own in the bottom of the frame. Boudreau singled to lead off the fourth, and scored when Ken Keltner hit a 3-run homer a few batters later. Galehouse was shown to the showers. Kinder gave up a run, and another Boudreau solo home run in the fifth. It was 6-1, Cleveland, before Bobby Doerr rekindled Bosox hopes with a 2-run homer in the sixth. It was too little too late. The final score was 8-3. They hadn't stood a chance. For the second time in three years, the Red Sox lost a final sudden-death game. "I remember Dave Egan later wrote a column saying that no one wanted to pitch that game," says Parnell with a trace of bitterness. "That was false. Everyone would have welcomed the opportunity to pitch that game."

Wait till next year.

"I was known as a Yankee killer. My best year against them was 1953. I beat them five times and shut them out four times. You just played a little harder against them." —Mel Parnell

1949—Beaten on the final day of the year, in New York

Though they didn't have a winning record until May 23, when they were 15-14, the Sox closed strongly, winning twelve of the last thirteen games they played in September. They'd won their last four meetings with the

Yankees, and at the end of the month held a one-game lead over New York with but two games to play—in New York. Should the Sox win either game, the pennant was theirs.

The October 1st game got off to a great start, from Boston's perspective. The Sox scored once in the first, then scored three more in the third; it was so bad that both Al Zarilla and Billy Goodman drew bases-loaded walks. Things were falling apart rapidly for the Yankees, but New York rarely goes down without a battle. They find a way to win so often, it's almost expected. The Yanks tied it up with a couple of runs in the fourth, and another pair in the fifth. 4-4 after five. So it stood until the bottom of the eighth, when Johnny Lindell banged a line drive home run down the left field line off Joe Dobson. Joe Page, pitching 6⅔ innings of relief, held the Sox scoreless in the ninth, and the Yankees lived to fight another day. Both teams now sported identical 96-57 records, tied for first place.

As day dawned in New York on October 2nd, baseball fans didn't know what to expect. Both teams had strong pitchers going, but little or nothing to back them up in the bullpen. New York scored first, in the bottom of the first, but then six more innings passed with no scoring by either side. 1-0, Yankees, after seven. Boston was blanked in the top of the next inning, but then the Yankees pounced for four runs and a 5-0 lead in the bottom of the eighth. Tommy Henrich hit a homer to kick off the scoring, but the crushing blow was Jerry Coleman's bases-clearing double. The hard-drinking Ellis Kinder had beaten the Yankees four times in '49, had won 13 in a row, and hadn't lost a decision in 21 straight starts. His streak had finally run out. Ted Williams misplayed a ball, leading to a run in the first, made an error on another play in the eighth, and failed to get a hit, though he did manage to work a couple of walks.

Bobby Doerr tripled in two in the top of the ninth, and scored on Billy Goodman's hit, but the three runs were two too few. Now it was two years in a row, and three of the last four that Red Sox hopes died on the final day of the year. Was this team cursed? Wait till next year? Not quite. "Wait till 1967!" should have been the cry. Eighteen more years would pass into the record books before they came to this point again.

"The majority of American males put themselves to sleep by striking out the batting order of the New York Yankees."—James Thurber

1967 — An Impossible Dream

No one expected the Red Sox to compete in 1967. They'd finished with one foot on the cellar stairs in 1966, deep in ninth place, 26 games out of first. The only team that performed worse was the New York Yankees, who were 26½ games out. Even Dale Carnegie would have been hard-pressed to think positive thoughts about the pennant hopes of this team. Anyone crazy enough to predict that the Sox would win it all in '67 would have been facing committal to a maximum-security mental health facility for their own protection. It was an Impossible Dream.

But it was a dream that came true thanks to a truly impossible season by the man called Yastrzemski. It was a tight race, but they did it thanks to daily heroics by Yaz and a strong supporting cast. Everything seemed to come together in this Year of Yaz. Captain Carl even won the Triple Crown, the last time any player in either league has accomplished the feat.

The Red Sox clinched on the afternoon of October 1, scoring five runs in the bottom of the sixth for a 5-3 win over the Minnesota Twins. That eliminated the Twins from competition. Check the standings—the Twins and the Tigers tied for second place, both just one game behind the Red Sox. The Yankees improved from .440 to .444, and worked their way up the ladder to ninth place. These were uncharacteristically tough times for the Yanks—from 1965 to 1972, they failed to finish better than 15 games out.

The World Series was a reprise of the 1946 October Classic, pitting Boston against the Cardinals some 21 years after St. Louis had come out on top. Both teams had monster starting pitchers: St. Louis' staff was anchored by the glowering Bob Gibson and Boston's by the glowing Jim Lonborg.

Gibson held the Red Sox to one run in Game One, their only tally a surprise home run by Bosox starting pitcher Jose Santiago, who allowed only two runs but had to absorb the defeat. Lonborg shut out St. Louis in Game Two as Yaz stroked two homers. St. Louis won Game Three, 5-2. Gibson didn't allow Boston a single run in Game Four, and the Cardinals had a 3-1 edge in the Series. It was Gentleman Jim Lonborg back on the mound for Boston in Game Five and the man who would later become a dentist anesthetized the Cardinal bats. St. Louis managed only one run and lost, 3-1. Boston evened the Series at three each with a win back in Beantown, 8-4.

It was down to Game Seven. Both managers had saved their aces, and it was Gibson against Lonborg at Fenway. Gibson threw a 3-hitter and let in two runs; Lonborg wasn't sharp. He gave up seven runs on 10 hits, including a home run by Gibson that proved to be the game-winning hit. St. Louis won, 7-2. Just as in 1946, Boston brought it to the final game. Just as in 1946, the Sox fell short to St. Louis.

1972—Not heads-up ball

Both Boston and New York pretty much stunk in the seasons '68 through '71, but in the strike-shortened year of 1972, Boston almost pulled out another pennant. Way back in April, when the strike was settled, it was agreed that the teams would all play out their schedules and that should they wind up the season having played an unequal number of games, then so be it. That would be that. It had been nip and tuck between the Tigers and the Red Sox for some time, but when September ended, the Red Sox held a 1½ game lead over the Tigers. There were four games to play and, as fate would have it, the last three were face to face. Baltimore beat Boston, 2-1, on October 1, when a double play let Mike Cuellar escape despite having served up back-to-back singles in the top of the ninth. And the Tigers mellowed out Milwaukee, 5-1. Detroit was now just a half a game behind Boston, who came to Tiger Stadium for the last three games of the season.

In effect, it became a short best-of-three series. Whichever team won two took the title. The Tigers scored first, one run on Al Kaline's home run in the bottom of the first. Detroit's Mickey Lolich struck out Boston pitcher John Curtis in the third, but Tommy Harper singled and then Luis Aparicio did the same, sending Harper to third. Carl Yastrzemski tripled to center field. Harper scored easily, but—wait—Aparicio stumbled, twice, and decided to scramble back to third base where he met up with his teammate, Yaz , who was there, too. Captain Carl had his head down, running hard, and hadn't seen Aparicio's slip. The relay 8-6-1-5 resulted in Yaz being tagged out; he had to settle for a double in the books. Only one run scored, not two, and there were now two outs, not one. Lolich struck out Reggie Smith.

An Aurelio Rodriguez home run in the fifth was Detroit's game-winning hit; the final score was 4-1. The date was October 2. Nothing good ever seemed to happen to the Red Sox on October 2. See, for instance, 1949 (above) and 1978 (below).

When the Red Sox lost again the following day, 3-1, it was all over and even their 4-1 win on October 4 couldn't make up the difference. If the Sox had had the chance to play the same number of games as Detroit, they might have won the "missing" game. As it was, the season ended with both teams having lost 70 games, but whereas Boston won 85, Detroit won 86. The Tigers flew to Oakland for the ALCS. The Red Sox flew home and dispersed. At least this time it didn't come down to the last game, but in a sense the last game *never happened*, due to the way the strike left the season unequal. No matter how you look at it, the official record showed the Tigers in first place and the Sox in second, half a game back. Curse the strike!

1975—When Game Seven was anti-climactic

Many feel the 1975 World Series was the greatest Fall Classic ever played, though 1912, 1924, and 2001 have to rank right up there. This time, it was the Red Sox pitted against Cincinnati's Big Red Machine. To get to the Series, the Sox had to win the Division and then capture the AL pennant. The capture of the A.L. East crown was never in question; they maintained a halfway comfortable lead from mid-July on. Winning the ALCS was even easier; they swept Oakland in three games, out-hitting and out-pitching the A's by pretty wide margins. In the Series, they were evenly matched. The Red Sox, nevertheless, sorely missed Boston strongman Jim Rice, whose wrist was broken in a late September game.

Luis Tiant shut out the Reds in Game One, 6-0 as the Sox scored all six runs in the bottom of the seventh. The rest of the games were closer. The Reds took Games Two and Three, 3-2 (scoring two in the top of the ninth) and 6-5 (winning at home in the bottom of the tenth).

Five runs in the fourth inning of Game Four gave Boston their second win. In Game Five, Cincinnati won handily, 6-2. The Reds were ahead in the Series, three games to two, and the Series shifted back to Boston.

Game Six was the big one. Finally getting underway, with everyone rested but antsy after three straight rainouts, Boston got three runs in the bottom of the first on Fred Lynn's 3-run homer. There the score remained until the top of the fifth, when Cincinnati tied it up. Then the Reds moved closer to the world championship by jumping ahead by two runs in the seventh, and adding one more for a three-run lead in the top of the eighth. The Sox got the first two runners on in the eighth but seemed about to leave them stranded when Evans struck out and Burleson lined to left field. The Reds were just four outs away from wrapping it up. The Fenway faithful were struck silent until pinch-hitter and future hairdresser Bernie Carbo hit a tremendous shot into the center field bleachers, tying the score. It was a brand new game.

There was no scoring in the ninth, nor the tenth, nor the eleventh. The Sox got a single in the ninth and the Reds got one in the tenth, but there wasn't much happening offensively for either team. Rick Wise came in to pitch for Boston and Cincinnati singled twice in the top of the twelfth, but Wise got out of the inning otherwise unscathed, the score still tied at 6. First batter up in the bottom of the twelfth, against Pat Darcy, was Red Sox catcher Carlton Fisk. Any halfway attentive fan of baseball has seen the film clip at least a dozen times. Fisk hit a towering fly right down the left field foul line, and the TV camera positioned inside the Green Monster caught Fisk leaping up, leaping up, using eloquent body English to try to wave the ball fair. It was a matter of inches, but those inches saved the day. Fisk hit a walk-off home run and sent the crowd home on such a high that Game Seven was almost anti-climactic.

Boston started the scoring once again, staking starter Bill Lee to a 3-0 lead in Game Seven. After five full innings, the score remained 3-0 in the Red Sox' favor. Then Tony Perez hit a two-run homer in the top of the sixth, to bring the Reds within a run. They tied up the game with another run in the top of the seventh and had the bases loaded but reliever Jim Willoughby came in and got Johnny Bench to pop out foul. Willoughby set down the Reds 1-2-3 in the eighth. After eight innings, it was Boston 3, Cincinnati 3. With two outs in the bottom of the eighth, manager Darrell Johnson had put in pinch-hitter Scott Cooper to bat for Willoughby. Cooper fouled out, just as Bench had done.

The whole season came down to the final inning of the final game of the World Series. Would it go extra innings again?

In the top of the ninth, with Jim Burton taking over for Willoughby, Ken Griffey walked and was sacrificed to second by Geronimo's bunt. Driessen made the second out on a grounder to second base, but Griffey moved up to third on the play. Pete Rose walked. Then Joe Morgan lofted a soft bloop hit into centerfield, scoring Griffey and giving the Reds the lead. Morgan took second on a throw in to third base, but the Reds had runners at second and third. Bench walked to fill the bases, and Perez flied out to left. For years afterward, Sox fans bemoaned the ninth inning turn of the screw, asking rhetorically of Johnson: "Why did you take out Willoughby?"

McEnaney came in and shut the Sox down 1-2-3. Game over. Series over. The Red Sox had been eliminated in a Game Seven for the second time in a row in front of the Fenway faithful.

1978—Dent over the Wall

The Red Sox played strong baseball for the first half of the season and, as of July 19, a week after the All-Star Game, the Sox held a 14-game lead over the Yankees. The Yankees were in fourth place, with the Brewers nine games behind Boston and the Orioles 12½ games back. Then the slide began; Boston lost nine of their next ten games, while New York won seven out of eight. By the 27th, the Yankees had picked up six full games. The Sox season stabilized, and for nearly the next month, the standings were more or less static between the two clubs. As late as August 21, the Yankees still trailed the Red Sox by 8½ games. And most ballclubs wouldn't mind seeing a 6½ game lead on September 1. Boston won six games in a row at the end of August. Things just didn't look that bad.

Then they lost five out of seven, while the Yankees made up ground. Those very same Yankees turned up at Fenway for a four-game series, only four games behind on September 7. The Yankees took the first game, 15-3. Oops. They took the second game, 13-2. This was starting to look serious. The third game was a 7-0 shutout, and the Yankees were just one game from being tied. With a September 10 win (7-4) on the fourth and final day of what was to become known as the "Boston Massacre," New York surged to a first-place tie with the Red Sox. In the four games, the Yankees had outscored the Red Sox 42-9. Boston's big 14-game balloon had burst. Was this team really cursed?

The worst wasn't over yet. A mere collapse would be one thing, but the way to really torture your fans is to revive them and to see their hope rekindled—only to snuff them again. The Sox got the lead back the next day, but New York was in sole possession of first place on the 13th and led Boston by 3½ games by the 16th. A week later, on the 23rd, Boston battled back to just one game behind. For one full week, that held—the Yankees won six in a row and the Sox matched them game for game. Finally, on October 1, the final day of the regular season, Catfish Hunter imploded, allowing 5 runs in 1⅔ innings and New York lost to the Indians, 7-2. Meanwhile, Luis Tiant was in Boston working on a two-hit, 5-0 shutout of the Blue Jays, which wrapped up just moments later. The scoreboard watchers knew the Yankees had lost; when the Sox game concluded, the Fenway Park ticket office announced that tickets for the one-game playoff for the following day were on sale, and half the crowd left their seats to stand in line and snap up the precious ducats.

OCTOBER 2, 1978

"Louisiana Lightnin' " Ron Guidry against former Yankee Mike Torrez. Guidry got touched first, when Yaz homered to lead off the second. Boston added another run on a Rick Burleson double, a Jerry Remy sacrifice bunt, and a single to center by Jim Rice. After six, it was Boston 2, New York 0.

With one out in the top of the seventh, Chris Chambliss singled, then Roy White did the same. Jim Spencer flied out to left. Two down. Bucky Dent stepped into the batter's box. The guy had four home runs on the season, 37 RBIs. This was no bench player, however; he'd been in 122 games to this point in the season, batting .239. But it was no accident that he was batting ninth in the order. If anything, he was expected to do what he did his next time up—strike out. He was 0-for-2 in the game, a routine fly ball and a routine grounder. Torrez tried to sneak one by him, and normally it would have worked. Not this day. Dent's high drive just barely cleared the Wall in left field. It wouldn't have dented it; it wasn't hit that hard. The score was, suddenly and unexpectedly, 4-2. Around New England, for decades afterward, Bucky Dent became known as Bucky F***ing Dent, so if the Red Sox were cursed, so, quite literally, was he.

The Yankees got one more run that inning, and another in the eighth when Reggie Jackson homered. With one out in the bottom of the eighth, Jerry Remy led off with a double. After Rice flied out, Yaz singled to center, scoring Remy. 5-3. Fisk singled, and so did Fred Lynn, scoring Captain Carl. 5-4. But Hobson and Scott both made outs. Would parallel construction win out here? Sox up, then down, only to pull even at the final moment? The Yankees didn't score in the top of the ninth. Dwight Evans pinch-hit and flied out to left, but then Burleson walked and Remy singled. The Red Sox had runners on first and second, with Jim Rice (who'd reached 400 total bases in 1978) up next, and Carl Yastrzemski after him. Rice flied out to right, but there was still a glimmer of hope as Burleson tagged up and went to third base. The drama was intense, but then suddenly deflated as Yaz popped up to Graig Nettles at third base. The notion of a curse sank its fangs deeper into the New England psyche.

"When the Yankees lost Don Zimmer in the off-season, they lost the man who was instrumental to their World Series victories in 2000, 1999, and 1978." —Conan O'Brien

1986—Don't blame just Buckner

Seventeen other teams made the post-season over the next eight seasons, but not the Red Sox. The next time the Sox reached post-season play was in 1986. The California Angels crushed Roger Clemens and the Red Sox in Game One of the ALCS, but Bruce Hurst limited the Angels to two runs in Game Two, and Boston won handily, 9-2. Old warhorse Bill Buckner singled and came around to score the winning run in the fifth; he scored again and hit a sacrifice fly to drive in a third run. Oil Can Boyd started Game Three, driven from the mound by two homers in the seventh as the Angels took the series lead. In Game Four, the Angels were down 3-0 heading into the bottom of the ninth. After a homer and two singles, Clemens was relieved by Calvin Schiraldi. A double, an intentional walk, and finally a hit-by-pitch drove in the final run, and the Angels had tied it up. A single, a sacrifice, another intentional walk, and then a single by Bobby Grich won it for California in the bottom of the eleventh. The Angels now had a 3 games to 1 lead.

The Angels took a 5-2 lead into the ninth inning during Game Five in Anaheim. In the sixth inning, Red Sox outfielder Dave Henderson had a Bobby Grich ball glance off his glove and go over the fence for a home run. It was the go-ahead run, and Henderson looked to be the goat. A two-run HR by Don Baylor in the top of the ninth cut the lead to 5-4. There were two outs. Needing to get just one batter out, Gary Lucas came in to relieve

Bobby Witt, and promptly hit Rich Gedman. Angels manager Gene Mauch yanked Lucas and put in Donnie Moore. Dave Henderson, making dramatic amends for his earlier embarrassment, hit a home run off Moore, and the Sox had a 6-5 lead. But wait. The Angels got one in the bottom of the ninth to send the game into extra innings. Moore hit Baylor to lead off the eleventh. Baylor, a specialist at getting hit by pitches, promptly did so; he was hit 35 times during the 1986 regular season. Two singles moved Baylor to second, and then to third. Then Dave Henderson came through again, hitting a sacrifice fly to drive him in. The Sox won, 7-6.

When Kirk McCaskill allowed the Red Sox to post seven runs in 2⅓ innings, it was all over in Game Six and the Sox had tied the ALCS at three games apiece. Boston walked all over John Candelaria for seven runs in 3⅔ innings in Game Seven. The two games were 10-4 and 8-1. It was Game Five that held all the drama.

The New York Mets were the pennant winners in the National League, and the Series opened strangely. Boston won the first two games in New York, and New York won the first two games in Boston. Game One was a tight 1-0 win, Bruce Hurst facing Ron Darling. The only run was unearned, in the seventh inning. A walk, a wild pitch, a grounder, and an error by second baseman Tim Teufel resulted in the lone score. Hurst won Game Five, the first time in the Series that the hometown fans got to see a win. It wouldn't be the last; New York fans soon had that pleasure.

Game Six started with a run for the Red Sox in the first, and another run for the Red Sox in the second. The Mets tied it up in the bottom of the fifth, the second run scoring as Boston pulled off a double play. Boston benefited from an unearned run in the seventh, and the Mets tied it back up with a sac fly in the bottom of the eighth. The game went into the tenth, tied 3-3. ALCS hero Dave Henderson homered to lead off the tenth. With two outs, Boggs doubled and Marty Barrett singled to drive him in. 5-3, Red Sox, going into the bottom of the tenth. If they could only hold on and win, the Red Sox would capture their first World Series since 1918. But even though this wasn't the Yankees, this was New York, and these were the Red Sox. Calvin Schiraldi had hit for himself in the top of the tenth. He was clearly the pitcher for manager John McNamara. McNamara didn't change his defense either; he left Bill Buckner in to play first base.

Schiraldi got the first two outs in the tenth. One out from a World Series win, the first time in 68 years. Then Carter singled. Then pinch-hitter Kevin Mitchell singled. Then Ray Knight singled, scoring Carter while Mitchell took third. Bob Stanley was brought in to relieve the shaken Schiraldi. The Maine native threw a wild pitch (some argue that Gedman should have been charged with a passed ball) and Mitchell scored the tying run. Mookie Wilson then hit an easy skittering inning-ending grounder right to Bill Buckner, who was guarding the line at first base. Except . . . the ball went right through Buckner out into right field and infamy, and Ray Knight scored on Buckner's error, an error that he will never and can never—some would even say should never—live down. The Mets win forced a Game Seven.

Why was the gimpy Buckner playing first base with a two-run lead? Ask John McNamara. In Game One, with the Red Sox ahead, Dave Stapleton replaced Buckner for defensive purposes in the eighth inning. In Game Two, Stapleton ran for Buckner and stayed in at first for defense. The Mets had handy leads in Games Three and Four, so Buckner stayed in the line-up for his bat (he had 102 RBIs in 1986). In Game Five, Stapleton replaced Buckner in the ninth. Back in the ALCS, Stapleton had spelled Buckner in Games Two, Four, Five, Six, and Seven. So there was a firm managerial precedent. McNamara ignored the precedent, or perhaps was too senti-mental, thinking Buckner should be on the field to celebrate the win. Thanks a lot, Mac.

The Red Sox did have another shot at the title in Game Seven. It was Hurst against Darling again, and Hurst looked to be set for his third win of the Series as the Sox stepped out first with three runs in the second. They held a 3-0 lead after 5½, but the Mets strung together three singles and a walk and scored a pair of runs, tying the game when a third run crossed the plate on a force play. They added three more in the seventh when the Sox sent in Schiraldi, who totally imploded. The only out he recorded was on a sacrifice. Boston crept back to within a run, scoring twice in the top of the eighth but the Mets put the final nails in the coffin with two more of their own in the bottom of the eighth. The Curse was born.

1988—Eckersley and Canseco were on the wrong team

Boston made the post-season, but was swept by Oakland in four straight games. Dennis Eckersley saved all four games. Jose Canseco hit three home runs for the A's. Gene Nelson—who?—won two Series games. The Sox batted .206 as a team. We'd rather not say any more about this.

1990—Boston scored but one run in each game

Boston made the post-season, but this time the Sox only batted .183 while the A's played small-ball and swept in four straight games, despite only making four extra-base hits—all doubles. Clemens allowed his anger to take him out of Game Four, exploding in fury at calls from the home-plate umpire and getting himself tossed from a game the Sox could not afford to lose. They lost. No further comment needed.

1995—Vaughn and Canseco, 0-for-27

Boston made the post-season but, despite a thrilling 13-inning first game, was swept by Cleveland in three straight games. The Sox improved their post-season team average from an anemic .183 in 1990 to a lusty .184, but sluggers Mo Vaughn and Jose Canseco (now with Boston) combined to go 0-for-27, striking out nine times between them. With men in scoring position, the Sox had two hits in 28 tries.

Beginning to detect a pattern here? With the loss of the last two games in the 1986 World Series, and three consecutive sweeps, the Red Sox lost thirteen straight post-season games. This was no longer a curse of being eliminated at the last minute, but another kind of curse altogether—to win the division, but to have the door slammed in your face the minute you hit the playoffs. There was no post-season in 1994, or who knows what would have

---

"If a bullet is ever fired at New York City Detective Tony Petrocelli's chest the lead would have to pierce a Red Sox patch sewn directly over the center of his Kevlar vest." So wrote Michele McPhee in a December 27, 2004 article in the *Boston Herald* about Rico's nephew, a 19-year veteran of the New York Police Department. He may be the only Red Sox fan among the 36,000-strong department of New York's finest.

"I am in enemy territory every day," Petrocelli, 41, told McPhee. "I walk into work with this patch on and defy my fellow cops to shoot me.

I have to keep my vest well-guarded 'cause they all want to rip the patch off," he laughed. "I tell 'em, touch my vest, I'll shoot you."

happened there? Actually, not much of anything for Boston. The Sox were seventeen games out when a work stoppage brought the season to its finale and Major League Baseball called off the World Series.

1998—Sox jump start the short series, but Cleveland closes it out

In '99, Boston broke the drought and tasted victory for the first time since Game Five, 1986, beating the Cleveland Indians handily, 11-3 in the first game of the best-of-five ALDS. Two Mo Vaughn homers and one by Nomar Garciaparra gave the Sox an 8-0 lead after 5½. Pedro Martinez won the game, with a little help from Jim Corsi. Then . . . well . . . then the Indians won the next three. Still . . . the Sox finally did show they could win a post-season game.

1999—Sox vs. Yanks for the first time in post-season play

A rematch with the Indians in the Division Series, and it seemed like a retread. The Indians won the first game, though it was a close one (3-2) and the winning run scored with one out in the bottom of the ninth. A guy named Manny Ramirez who'd been hit by a Derek Lowe pitch moved up on a single, moved up on a walk, and scored on Travis Fryman's single to left field. The Indians won the second game, 11-1. Not a pretty game for either Saberhagen or Wasdin. After losing five in a row to the Indians, and therefore 18 of their last 19 post-season games, the Sox traveled on to Cleveland and broke out the bats. Valentin's double and Daubach's homer helped the Sox score six times to break a 3-3 tie in the seventh inning. Final score, 9-3.

Game Four was a slugfest. 23-7, Boston. Game Five, the deciding game, was a 12-8 victory. It was 5-2 for the Tribe after the first two innings, but Troy O'Leary's grand slam in the third (after the Indians walked Nomar intentionally to get to O'Leary) put Boston in the lead, 7-5. The Indians scored three times in the bottom of the third to take a slim 8-7 edge. A sac fly brought in an unearned run for Boston in the fourth. 8-8, and so it stayed until the seventh. John Valentin singled to lead off, and moved to second base on a ground-out. Nomar was walked intentionally to get to O'Leary. Deja-vu all over again: O'Leary homered, this time a three-run shot. 11-8, for Boston. In the top of the ninth, with a man on second and one out, Nomar was up again. Walk him to get to O'Leary? No, pitch to Garciaparra. Garciaparra doubled. 12-8. O'Leary was the one walked intentionally this time, and fortunately for Cleveland Mike Stanley struck out and Varitek's grounder forced O'Leary at second. But the damage was done. The win allowed the Sox to move on to the ALCS and face the New York Yankees in the best-of-seven battle for the pennant.

At Yankee Stadium, the Yankees won two close ones, 4-3 (in 10 innings) and 3-2. An early 3-0 Red Sox lead went for naught as New York nibbled and clawed back with two in the second and the tying run in the seventh. The game went into extra innings, but the first batter up in the bottom of the tenth, facing new Sox reliever Rod Beck, was Bernie Williams and he hit a walk-off homer to win Game One. New York won the second game, another close game, 3-2. The two teams moved to Boston for the next three games.

Game Three was billed as a pitcher's duel between two of the greatest pitchers of the late 20th century—five-time Cy Young Award winner Roger Clemens, hated in Boston for joining the Yankees, against Roger's replacement, Pedro Martinez, who'd already won the Cy Young in the National League and (with his 23-4 mark and 2.07 ERA) was clearly going to win it this year in the American League. Pedro pitched well, giving up just two hits in seven innings, while striking out 12 Yankees. Roger, well, he didn't get past the second inning, hit hard for five runs on six hits. The Red Sox won in a lopsided laugher, 13-1.

The laughter was short-lived, though. The Yankees beat Boston easily the next day, 9-2, and easily again the day after that, 6-1. New York got the last laugh, taking the ALCS four games to one, and then sweeping the Atlanta Braves in the World Series to win their 25th World Championship.

2003—Little knowledge can be a dangerous thing

For a while, it didn't look like the Sox would make it past the first round. In extra innings, Oakland finally beat the Red Sox, before the home crowd on the less sung about side of the Bay. In the first game, the A's were down by one but tied it in the bottom of the ninth. It took 12 innings, but they won, 5-4, on a Ramon Hernandez bases-loaded single. They got five runs in the second inning and also won the second game, 5-1.

The first game in Boston presented the spectre of elimination for the Red Sox, Ted Lilly against Derek Lowe. After ten innings, the score was 1-1. The low score was deceptive; it was a bizarre game, with poor baserunning robbing the A's of opportunities. Byrnes seemed to score from third on a fielder's choice and a wild throw to home plate, but Varitek blocked the plate effectively and Byrnes focused more on his hurt ankle, perhaps not realizing he'd failed to touch the plate. He wandered away, giving Varitek time to retrieve the ball, chase him down, and tag him out. Two batters later, after Hernandez reached on a Nomar error, Sox third baseman Bill Mueller and Miguel Tejada got tangled up and Tejada was convinced it was obstruction. Incredibly, he stopped to argue the point, rather than running home. As a result of choosing debate over de base, he was tagged with the ball and declared out. There was obstruction, the umpires ruled, but it was prior to Tejada reaching third. He was therefore awarded third base, but when he left third base to go halfway home, that was at his peril and he was ruled out. With all that happening in one inning, the A's got just one run. It tied the game, though, and it stayed tied through the top of the eleventh. With Mirabelli on base, Trot Nixon hit a walk-off homer and Boston won, 3-1.

Boston edged Oakland in Game Four, 5-4, a David Ortiz two-run double in the bottom of the eighth the deciding blow. Traveling back across the country for the deciding game in the best of five ALDS, a Varitek homer and a three-run Manny Ramirez homer gave the Sox four runs in the top of the sixth. The A's got a run in the sixth and a run in the eighth, but it was another one-run Red Sox win and the A's failed to get past the first round of the playoffs for the fourth straight time.

The Red Sox had now advanced to the ALCS, earning the right to go against the New York Yankees. Boston took the first game, at Yankee Stadium, 5-2, on the strength of a monster third-deck homer by Ortiz, a controversial homer by Todd Walker first called foul but then overruled after an umpire's conference, and a Ramirez roundtripper. And a strong start by Tim Wakefield. In Game Two, Derek Lowe let New York score six times, and the series was evened thanks to a 6-2 Yankees win. New York took the first game at Fenway, Clemens beating Pedro Martinez. When Pedro hit Karim Garcia in the fourth inning, some shouting and gesturing followed, and when Ramirez thought a Clemens pitch came a little too close to him, he moved toward the mound. Soon both benches had cleared. Yankees coach Don Zimmer spotted Martinez a bit off to the side of the scrum and charged him; Pedro dodged him, grabbing Zimmer's head and throwing him to the ground. In the ninth inning, fighting broke out once more, but this time it was in the Yankees bullpen. Complaining that a groundskeeper was too demonstrative in his support of the Sox, Yankees pitcher Jeff Nelson tangled with him. Right fielder Garcia hopped the bullpen fence and got into it, too. The groundskeeper was hospitalized and in a trial nearly a year later, the two Yankees were found guilty and sentenced to community service. It was a night filled with fireworks, but New York won the game, 4-3.

Game Four was another big win by Wakefield. Red Sox 3, Yankees 2. New York took the lead in the series, though, winning 4-2 the next day. Game Six was a little embarrassing for New York, with the lead switching a couple of times. An error and two wild pitches in the Red Sox seventh gave Boston four runs and enough of a margin to ultimately win the game, 9-6, and force a seventh game. It was the first time the Red Sox and Yankees had faced each other in a final elimination game since the single-game playoff in 1978. Appropriately, it went into extra innings.

It was another Pedro versus Roger matchup. The Red Sox scored three times in the second, and Clemens was gone after three. At the halfway point, it was Sox 4, Yankees 0. A Giambi homer in the bottom of the fifth gave New York its first run. When Giambi homered again his next time up, in the seventh, the Yankees got another run, but Pedro got out of the rest of the inning without further damage. He'd pitched well, and as he left the field, he pointed to the heavens and accepted hugs from his teammates after he came down the dugout steps. David Ortiz answered Giambi's second solo shot with one of his own. Sox 5, Yankees 2. When the Yankees came up in the bottom of the eighth, Red Sox pitching just needed to get six outs.

The bullpen was rested and had excelled throughout the series. Sox fans were stunned to see Pedro come out to pitch. Manager Grady Little abandoned the pattern he'd followed throughout the season, ignoring Pedro's pitch-count evidence, preferring to stick with his starter. Pedro was already out of the game psychologically; now he was asked to put his game face back on, gear back up again mentally, and get some more outs. He got Nick Johnson to pop up to the shortstop. Five more outs. Then a double, a single, a double, and a third double—and the Yankees had three runs to tie the game. Grady Little finally emerged and took Pedro out. The bullpen did the job, finishing the inning, and retiring New York in the ninth and tenth as well. Wakefield had pitched the tenth. The first batter up in the Yankees' eleventh was Aaron Boone, and he homered off Wakefield. The game was over that suddenly, and Red Sox fans had to listen to the taunting "19-18" chant for yet another season.

The Curse

On the morning of the sixth game of the 1986 World Series, Vecsey wrote of a "haunted franchise" and "the ghosts of Pesky and Yaz and Lonnie and Torrez." The following morning, after the Mets snatched a Game Six victory away from the Red Sox, Vecsey wrote in passing that "Harry Frazee incurred the Curse of Babe Ruth by selling the slugging pitcher to the Yankees early in 1920." The following day, the *Times* headlined Vecsey's column, "Babe Ruth Curse Strikes Again." He wrote, "All the ghosts and demons and curses of the past 68 years continued to haunt the Red Sox last night . . . .there is no denying that the Boston Red Sox have been playing under a cloud ever since their owner, Harry Frazee, sold off Babe Ruth early in 1920, and that cloud settled over them in this Series."

Years later, near the end of the 2004 season, Vecsey allowed, "Back in 1986, hours before the sixth game of the World Series, I wrote an early-edition Sunday column that toyed with the concept of some cockamamie curse involving Babe Ruth and the Red Sox." He tells readers that, according to historian Glenn Stout, "My 1986 column was the first time anybody had ever written about a curse involving Frazee and '*Nanette*' and Ruth," to which he adds, "Personally, I don't think I'm that creative. The image of a franchise haunted by Frazee had been scuttling around in sportswriter minds for decades. Whatever. Four years later, my esteemed colleague at *The Boston Globe*, Dan Shaughnessy, wrote a book called *The Curse of the Bambino*. So now it's history."

What is fact and what is fiction? The modern scientific mind rejects the notion of otherworldly curses, yet the cumulative history does give one pause. There are more things in Heaven and earth, Horatio . . .

From 1914 to 1919, Babe Ruth was a mainstay of the Red Sox starting rotation, boasting an 89-46 win-loss record. His lifetime earned run average
was 2.28. (Ruth also saw limited action on the mound in New York.) As a
part-time outfielder, he also led the American League in home runs in 1918
with 11 and set the baseball world on its ear in 1919 with the unheard-of
total of 29 round-trippers.

The legend says that soon after the 1919 season, Red Sox owner Harry
Frazee, a New York theatrical entrepreneur beset with financial difficulties,
began to see Ruth as a way out of the straits. Frazee was trying to raise
money to finance his Broadway production *No, No, Nanette,* and the
Yankees had the money. During the holidays, Frazee sold the Babe to the
Yankees for $100,000 cash and obtained the loan of another $300,000
through granting the Yankees owners a mortgage on Fenway Park. Yes, the
New York Yankees had a claim on Fenway Park itself. (Interestingly
enough, the contract itself was put up for auction in November 2004, and
drew 206 bids, driving the price up to $470,000. The mere paper was
deemed to be worth more than the cash and loan for Ruth himself. The
seller apparently wanted more, and the contract did not sell since bidders
had not reached the reserve amount.)

The ensuing decades of Red Sox disappointment, frustration, and
downright ineptitude have come to be attributed—at least through folklore—throughout New England to the "curse of the Bambino."

What seemed a curse for the Red Sox was a blessing for the Yankees.
Ruth quickly made New York a powerhouse, and even enabled the city to
build a ballpark worthy of their new star. Yankee Stadium became the
"House that Ruth Built." It was in New York, media center and myth-maker
and hero creator, that Ruth became larger than life. With articulate writers
and reporters churning out daily accounts of his exploits, Ruth soon became
a national and international icon. In New York, Ruth's pitching skills
became incidental at best. He was put on earth to hit and he hit with power
never witnessed on a ballfield before or since. Ruth still holds the highest
lifetime slugging percentage of any player to play the game. With the ball
enlivened, he could showcase his talent. Ruth went on a rampage of hitting
that had old-time ballplayers shaking their heads in disgust at what had

become of their finesse game of station-to-station baseball. Ruth hammered 54 home runs the first year; 59 the second; then totals of 35, 41, 46, 25, 47, 60, 54, 46, 49, 46, 41, 34, 22, and 6. 714 home runs in all—and one can only imagine how many more he would have added playing every day in Boston instead of toeing the rubber on the mound.

Ruth's arrival in New York was not only a blessing for that metropolis but for all of baseball. Ted Williams put it best: "No wonder America loved Ruth. He did more for baseball than probably any other individual. He was baseball's most significant figure. He brought it back after the [1919 World Series] Black Sox gambling scandal and he rejuvenated the game. He was a tremendous drawing card, a charismatic type of individual who was just perfect for the job. The game of baseball pretty near catered to what he could do. They livened up the ball. They built Yankee Stadium because of him. They did everything." [Ted Williams and Jim Prime, *Ted Williams' Hit List*]

Ruth wasn't the only player sold or traded to New York. Frazee funneled quite a number of players to the Yankees. In fact, the first time the Yankees won the World Series, 11 of their 24 players had come from the Red Sox. [See sidebar on p. 55]

It was, however, the "snatching defeat from the jaws of victory" seasons beginning in 1946 that gave birth to the legend of the Bambino's curse. If Boston had played mediocre ball, that would have been one thing. The pain felt by fans and Bosox alike grew from being so close, so many times, but never completing the final step.

Ben Walsh, contributing to a Society for American Baseball Research chat list, wrote, "The Boston faithful have endured a fate worse than any the Greek gods came up with. Sisyphus forever rolling a boulder up a hill, only to have it roll down again at the summit. Tantalus, eternally tempted and tortured by cool water and fruit just out of his reach. These guys have nothing on the Red Sox fan. It didn't even take Ulysses 83 years and counting to get home. That's why it's a Curse—it's far more than just not succeeding. Any team can fail. It's failing when the prize is so close you can touch it that is the mark of the Curse."

"The Red Sox is the team of choice for romantics. Can you imagine a poet writing an ode to the Yankees?" —Stephen King

It really provides a great tale, though—the Curse of the Bambino. Media people loved the hook. "I root for stories more than teams," says Buddy Martin, a sports columnist and managing editor for the *Charlotte Sun*. In the wake of the 2004 World Series win by the Red Sox, it's going to be interesting to see what the media gloms on to next. Some diehard Yankees fans, immediately and predictably, began to talk of the next Red Sox championship being in the year 2090—after another 86-year drought.

Dan Shaughnessy's popularization of the legend in the 1990 book *The Curse of the Bambino* struck a responsive chord and has been a steady bestseller for more than a dozen years. From a story that was "scuttling around in sportswriter minds" for years, it became one of the more familiar phrases across New England. Any Red Sox fan worth his or her salt has heard of the Curse of the Bambino. Many have also *felt* it in a very real way.

Bill Simmons, The Sports Guy, writing for ESPN.com, called for a more objective perspective: "Curse Schmurse. I mean, think about this rationally . . . do you really think Babe Ruth is devoting his afterlife to haunting the Red Sox franchise? Wouldn't he devote his energies to haunting Roger Maris and Hank Aaron, or taking revenge on William Bendix's extended family after seeing Bendix's swing in *The Babe Ruth Story*? Why would the Babe even care about the Red Sox? Being sold to the Yankees was the best possible career move for the Babe, wasn't it?"

Even if one doesn't believe in curses, was the underlying story about Frazee itself accurate? Was Harry Frazee the real demon in the Red Sox' decades of defeat?

Or was the whole thing just an easy excuse? Phil Reisman, writing in Westchester County's *Journal-News* in early May 2002, said "I don't care if the Boston Red Sox are in first place. It's only May, and they will find a way to lose. The Red Sox stink. Even when they're good, they stink. They have always stunk. They haven't won a World Series since 1918. . . . For a Yankee-watcher like me, a man who mightily suffered through the 'Horace Clarke years,' an era of depressing mediocrity in the Bronx, it's great fun to watch the rival Red Sox lose and lose and lose. Red Sox fans over the years have conveniently excused their team's historic ineptitude by evoking the 'Curse of the Bambino.' "

In *Red Sox Century*, Glenn Stout and Richard Johnson note the legend but argue, "This popular account is almost pure fiction, an incomplete story that leaves an entirely false impression and ignores ample evidence to the contrary. Frazee never had a run of theatrical failures and was never in serious financial trouble. And his many deals with the New York Yankees were neither one-sided nor part of some fiendish conspiracy." [*Red Sox Century*, p. 137]

In the last few years, a revisionist legend of its own has grown up, suggesting that Dan Shaughnessy was responsible for misstating the facts. *No, No Nanette* wasn't even staged until 1925, so how could Shaughnessy say that Frazee sold Ruth to finance its production? Frazee actually had other motives, among them his reaching the end of his rope with Ruth. The Babe was constantly asking to renegotiate his salary. He more than once hopped the club, seeking paying jobs for company teams. He was viewed by many as a growing embarrassment with his incorrigible drinking and womanizing. Frazee was fighting battles with American League president Ban Johnson as well, the revisionists argue. Perhaps revealing a hint of envy, the insinuation from some is that Shaughnessy over-simplified the story so he could cash in on the long history of Red Sox defeats.

As always, the truths are probably somewhere in between—matters we can not yet fully resolve. Sure, Shaughnessy's book sold well. It's a damn good book, and it tapped into a receptive market. He never said that *No, No Nanette* benefited directly from Ruth's sale; he recognizes that *Nanette* was not staged until 1925, and points out that if anything it was the play *Madame Sherry* which followed most closely on the Ruth sale. Shaughnessy does say that Frazee "used the blood money to keep himself on his feet." A little hyperbole there, but, then again, the book is meant to be one with a sense of humor. Back cover copy for the paperback edition describes it as "baseball folklore at its best." Shaughnessy never once states there is any true curse. That conclusion may have been drawn by readers, but his baseball research is respectable (Stout has dug more deeply in subsequent years) and he himself asks the question a couple of times near the end of the book: "Is there such a thing as a baseball curse?" "Are the Red Sox cursed? Will the Red Sox ever throw off the curse and win another World Series?" He leaves his questions hanging. That makes for better drama.

In a way, the Curse was all good fun—though hard to bear for diehard Sox fans who suffered each blow as another manifestation of the alleged Curse. The notion of a curse, though, may have grown to the point that it truly did undermine Red Sox play on the field. It's always harder to play when burdened with expectations. No matter how many times modern ballplayers discounted the idea of any curse, there were those both on the Red Sox and on opposing teams who talked of the "ghosts" that haunted the Red Sox. Does perception sometimes become reality? Does the experience and even the idea of failure become a self-fulfilling prophecy?

Sports psychologists say that "confidence helps players concentrate and to let go of what's around them . . . .Concentrating relaxes muscles, keeps the body using long-honed instincts, and keeps the brain from thinking too much." But, if players "are surrounded by media stories, by fan reactions, or even by relationships with team officials that reflect a history of low success, then they will quickly meet the expectations that others have of them," said Mark Anshel, a sports psychology professor at Middle Tennessee State University. [Nicholas Thompson, "Winners: Science shows failure is self-fulfilling prophecy," *Boston Globe*, July 22, 2003]

Red Sox players of days gone by didn't feel an oppressive curse on their backs. Bob "Lefty" Cremins pitched for the Sox in 1927, and even faced the Babe in Ruth's biggest year, 1927. Phil Reisman asked him about the Curse. Cremins' reaction" "Well, I don't know, what the heck," he said. "I just wanted to play baseball. That's all I cared about." He retired Ruth. "Two pitches and he grounded out to first base. I was glad to get rid of him."

Billy Werber was in the Yankees' system and made a few appearances both in 1930 and early in 1933. He came over to Boston for most of '33 and was a regular the next three seasons, too. On the final day of 2001, he said, "Yankee-Red Sox rivalry? I don't recall much of a rivalry then. I don't recall any particular rivalry or animosity going into Yankee Stadium. It was just another ballgame. They've always had a good ballclub. Good organization. It makes you wonder how much of it was a media creation. Or maybe there just wasn't a lot of rivalry in the late '20s and deep into the '30s—after all, what was there to be a rivalry about? The Red Sox stunk and the Yankees were on top of the world!" [Interview by Bill Nowlin, December 31, 2001]

Jim Lonborg, ace Red Sox pitcher in the 1967 Impossible Dream season, said that he had never heard of any curse or jinx until Dan Shaughnessy started including it in his stories. Then it began to take root, in the media at least. Once implanted in the consciousness of fans and players alike, the idea of the Curse just wouldn't go away.

"Fan expectations, which can be very negative in Boston. In tight situations, the fans 'are waiting for something bad to happen,' said former pitcher Calvin Schiraldi, who was the losing pitcher for the Red Sox in the

Which Series-winning team had the most players who had previously been with one other team?

It would be hard to top the 1923 Yankees, who used 17 players in the Series—and TEN of them (59%) were ex-Red Sox players. There were 13 regulars, and eight of those (61.5%) had come directly from Boston to the Yankees. Perhaps the record books should be revised to give the Red Sox credit for winning in 1923, albeit while wearing pinstripes.

Pitchers:

Joe Bush—after four years with the Red Sox, joined the Yankees directly from Boston in time for the 1922 season

Waite Hoyt—after two years with the Red Sox, joined the Yankees directly from Boston in time for the 1921 season

Sad Sam Jones—after six years with the Red Sox, joined the Yankees directly from Boston in time for the 1922 season

Herb Pennock—after eight years with the Red Sox, joined the Yankees directly from Boston in time for the 1923 season

Bob Shawkey—acquired from the Philadelphia Athletics in 1915

In the six-game Series, Bob Shawkey's Game Four start was the only Yankees pitcher who had not come directly from the Red Sox.

Starting lineup:

Joe Dugan, 3b—after half a year with the Red Sox, joined the Yankees directly from Boston partway through the 1922 season

Bob Meusel, of—the rare Yankee who actually began his career as a Yankee

Wally Pipp, 1b—joined the Yankees from Detroit

Babe Ruth, of,1b—after six years with the Red Sox, joined the Yankees directly from Boston in time for the 1920 season

Wally Schang, c—after three years with the Red Sox, joined the Yankees directly from Boston in time for the 1921 season

Everett Scott, ss—after eight years with the Red Sox, joined the Yankees directly from Boston in time for the 1922 season

Aaron Ward, 2b—with Meusel, the only other regular to begin his career as a Yankee

Whitey Witt, of—native of Massachusetts, came to New York from the Athletics

Bit players:

Hinky Haines—had one AB in Series (joined with Hendrick as "Gink and Hinky")

Harvey "Gink" Hendrick—had one AB in Series

Fred Hofmann—had one AB in Series (Hofmann went the reverse route, and left NY after the 1925 season. He played for Boston for two years.)

Ernie Johnson—appeared but did not have an official AB in Series

Other Yankees on the roster, who did not play in the 1923 World Series:

Benny Bengough—broke in with Yankees mid-1923

Mike Gazella—broke in with Yankees mid-1923

Carl Mays—after four and a half years with the Red Sox, joined the Yankees directly from Boston in mid-1919

Mike McNally—after six seasons with the Red Sox, joined the Yankees directly from Boston in time for the 1921 season

George Pipgras—broke in with Yankees mid-1923

Oscar Roettger—broke in with Yankees mid-1923

Elmer Smith—after a partial season with the Red Sox, joined the Yankees directly from Boston mid-1922 last two games of the 1986 World Series. 'I think they are in love with this curse thing.'

"Player expectations matter a great deal, too, and, at the least, the history of the Red Sox increases confidence among opponents. 'When you were with the Yankees, you just handled the Red Sox,' Reggie Jackson, a longtime Yankees star, said to a *Globe* reporter in 1993. 'You knew you were going to beat them.'

"Current Red Sox players deny that low expectations, or talk of a curse, affect them. Pitcher Derek Lowe said, though, that he understands fan unease: 'They are diehard fans and the team hasn't won in 80 years.'

"Bob Tewksbury, a former all-star pitcher now studying sports psychology at Boston University, noted that some players can thrive well in tough environments such as Boston. But, he said about the Red Sox, 'Every year that goes by without winning the championship, the burden gets heavier and heavier.' " [Thompson, op. cit.]

Current relief pitcher Alan Embree scoffs at the Curse, but said he was asked about it "within 30 minutes of being traded to the team." [Ibidem]

The Red Sox lost in dramatic fashion once more in October 2003. The Curse cropped up numerous times. After winning Game Five, Yankees southpaw David Wells invoked it. "I believe in it," he told reporters. When the Red Sox came back to win Game Six, Sox centerfielder Johnny Damon said, "We know if we want to get to the World Series we have to get through the Curse and the Yankees. We feel pretty good we can do that. We're going to have a couple of cocktails, get some rest, and be ready to take on the Babe and the rest of the Yankees."

Then came Game Seven. After his game-winning leadoff, walk-off homer in the 11th inning, Yankees third baseman Aaron Boone said, "Like Derek told me, 'The ghosts will show up eventually.' " Derek Jeter and other players were very well aware of all the talk about the Curse. New York's former mayor Rudy Giuliani said, "I've never believed in the Curse, until 2003."

For several years, it had become *de rigeur* for new Sox signings to state that the past is the past, and that any supposed curse from years gone by would have no bearing on their play. Things happened, though. And until 2004, it was easy enough to find explanations in the supernatural. The spread and acceptance of sabermetrics had become so profound, however, that by the end of the 2003 season, a large percentage of Fenway Park fans knew that Pedro Martinez began to weaken after his 100th pitch, and specifically after his 105th pitch. Because they could so plainly see Pedro's statistical record, when Grady Little sent his star pitcher back to the mound to pitch the eighth inning of Game Seven, a great many fans were stunned, dismayed, and even angered—even before he faced the first batter. But when the Yankees scored and tied it up, it was also clear that this was not the intrusion of supernatural forces into the game, but simply a bad managerial mistake.

Yet Little himself invoked thoughts of ghosts when, almost immediately after the ALCS, it became evident that he might be relieved of his responsibilities—fired. "That's not my problem," he said. "Just add one more ghost to the list if I'm not there, because there are ghosts. That's certainly evident when you're a player in that uniform." He added, "If Grady Little is not back with the Red Sox, he'll be somewhere. I'll be another ghost, fully capable of haunting." [*Boston Globe,* October 23, 2003]

For Derek Jeter, for Aaron Boone, and for Grady Little, this is evidence that, on some level, they'd internalized the notion of ghosts at Fenway Park. The idea of a curse can easily become a self-fulfilling prophecy. Many Red Sox fans watched with timidity when key games were being played. Many sought to protect themselves against disappointment by wondering with cynicism: "OK, how are the Sox going to screw it up *this* time?" In their fearful heart, they knew it *would* get screwed up; the only drama was in speculating how.

The legend of the Curse ballooned with each year. Buddy Martin may have loved a good story, but this was becoming media overkill. More and more, experienced writers simply became irritated by the incessant recycling of Curse talk. Peter Gammons, commenting for ESPN, said, "It's a silly, mindless gimmick that is as stupid as the wave." One can only imagine how the players felt. Traded to Boston, or signed by the Red Sox, a perfectly innocent player walks into a drama where he's peppered with questions about a curse dating from the days before women had the right to vote, before radio's first baseball broadcast, and before the invention of television.

At the beginning of September 2004, when the Red Sox were just beginning to seem to come back to life from a season squandered through mediocre .500 play in June and July, the sometimes light-hearted idea of the Curse took a more serious twist as Glenn Stout wrote a cover article for *Boston Baseball*, entitled "Nothing But the Truth." Stout's research indicated that a misdirected anti-Semitism may have fed into the demonization of Frazee, though the assumption he was Jewish may have surprised the man himself, an Episcopalian.

Vecsey's column "inadvertently provided a villain to a franchise that needed one—Harry Frazee," argues Stout. Vecsey himself saw it as just "a device." When he read Stout's article, Vecsey submitted an entire column in the September 24, 2004 *Times*, headlined "A Myth That Should Not Be Perpetuated." He begins, "We must all take a new look at why Harry Frazee has been such a scapegoat for decades. It is not a pretty story. The alligators-in-the-sewers legend is that Frazee, who owned the Red Sox, sold Babe Ruth to the Yankees after the 1919 season to finance a new show called 'No, No, Nanette.'

"Only in the past few years has it been drummed into our brains that 'Nanette' did not appear on Broadway until 1925. The demonizing of Harry Frazee only gets worse. Recent scholarship by Glenn Stout, a writer in New England, has revived the fact that Frazee was involved in a feud with the powers of the American League. Because Frazee was a New Yorker and a showman, he was apparently fair game to be labeled as Jewish."

Vecsey notes Stout's research, particularly the September 10, 1921 *Dearborn Independent*, which, in a piece titled "Jewish Degradation of American Baseball", asked how the Red Sox had been "placed under the smothering influences of the 'chosen race.'"

Vecsey admits to feeling guilty "for advancing the image of Frazee as a craven loser. All I can say is that I don't want to be a part of the Frazee legend. My chronology about 'Nanette' was wrong . . . .I had no glimmer of any ancient anti-Semitic link to Frazee, a prominent and popular New Yorker who had serious enemies in other parts of the country . . . . Enough. The Red Sox may indeed be haunted by some miasma dating from the sale of Babe Ruth, who turned out to be the epochal player in baseball history." It was not, however, attributable to Harry Frazee.

There can't be any doubt that the Ruth-less Red Sox fared poorly, but how explain the decades of Sox shortcomings that followed Ruth's retirement? Probably a better explanation for the failures of the last half of the twentieth century would be Boston's painfully slow racial integration, writes Stout. Howard Bryant's book *Shut Out* documents the history of Red Sox racism, and credits GM Dan Duquette for finally overcoming the legacy, at least as regarding on-field personnel.

Allen Barra writing for slate.com was not so generous. "Curse of the Bambino, my butt; the Red Sox *passed* on a chance to sign Willie Mays. . . . The Red Sox are the team God dislikes; the Cubs are the team God merely forgot about."

The Red Sox were the last team to have an African American on the team—Pumpsie Green in 1959—a full two years after Jackie Robinson retired, having played ten full years of major league ball. Which was the next-to-last team integrate? The New York Yankees were "perhaps worse in their resistance" precisely because other teams at all levels emulated the Yankees and Yankees GM George Weiss was "openly racist." [Howard Bryant, *Shut Out*, p. 50] The first African American Yankee was Elston Howard in 1955.

The notion of a Curse grew, force-fed to the point of gluttony each time the Sox saw victory slip away. When Grady Little left Pedro Martinez in too long in Game Seven of the 2003 American League Championship Series and the team blew a decent lead, it reared its head once more. Brigham's developed a "Reverse the Curse" ice cream. Break the Curse Cookies were created by the Dancing Bear Cookie Company. A prominent traffic sign on Boston's Storrow Drive which warned motorists of a reverse curve ahead was altered with paint, repeatedly. And dozens of remedies were attempted, all with the goal of breaking the Curse. Many of these are detailed below. Stout saw it as a sort of reverse opiate of the people, one that offered despair rather than hope. "The curse was narcotic," Stout wrote. "The curse explained everything. The curse *worked*. See, it was somebody else's fault after all." Frazee, he told HBO, became the perfect patsy, in part because he was from New York and in part because he was, conveniently, dead.

Curse schmurse. The Red Sox winning the 2004 World Series may put an end to the Curse, but it won't put an end to the rivalry between the Red Sox and the Yankees. If anything, it may intensify.

For many years now after NFL football games, several players from both teams gather at midfield on the 50-yard line and go down on one knee for a joint prayer ceremony. This joining together is something we doubt we'll ever see after a Red Sox-Yankees game. The rivalry is even too bitter for a simple "2—4—6—8, who do we appreciate."

Yankees owner George Steinbrenner doesn't like losing, and will press his people to greater heights. Manny Ramirez poured gasoline on the fire by carrying a sign handed him by a fan in the Red Sox victory parade. The sign read, "Jeter is playing golf. This is much better." Alex Rodriguez will no doubt be looking to redeem himself as well, and maybe finally get the ring he's been seeking. Having vanquished the Evil Empire once, the Henry/Werner/Lucchino/Epstein team will be looking to repeat. Simply having won more World Championships (one more) than the Yankees in the 21st century is not enough.

The blessings of victory may spread across New England. Dr. Jim Recht, who teaches psychiatry at Harvard Medical School, explained, "In a tiny way, but in a great way, kids are more likely to have more potential to overcome adversity. I think that kids now are going to have a 1 percent extra sense of their potential in life." Not rigorous science, but Recht no doubt has a point. "You think about these guys whose whole conception of their possibilities in life was so severely limited, so depressingly limited and boxed in." Seeing the Red Sox win, after 86 years of failure, demonstrates the possibility of success. Carolyn Y. Johnson, writing for the *Boston Globe*, said "The victory could empower an entire generation of New Englanders, putting cracks in the foundation of a personality forged hundreds of years ago by Puritans who faced bitter winters and accepted fate without question." [Carolyn Y. Johnson, "Number 2 no longer: Nation needs a new self-image", *Boston Globe*, November 2, 2004] Well, OK. If nothing else, it was an exciting October.

Interlude
Trading with the Enemy

The Red Sox helped to fuel the development of the Yankees in the years when they first began to accumulate pennants and world championships. Many early Sox stars went to New York and helped to build the dynasty. The best known was Babe Ruth but there were numerous others. George Sullivan reminds us that "The Yankee dynasty of the twenties was three quarters the Red Sox of a few years before." [George Sullivan, *Picture History of the Boston Red Sox*, p. 62] There is a history of other trades between the two teams.

In 1903, during December, the Bostons sent pitcher "Long Tom" Hughes to New York for pitcher Jesse Tannehill. Hughes had won 20 and lost 9 for the World Champion Boston team, though he took a Series loss for the two earned runs he surrendered. He went 7-11 for New York, before he moved on to Washington partway through the 1904 season. He finished up 1904 and then played eight more seasons for Washington. For Boston, he won 62 and lost 38 with excellent earned run averages. The deal has been said to be one engineered in part by Ban Johnson, who was trying to help strengthen the brand-new New York ballclub. If so, it backfired. Boston got the better deal.
ADVANTAGE: BOSTON

In 1904, outfielder Patsy Dougherty was traded to NY for utilityman Bob Unglaub—a swap almost certainly prompted by Ban Johnson. "It was one of the worst trades in team history," write Glenn Stout and Richard Johnson. This trade "precipitated a decline on the field far worse than that which was later blamed on the sale of Babe Ruth sixteen years later."

Why was the Boston club so hot to trade for Bob Unglaub? They were the reigning World Champions and they were willing to give up one of their more popular players—Dougherty, their left fielder, who'd led the league in both hits and runs the year before. He'd hit .342 and .331 in his two seasons with Boston but had fallen off to .272 after his first 195 at-bats. Maybe it was just another Ban Johnson-orchestrated trade designed to bring competitive balance to a new league. Stout and Johnson argue that New York was so upset about how the Hughes/Tannehill deal had worked out that the Unglaub for Dougherty deal may well have been meant to compensate. Boston traded Dougherty in June for Unglaub, who was just 22 and may have shown some potential. But Unglaub hadn't played much in 1904 (just 13 AB, .154) and he hit just .233 in limited action in 1905. Out for all of 1906, he played a full year at first in 1907, hitting .254. Unglaub even managed Boston for 29 games that year, the summer he turned 25 years old, the team going 9-20.

Dougherty played well enough for New York, hitting .283 and .280 but then he had another slow start in 1906 and was traded to Chicago where he played for 5½ years, with a quite respectable career. He finished with a lifetime .284 mark.

ADVANTAGE: NEW YORK

October 13, 1907: New York, Boston, and the White Sox pull off a three-way trade. Jake Stahl, who'd been on the 1903 World Championship team for Boston, was sent to New York by the White Sox, who forwarded Frank LaPorte to Boston. Chicago received shortstop Freddy Parent from Boston. LaPorte played 62 games for Boston (.237), then finished the 1908 season for NY (.262). He knocked in 15 runs for both teams. Parent only hit .207 for the White Sox; the record shows his better days were behind him. Stahl played 75 games (.255, 42 RBIs) for New York, then was purchased by Boston on July 10, and he played another 78 games for the Red Sox (.244, 23 RBIs.)

ADVANTAGE: NEW YORK, if salary levels were comparable

An outright sale was consummated in 1909. New York sold Happy Jack Chesbro to the Red Sox for cash. Chesbro's wild pitch had lost the dramatic deciding game of the 1904 season, enabling Boston to beat New York and win the 1904 pennant. New York never would have been close without Happy Jack, though—he won 41 games and lost 12 in 1904, pitching a staggering 454⅔ innings. Surprisingly, his arm held out and he won another 66 games for New York over the next few years, and continued to eat up some innings. In 1909, he was 0-4 with New York, though, with a 6.34 ERA. When he was put on waivers, Boston bit and bought him for the waiver price of the day. His record for the Red Sox, before retiring from major league ball, was 0-1. Cash in the pocket was better than that.
ADVANTAGE: NEW YORK

Red Kleinow was the catcher on that final day in 1904, when Chesbro uncorked his wild pitch and the Highlanders lost the pennant to Boston. The ball sailed over his head; some felt he should have made the catch. In May 1910, Kleinow followed Chesbro as the next player sold to Boston. He saw a lot more action, but he didn't help Boston much—batting but .150 in 147 at-bats, and driving in only 8 runs. He appeared in eight games in 1911, not driving in a single run, then made his way to the Phillies where he got into four more games but still failed to get even one RBI.
ADVANTAGE: NEW YORK

Four years later, in 1914, New York—now the Yankees—bought Sox catcher Les Nunamaker. He cost them $5,000. Two weeks later to the day, the Red Sox bought pitcher Guy Cooper from New York. "Rebel" Cooper from Rome, Georgia appeared in nine games for the Red Sox, winning 1 but losing nary a game. He threw 22 innings, and posted a 5.32 ERA. The next year, he threw just two innings in one game and then disappeared from the major league scene. Nunamaker was a steal. Bringing a career .247 average with him to New York, he became the Yankees' main catcher through 1917. In over 1000 at-bats, he hit .262, driving in an even 100 runs. That first year with New York, he did something no other catcher has done for over 100 years—threw out three baserunners all in the same inning, as all three Tigers tested his arm.
ADVANTAGE: NEW YORK

In 1918, after the World Series was over, with the Red Sox triumphant, they traded pitchers Ernie Shore and Dutch Leonard, and leftfielder Duffy Lewis to New York for pitchers Ray Caldwell and Slim Love, catcher Roxy Walters and outfielder Frank Gilhooley, as well as some $15,000 in cash. Shore was in the service in 1918, but had been on the World Champion 1915 and 1916 Sox teams. For Boston, he'd posted ERAs of 2.00, 1.64, 2.63, and 2.22—and threw a perfect game, winning 58 in all and losing 33. When he got to New York, he saw limited duty (139 innings over two seasons) with ERAs over 4.00 both years. Dutch Leonard had been with the Sox for six years, with 92 wins and 63 defeats. His best year was 1914, 19-5 with a league-leading ERA of 0.96. He'd not pitched nearly as much in 1918, either. He never did pitch for New York. Maybe he just didn't like the Yankees. He refused to report. Things were worked out and he pitched five more years—for the Detroit Tigers. His ERAs were much higher and his won-loss record an even 49-49.

Duffy Lewis had eight seasons under his belt and was a left-field fixture at Fenway, having made the transition over from the old Huntington Avenue Grounds. The inclined slope in Fenway's left field was dubbed "Duffy's Cliff." He'd been on three pennant-winning teams for Boston and always done well, but due to the World War, he didn't see a day of baseball in 1918. When he returned from service in the U.S. Navy, he was traded to the Yankees. His better days were behind him. For New York, he hit .272 in 1919 with 89 RBIs and then .271 the next year.

Caldwell had served nine years with New York, with pretty good ERAs (and a won-loss record of 95-99). He started 1919 for Boston and went 7-4 with a 3.96 ERA but was traded to Cleveland midyear where he actually did pretty well in the next 2½ years (31-17). No love lost? Slim Love from Love, Mississippi, was 21-17 over three years with New York, but he never played for Boston. He went on over to Detroit with Dutch Leonard and finished his career over there (6-4), with just 93 innings in two seasons.

Roxy Walters hadn't shown much in New York, declining each year over three years. With Boston, his average continued to slide but he stuck with the team for five seasons and he finally had a decent year again in the fifth and final year, getting his average up to .250. That may have helped make him more marketable; he was shipped off to the Indians after that 1923 season. Frank "Flash" Gilhooley had an up-and-down career with the Cardinals and Yankees, but he was around a .275 hitter overall. For Boston,

though, he hit just .241 and was gone after 1919.
ADVANTAGE: NEW YORK

The Yankees sold Good Time Bill Lamar to the Red Sox on June 13, 1919. Lamar, an outfielder, was hitting just .188 for the Yankees, coming off seasons of limited action where he'd hit .244 and .227. For Boston, he appeared in 48 games and hit a strong .291.
ADVANTAGE: BOSTON (if they didn't overpay)

In late July 1919 the Red Sox completed a trade with the New York Yankees that sent pitcher Carl Mays to New York in exchange for pitchers Allan Russell and Bob McGraw. Mays was an exceptional pitcher with Hall of Fame potential, who is sadly remembered today for one bad pitch—the fatal beaning of Indians shortstop Ray Chapman in August 1920. Mays also had a reputation as a mean pitcher, who had little regard for others—there was considerable speculation that he often hit batters intentionally. With Boston, he'd pitched well (77-51) with an ERA that never exceeded 2.60—the mark in his rookie year of 1915. He'd helped the Red Sox to Series titles in 1916 and 1918, but was off to a disappointing 5-11 record when traded in 1919. The Red Sox were not the champion team of the year before. Upset with sloppy fielding behind him, he'd already walked off the mound and left the park in the middle on one game on July 13. The trade was, in part, simply the getting rid of a petulant pitcher who'd become too much of a thorn in the side of the Sox.

Happier in New York, he won 9 and lost just 3 that year, and went on to win 26 games in 1920 and a league-leading 26 in 1921. Whatever trauma the 1920 beaning might have induced may have affected opposing batters stepping into the box more than it did Mays. He gave the Yankees 80 wins against 39 losses before going on to Cincinnati and, at the tail end of his career, the Giants for a year.

In exchange for Mays, Boston acquired pitchers Bob McGraw, Allan Russell and a PTBNL (player to be named later), plus the not-inconsiderable sum of between $25,000-$40,000. McGraw had begun his career with the Yankees but only appeared in nine games and was 1-2. When he came to Boston mid-season in 1919, he went 0-2 with a 6.75 ERA and found himself back in New York the following year, where he did practically nothing (0-0, 15 IP). He saw more action in the National League, beginning a second career after four years out of the majors, in 1925. Russell was called "Rubberarm" and he did log some innings. With New York, he'd won 26 and lost 36 since breaking in late in 1915, always with a decent ERA. What did he do for Boston? He served 3½ years, going 10-4 that first year and 27-28 overall. Not that bad, considering how pathetic the Ruth-less Red Sox became (see the 1920 entry)—but he was no Carl Mays.

ADVANTAGE: NEW YORK

In 1920 the Red Sox sold Babe Ruth to the Yankees for a $300,000 loan and $100,000 in cash. Ruth subsequently helped lead the Yankees to seven World Series appearances and compiled offensive statistics that defy the imagination. They traded the greatest slugger in history—who was a superlative pitcher as well—for money. Talk about an investment! How many pennants has New York won since then? How many World Series titles do they hold? The cash served Frazee well; it did not serve the Red Sox well. Ruth went on to dominate the game with an international stature never matched since. If Frazee put any of the money received into building the Red Sox, it nowhere approached the return the Yankees received on their investment.

ADVANTAGE: NEW YORK

Also in 1920, in December, the Sox sent pitchers Waite Hoyt, Wally Schang, and Harry Harper, along with infielder Mike McNally to the Yankees for second baseman Del Pratt, outfielder Sammy Vick, pitcher Hank Thormahlen and catcher Muddy Ruel.

Hoyt hadn't seen much duty with Boston (10-12, in 226⅔ innings over two seasons) but in nine-plus seasons wearing the Yankees uniform, Hoyt was 157-98 and pitched in six World Series for New York. He is a member of the Hall of Fame. Harper had been a Senators pitcher for seven seasons, and a Red Sox for one (5-14, 3.04 ERA). With New York, he played just one year (4-3. 3.76 ERA but he got himself into a World Series game, starting Game Six against the Giants.) Unfortunately, he only lasted 1⅓ innings and earned himself a 20.25 ERA. Schang had done well for Boston, hitting over .300 the last two years he'd been with them. For New York, he did even better his first two and finished five seasons with the Yankees, playing in the 1921, 1922 and 1923 World Series hitting .271 in Series competition. McNally saw four years of part-time play with New

York, averaging .252. He saw Series duty in '21 and '22 and got four hits in 20 at-bats.

Who did the Red Sox get in trade? Del Pratt, a nine-year veteran infielder with the Browns and the Yankees coming off his best season (.314 with 97 RBIs). For Boston, he did even better (.324 and 102 RBIs) his first year and hit .301 with 86 RBI the next. He finished his career with two more years in Detroit. Sammy Vick had been with New York for four seasons, but only played much in 1919, when he hit .248. For Boston, he only saw 77 at-bats. He hit .260. He wasn't back in 1922. Muddy Ruel was the catcher they picked up, having included Schang in the trade. Ruel had hit .240 and then .268 the prior two seasons with New York. With Boston he saw much more duty and hit .277, but then dropped to .255. He was traded on to Washington where he played eight years, getting into a couple of World Series (he didn't do well at all in 1924 but went 6-for-19 in the 1925 Series). Ruel revisited Boston and put in 33 more games as a Red Sox early in 1933 (hitting .301) before being shipped off to Detroit. Pitcher Hank Thormahlen had accumulated 28 wins for the Yankees and lost 20. For Boston, in just one year's service, he won just one game but lost seven.

ADVANTAGE: NEW YORK

After the 1921 season, on December 21, the Yankees got another passel of players from Boston. They picked up veteran shortstop Everett "Deacon" Scott and pitchers Sad Sam Jones and Joe Bush. Scott had been eight years with the Red Sox and played in three World Series. He'd started out a weak hitter but improved considerably over his last three years. His play for New York was at about the same level and he served three-plus years before heading on to other teams. "Sad Sam" Jones starred in 1918, with the best winning percentage in the league, at 16-5. He'd thrown five shutouts in 1921 for Boston, also leading the league. Jones had won 23 games for Boston in 1921, a year in which the entire staff only notched 75 victories. He pitched the next five seasons for New York, appearing in three World Series. "Bullet Joe" Bush was anything but bush himself. He pitched six years for the Athletics and four for Boston, winning 31 games his last two years with Boston. For New York he won 26 and lost only 7 in 1922, the best won-loss percentage in the A.L.. In his three seasons with New York, he won 62 games for them and was only charged with 38 defeats. He won one Series game in 1923, but lost three between the '22 and '23 Series, but he did hit 3-for-7 at the plate in 1923.

For these three prime players, the Red Sox obtained shortstop Roger Peckinpaugh, and pitchers Rip Collins, Bill Piercy and Jack Quinn. Collins had been 25-13 for the Yankees in two seasons. For Boston he played just one year, but won 14 and lost 11. He played eight more years for the Tigers and Browns, and was 108-82 lifetime with a 3.99 ERA. Piercy had been 5-5 over the same two seasons for New York, but with a much better ERA than Collins. He stuck with the Red Sox for three years, pitching occasionally well (16-33). Quinn was an 11-year veteran (including two years with Baltimore in the Federal League) and was in his second stint with New York. In the three years before, he had won 41-31. He pitched three-plus years in Boston and won 45 games—but lost 54. Still, these were dismal years for Boston. Quinn ended a 23-year career with a 3.29 ERA and a 247-216 record. He was a good pitcher and the trade overall was not as absurd as it is may have seemed at first glance.

Less than three weeks later, on January 10, 1922, the Red Sox dealt Peckinpaugh in a three-way trade to the Senators. Bing Miller and Jose Acosta went from Washington to Philadelphia, and the Red Sox picked up Jumping Joe Dugan from the A's. Just as Peckinpaugh never played for the Red Sox, Acosta never pitched for the Senators; he was sold to Chicago a few weeks later. Dugan appeared in 84 games for Boston, but was traded mid-season—to the Yankees. For Boston, he hit .287. For the balance of the year, 60 games with New York, he hit. 286.
ADVANTAGE: NEW YORK

In 1922, Boston sent Jumping Joe Dugan and Elmer Smith to New York, for John Mitchell, Elmer Miller and Chick Fewster and a PTBNL, who turned out to be Lefty O'Doul. It was a six-player, two-Elmer trade. The Yankees needed a third baseman. "Home Run" Baker was 36 years old and, though still hitting well, it was his last year. Dugan had been with the Athletics for five seasons and matured to become a very solid hitter. Newly acquired by the Red Sox for the 1922 season, he was hitting .287 and the Yankees liked his looks. In these years, all they had to do was ask and Frazee complied. Dugan finished out the year and played six more seasons for New York, hitting for good average. Boston threw in Elmer Smith as well. Smith was also a new acquisition for 1922, with seven years of prior experience, primarily with the Indians. The outfielder was kind of up and down with his hitting, though it had been up in '22 with .286 for Boston. He played out 1922 and all of 1923 with New York, seeing little action in 1922 but hitting .302 in 1923 (183 AB).

It wasn't as though Frazee walked away empty-handed. New York sent Boston four players, the best of whom was Lefty O'Doul. O'Doul finished up with a lifetime .349 average, leading the league with .398 in 1929 and .368 in 1932. Unfortunately for Boston, it was the National League he led both times—playing for the Phillies and Dodgers respectively. For the Yankees, he'd only had 37 at-bats. For Boston, he played just the one year (1923) and only had 35 at-bats, hitting .143. They didn't appreciate the potential; the next year O'Doul hit .319 for the New York Giants.

Mitchell had only 46 at-bats with New York. He got much more playing time in Boston but was basically a .245 hitter and just stuck through 1923. Miller and Fewster were outfielders. Miller had five-plus games with the Yankees, including a good .298 in 1921 playing in 56 games. He was hitting .267 when traded but only managed .190 for Boston and was out of the majors at season's end. Fewster also had five-plus Yankees seasons, hitting about .280 but was only at .272 when traded. Unlike Miller, he did better with Beantown (.289 that year) but then he, too, declined—hitting just .236 in 1923. By 1924 he was with another team.

ADVANTAGE: NEW YORK (but only because Boston failed to hold onto O'Doul)

In 1923 the Sox dealt pitcher Herb Pennock for outfielder Camp Skinner, pitcher George Murray, infielder Norm McMillan and $50,000. Pennock was 162-90 over eleven seasons in pinstripes. He twice won 20 games and was a perfect 5-0 in four World Series. He is in the Hall of Fame. Meanwhile Murray was 9-2 in two seasons in Beantown. Skinner was used very little (13 AB, 3 hits, 1 RBI) and lasted only one season with the Sox; it was his last major league season. McMillan was a regular, batting .253 and driving in 42 runs. It was his only season with Boston, too. He had a good year with the Browns in 1924, and played for the Cubs in 1928 and 1929.

ADVANTAGE: NEW YORK

In January 1923, pitcher George Pipgras was traded to New York for catcher Al DeVormer. The same day, Boston sold infielder Harvey Hendrick to New York for cash. Pipgras had not yet appeared at the major league level for Boston, but was apparently a pretty good prospect, and he stuck with the Yankees for eight years. For New York, Pipgras won 95 and lost just 64. He won one World Series game for the Yankees in 1927, another in 1928 and yet another in 1932. DeVormer only had 127 at-bats over three years when he reported to Boston, but hit .258 in 209 AB for the Red Sox. He didn't play major league ball in '24, '25 or '26 but reappeared with the Giants for a year in 1927. Hendrick had also never appeared in a game for Boston. He didn't really do all that much for the Yankees in 1923 or '24, but all told played 11 years in the majors and posted a lifetime .308 average. Boston got Pipgras back in 1933 but even though he was on the roster for three years, he won just nine games while losing nine.

ADVANTAGE: NEW YORK

Later in January, the Yankees came back for more. This time they gave the Red Sox a pitcher, an infielder, an outfielder and some more cash, all in exchange for veteran pitcher Herb Pennock. Pennock already had 10 years under his belt, for the Athletics and Red Sox (77-72). With the Yankees hitters on his side, Pennock won 164 while losing just 90. He's a member of the National Baseball Hall of Fame.

George Murray, the pitcher the Sox swapped for, had been 3-2 for NY but was 9-20 in two years for Boston. Infielder McMillan had hit .258 for NY in just 78 AB in 1922. He stayed just a year for Boston, got a full 459 AB and hit .253 with no home runs and 42 RBI. He was sent to the Browns after the season. The outfielder—Camp Skinner—didn't get much playing time at all (just 13 AB) but hit .231, better than the .182 he'd managed for New York. That was it for his career. The cash was no doubt welcome.

ADVANTAGE: NEW YORK

Late in 1924, the Red Sox acquired infielder Mike McNally for infielder/outfielder Howie Shanks. McNally had been traded to New York back in 1920. McNally never actually played for the Red Sox after 1920, though. The day after they reacquired him, they traded him to the Senators for third baseman Doc Prothro. In effect, from the Red Sox viewpoint, this was a Shanks-for-Prothro trade—and Prothro did very nicely for them in

1925, batting .313 with 51 RBIs in over 400 at-bats. The next year he was gone, to Cincinnati, where he only appeared in three games. In the late 1930s, Prothro managed the Little Rock team for the parent Red Sox, winning one pennant for them in 1937. Shanks, for the Yanks, performed pretty much as expected. The last two of his 11 years with Washington were his best, hitting .302 in 1921 and .283 in 1922. For Boston, though, he only hit .254 in 1923 and, in more limited service the following year, .259. For the Yankees, he only played in 1925. In 155 at-bats, he hit .258 and drove in just 18 runs. It was his last year in the majors.

ADVANTAGE: BOSTON

In 1925, Ray Francis and $8000 cash went to the Red Sox, who sent New York Alex Ferguson and Bobby Veach. In Francis, the Sox got a pitcher who'd gone 7-18 for the Senators in 1922 and 5-8 for the Tigers in 1923. He wasn't with any major league team in 1924 and had only thrown 4⅔ innings, giving up four runs, in 1925. What was the big attraction? For Boston, he went 0-2 giving up 29 runs in 28 innings, and never graced another major league roster. One needn't even look at the other side of the equation to know who made out better on this deal.

Alex Ferguson had been on the Yankees in 1918 and 1921, without anything to be proud of. For Boston, he'd eaten up a lot of innings building a 32-46 record but with decent ERAs. As a Yankee, he didn't even last the season, though he won 4 and lost 2. He was traded to the Senators and ended up 5-1 with them, helping Washington win the 1925 pennant. Ferguson won Game Three of the World Series but he lost Game Six (and the Senators' Walter Johnson lost Game Seven). Ferguson pitched four more years, mostly with the Phillies going 17-33.

Veach had played 12 years for the Tigers and then the one 1924 season with Boston. A lifetime .310 batter, 1925 was his last year. Following a .295 1924 with the Red Sox, he was traded to New York after just five AB in 1925. For the Yankees, he hit .353 in 116 AB, but then was traded (along with Ferguson) to the Senators.

ADVANTAGE: NEW YORK

Five years later, in 1930, the Red Sox traded pitcher Red Ruffing to the Yanks for outfielder Cedric Durst and $50,000. The Red Sox were dead last in 1922, 1923, 1925, 1926, 1927, 1928 and 1929. What broke the pattern in

1924? The White Sox were a half a game further down in the final stand-ings. What did a team destined to come in last (as they reliably did again in 1930 and 1932) need a pitcher like Red Ruffing for? Better to pocket $50,000. Owner Bob Quinn could use that. So when the Yankees offered him outfielder Cedric Durst, too, Quinn took the deal.

Durst hit .245, one point above his final lifetime .244 average, for Boston, but it was his last year in the major leagues. (Several years later, he turned up as Ted Williams' roommate when Ted was on the road with the Pacific Coast League San Diego Padres. Durst was intended to exert a sta-bilizing influence on the young tempestuous Ted.)

The Yankees got the best of this deal. Ruffing played for Boston for six years. He couldn't win many games on a perennially last place club, though. His record for Boston was 39-96. With the Yankees, though, everything changed. He won 231 games and lost just 124. He strung together four con-secutive 20-win seasons and was 7-2 in seven World Series with a 2.63 ERA. He even hit well, batting .269 in 1937 at bats. He'd hit over .300 for Boston in both 1928 and 1929, with over 100 AB each season. Ruffing is now in the Hall of Fame. The $50,000 is long since gone.
ADVANTAGE: NEW YORK

Earlier in 1930, the Yankees claimed Ken Williams from the Red Sox on waivers on January 29. Though he'd hit .319 in a 14-year major league career, and had hit well for Boston the prior two seasons, he was finished and never played a game for New York, released before the season began.
ADVANTAGE: BOSTON

In 1932, New York reacquired pitcher Wilcy Moore from Boston for the predictably-nicknamed "Dusty" Rhodes. Rhodes had only been in 41 games for New York since breaking in early in 1929. He'd won 7 and lost 9. The year the Sox got him, he won 1 game for them but lost 8. Rhodes actually won 12 games in 1933 and again in 1934 but he lost more. He was 27-45 for the Red Sox.

Wilcy Moore was a Yankees sinkerball pitcher on the 1927, 1928 and 1929 teams. He'd won 29 and lost just 15 and actually led the league in ERA and saves in 1927. He spent 1930 with St. Paul in the American Association, adding a curve ball to his repertoire. He was drafted and joined

Boston in 1931. He won 15 and lost 23 with the Sox, leading the A.L. in saves in 1931, perhaps somewhat remarkable on a team which only managed 62 wins all season long. Back with New York, he won 2 in 1932 and 5 more in 1933. He lost 6 in '33.

ADVANTAGE: BOSTON

Also in 1932, the Yankees traded two players for Danny MacFayden. Born in Massachusetts, he was a real Boston favorite and looked to be a star in the making. He'd won 53 games for Boston teams which finished in last place his first five years and improved to sixth place but still 45 games behind in 1931. 1932 saw the Sox headed straight back to the cellar and MacFayden was already a dispiriting 1-10 when New York dealt for him. He did OK for N.Y. in more limited opportunities, going 14-10 before being traded on.

The Red Sox got many more innings out of Ivy Andrews, who had only 11 innings' experience with New York before the trade. For Boston, he won 15 and lost 20—not bad at all given the team's overall performance in those years. Henry Johnson had been a decent hurler for New York over seven seasons, with a 47-36 record. For Boston, he was 16-15 in three years before moving on.

ADVANTAGE: BOSTON

In 1934, Lyn Lary donned a Red Sox uniform, traded by New York for Freddie Miller and $20,000. Young Yawkey was trying to buy up talent. The Yankees couldn't have thought they were getting that much in Miller. He'd played in 17 games in 1933 and early 1934, batting just .184—and in fact he never did play even one game for the Yankees. Hopefully, the $20,000 was put to good use.

Lary had two very good years in 1930 and 1931 (.280 with 107 RBIs in the latter year) but had fallen off to below .230 with few RBIs the next two years, but the Yankees now had Crosetti at short. For Boston, he filled in respectably until Yawkey acquired Joe Cronin in the offseason. Lary hit .241 with 54 RBIs.

ADVANTAGE: BOSTON

In the winter of 1935/1936, the Red Sox and Yankees pulled off what could be seen as an indirect trade via Washington. There's no indication it was intended as such, but the upshot of the hot stove season swapping was that the Sox traded star outfielder Roy Johnson and Carl Reynolds to the Washington Senators for infielder Heinie Manush. Johnson had hit .313, .320 (119 RBIs), and .315 in the preceding three years. Reynolds hit over .300 with 86 RBIs in 1934, but didn't play as much in '35. He still posted a .270 mark in 78 games. Manush was voted into the Hall of Fame in 1964, but the infielder's better years were behind him; he did manage a .291 average for the Red Sox in the one year before he moved on.

Johnson never played for the Senators. Traded to Washington in December, 1935, he and Bump Hadley were traded to New York for Jimmie DeShong and Jesse Hill one month later. DeShong won 18 games for Washington in 1936. Hill hit .305, not a bad pickup, either. Hadley served the Yankees well for five seasons.

Johnson saw only limited action with the Yankees, .265 in just 147 at-bats.

ADVANTAGE: TOSSUP

In February 1937, the Red Sox sold New York another Babe—Babe Dahlgren. He had a decent start with the Sox in 1935, hitting .263, but didn't play much in 1936 and, once acquired by the Yankees, just had one solitary (and unsuccessful) at-bat in 1937. There were only two seasons where he put in full years for New York but did not really distinguish himself, hitting .235 in 1939 and .264 in 1940. After 1940, he began an odyssey which saw him with six different clubs.

Whatever money the Red Sox got for him proved to their advantage in the short run, since the one at-bat was of no use at all to the Yankees and his .186 average over 43 at-bats in 1938 (with only one RBI) was not worth much, either. In 1939 and 1940, though, serving in place of Lou Gehrig, he drove in a combined 162 runs, despite more or less average batting averages. He doubled and homered, scoring two runs in the Game Two 4-0 World Series win against the Reds in 1939.

ADVANTAGE: NEW YORK

In 1962, after a long stretch in which the two teams did no business for a quarter-century, New York traded infielder Billy Gardner for Triple A Seattle veteran outfielder Tommy Umphlett. Gardner was an eight-year veteran, playing for the Giants, Orioles, Senators, and Twins before landing with the 1961 World Series champions in midyear. He hit .212 for New York; the highest he'd ever hit was .262 for the 1957 Orioles. With Boston, though, he blossomed, hitting .271 in 200 AB in 1962 before dropping sharply the following year to .190.

At least he contributed. Umphlett had been a real prospect in the Boston organization, hitting .283 in 1953 before going to the Senators where he followed with two years under .220. He was on the Seattle Rainiers roster at the time of the trade, playing under manager Johnny Pesky, but never did make it back to the majors.
ADVANTAGE: BOSTON

In 1967, the Yankees traded catcher Elston Howard to Boston in exchange for some always-useful cash, as well as two players to be named later, who turned out to be pitchers Peter Magrini and Ron Klimkowski. Howard had been named to nine All-Star teams and played in five. He'd also seen nine years of post-season play with the Yankees in his 12½ years with New York. Coming to Boston, he helped the Impossible Dream become a reality—and there he was in the World Series once again. His career had clearly wound down, though, and he only hit .147 for the Red Sox that year and only .241 the next, his final year.

The Yankees picked up some players with more upside potential. Klimkowski made the team in 1969 and threw 143 innings for New York in two stints. He won 6 and lost 10, despite a quite-good 2.65 ERA in 1970. Magrini had pitched 7⅓ innings for Boston back in 1966 and lost one game for them, with a 9.82 ERA. He never appeared in a game for the Yankees.
ADVANTAGE: BOSTON

In 1972, the Red Sox traded reliever Sparky Lyle to the Yankees for infielder/designated hitter Danny Cater, and Mario Guerrero. This has long been considered the worst trade the Red Sox ever made, perhaps partially for non-baseball reasons, in a fit of pique at Lyle for his habit of sitting on birthday cakes with his bare butt. Lyle twice led the A.L. in saves while in NY and totaled 141 over seven years. His win-loss record was 57-40. He appeared in three postseasons (a distinction which eluded Cater and Guerrero), winning three games and captured the Cy Young Award during his sojourn. In three lackluster seasons in Boston, Cater bated .237 his first year, stuck around for a couple of part-time years and then was gone.

Guerrero had his major league debut with the Sox in '73, and played part-time himself for two seasons, .233 and .246. He and Cater both traveled on together yet again—this time to the St. Louis Cardinals.
ADVANTAGE: NEW YORK

In 1977 Boston went the free agent route and signed Yankees pitcher Mike Torrez. Torrez compiled a respectable 60-54 record over five years in Boston but will be remembered most of all for delivering the pitch that Bucky Dent promptly hit over the Green Monster to win the 1978 A.L. playoff for the Yankees.

After the 1978 season, when the Sox fell to New York in the final play-off game, was it time for a housecleaning? GM Haywood Sullivan apparently thought so, and Stout and Johnson write he "wreaked the most havoc on a Red Sox roster since the reign of John I. Taylor." Within the next two years, the former catcher disposed of pitchers Bill Lee, Ferguson Jenkins, Rick Wise, Reggie Cleveland—and Luis Tiant. El Tiante wound up with the Yankees, through free agency. Tiant was 38. He loved it in Boston. He'd revived his career, with the Red Sox. He'd won 122 games for Boston and lost 81. He'd been in two All-Star Games and one World Series. In 1978, he had been 13-8—and that was the same record he posted for the Yankees in 1979; though his ERA was higher, it was still under 4.00. In 1980, he was 8-9. Red Sox fans are happy that he's now back in Boston to stay, a fixture at Fenway with his own eatery out on Yawkey Way.

In 1979, the Yankees used free agency to sign Bob Watson away from the Red Sox. Watson played three seasons in NY and helped lead them to two ALCS series. He hit .318 and homered twice in the 1981 World Series.

In 1986, the Red Sox unloaded DH Mike Easler in exchange for DH Don Baylor. Baylor had already put in 16 seasons and seemed to be at the tail end of his career, having declined in average for three straight years for New York: .303, .262 and .231—though he was increasingly productive in terms of runs driven in: 85, 89 and 91. In retrospect, the Yankees did him a favor, since in 1986 he was on a pennant-winning team with the Red Sox in a year the team came within one pitch of a world championship. He never reached the post-season with the Yankees. During 1986, Baylor knocked in 94 runs with 31 homers, though hitting just .238 for Boston. During the 1987 season, he was off to his next team.

Easler was a fair enough trade, though, hitting .302 with 78 RBIs for New York. He, too, was gone the next year, to Philly—though midyear he came back to New York and finished up his career with the Yankees. ADVANTAGE: BOSTON

In 1992, the Yankees signed longtime Red Sox star and hitting machine Wade Boggs. He played five seasons in New York and won a World Series with them in 1996. He wears a "B" cap in the Hall of Fame, though.

In 1997, catcher and DH Mike Stanley and infielder Randy Brown were traded to the Yankees for pitching prospect Tony Armas Jr. and a player to be named later who turned out to be pitcher Jim Mecir. The Red Sox less than a year later got Stanley back, via the Toronto Blue Jays, for two more pitchers: Peter Munro and Jay Yennaco. Stanley had played well for the Rangers, for New York and for Boston. He was hitting an even .300 when he was traded back to New York; he didn't get that much playing time for New York but hit .287 nonetheless to close out the year. He began the next season with Toronto, but was back with Boston for another couple of years and helped Boston get into the post-season both in 1998 and 1999. Randy Brown was a prospect who never made it; he neither saw time with Boston nor with New York. Tony Armas Jr. was a very good pickup and later figured with Carl Pavano in a trade the Red Sox made with the Expos to acquire Pedro Martinez. Jim Mecir was a good pickup as well. He was left unprotected, though, by the Red Sox in the expansion draft and was signed by Tampa Bay. ADVANTAGE: BOSTON

Since 1997, as the rivalry has intensified, there simply haven't been any trades between New York and Boston. Some players who had served with the Red Sox (Paul Quantrill and Tom Gordon, for example) later signed with the Yankees. Other players left New York and signed with Boston, such as pitchers David Cone, Ramiro Mendoza, and David Wells.

NEW YORK YANKEES TO BOSTON RED SOX FAN CONVERSION FORM

Thank you for your interest in becoming a member of the Boston Red Sox Fan Club.

Due to an unprecedented volume of requests, we are currently processing only fan conversion registrations for New York Yankees fans. Conversion requests from other teams will be taken in the order they are received, and only after all former Yankees fan requests have been processed. We expect this to take a number of weeks based upon the current backlog of Yankees fan requests.

Please take a few moments to fill out the conversion form below to help us get to know you better and pre-scribe any required counseling to recover from your previous fan experience.

Name: _____

Address: _____

Who's Your Daddy: _____

1.   **Please select your favorite recent Yankees new player acquisition:**
[ ]   Tom "Flush" Gordon
[ ]   Alex "A-****-Rod" Rodriguez
[ ]   Gary "Talk-It-Can't-Walk-It" Sheffield
[ ]   Javier "Grand Slam" Vazquez
[ ]   Kevin "Charlie" Brown

2.   **Which of the following would you most like to see as the most played YES Network "Great Moments in Yankees History" film clip in 2005:**
[ ]   Rivera's "shocking" blown save in Game 4
[ ]   Rivera's "shocking" blown save in Game 5
[ ]   A-Rod slapping the ball out of Arroyo's hand, causing Jeter to return all the way to first base instead of moving into scoring position on the play
[ ]   The Red Sox joyously spraying celebratory champagne on their ecstatic fans in Yankee Monument Park
[ ]   Vazquez's grand slam pitch to Johnny Damon in Game 7
[ ]   Vazquez's 2nd home run pitch to Johnny Damon in Game 7
[ ]   "Big Papi" Ortiz accepting MVP trophy at Yankee Stadium
[ ]   A-Rod crying like a little girl in the dugout after game 7

3.   **Please indicate the last book you read:**
[ ]   How to lose the ALCS in four very hard lessons
[ ]   Suicide Hotline—It's not just for Cubs' fans anymore
[ ]   The Heimlich Maneuver—What to do when choking
[ ]   None of the above. I don't read books. I was a Yankees fan.

4.   **Which recent Yankees personnel move did you enjoy most:**
[ ]   Hall-of-Famer Roger Clemens winning a 7th Cy Young Award in an Astros uniform
[ ]   Seeing Andy Pettitte in an Astros uniform
[ ]   Seeing Tino Martinez in a Devil Rays uniform
[ ]   Seeing Alfonso Soriano in a Rangers uniform
[ ]   Seeing David Wells in a Padres uniform, then switching it for a Red Sox one
[ ]   Seeing Manny Ramirez remain in a Red Sox uniform

5.   **Which following designation best describes Derek Jeter's performance in this year's ALCS:**
[ ]   Captain October
[ ]   Captain Underpants
[ ]   Captain & Tennille

6.   **Math: The Red Sox and the Yankees played 26 times in 2004. How many more games did the Red Sox win than the Yankees? (hint: the number is the same as the number in a four-game sweep)**

7.   **Please choose your favorite movie:**
[ ]   Anger Management
[ ]   Hunt for Red October
[ ]   Damn Yankees
[ ]   Still We Believe

8.   **Finish this sentence: "Alex Rodriquez is . . .**
a.   overrated
b.   overpaid
c.   overdue
d.   overly prissy
e.   over

9.   Please select your favorite recent Yankees moment:
[ ]   Bucky Dent throwing out the first pitch with more velocity and movement than Kevin Brown
[ ]   The pathetic A-Rod slavishly mimicking every Jeter move and gesture in the Yankees' dugout
[ ]   The Yankees wearing themselves out by scoring 19 runs when it didn't really matter, then losing 4
         straight while leaving 10 million potential game-winning runners on base
[ ]   Rivera failing to prevent unkempt hooligans and idiots from eating the Yankees' lunch and handing
         them their butts

10.   Math:
a)   How many times have the Yankees won the World Series in the last four years? (hint: less than one)
b)   How many times have the Yankees won the World Series in the current century?
c)   How many times have the Yankees won the World Series in the current millennium?

11.   Select the most vociferous, stupid, and annoying Yankees fan:
[ ]   Former New York Mayor and 9-11 profiteer Rudy Giuliani
[ ]   Current New York Mayor and former Red Sox fan Michael Bloomberg
[ ]   Washed up "comic" hack and Yanks personal ballwasher Billy Crystal
[ ]   Front-running celebrity phony Jack Nicholson
[ ]   Tim McCarver

12.   Are you ready to admit that:
a.   Ted Williams was better than Joe DiMaggio?
b.   Dom DiMaggio was better than his brother Joe?
c.   Carlton Fisk was better than Thurman Munson?
d.   Even Manny Ramirez is faster than Bernie Williams?
e.   Reggie Jackson was a better outfielder than Matsui?
f.   Gary Sheffield owes his stats to steroid abuse?
g.   No self-respecting parasite would invade Jason Giambi?
h.   The Yankees were unable to win the ALCS because ex-Red Sox manager Don Zimmer wasn't sitting
         next to Joe Torre making all the decisions?

13.   Please indicate your favorite moments in Yankees history (check all that apply):
[ ]   Alex Rodriquez is traded to the Yankees
[ ]   Don Mattingly never wins a World Series
[ ]   The Yankees let Roger Clemens get away
[ ]   The Yankees steal Contreras from Boston, at the cost of many millions, then have to pay millions
         more to send him to Chicago
[ ]   The Yankees let Pettitte get away
[ ]   Giambi's steroid abuse causes his BALCO body to collapse like a screen door in a hurricane.
[ ]   The Yankees let David Wells get away

**14.   Have you experienced any of the following after the embarrassing four game collapse? (Check
         all that apply)**
[ ]   Headache
[ ]   Uncontrolled Anger
[ ]   Heartache
[ ]   Holes punched in doors or walls
[ ]   Nausea
[ ]   Smashed TV screens
[ ]   Depression and Broken Dreams
[ ]   Avoided Red Sox fans for days or weeks
[ ]   Sympathetic asphyxia (choking)

Once you have completed this form, please forward it to Fenway Park. Then burn all your remaining Yankees
clothing, memorabilia, and associated reminders. After reviewing your request, the Red Sox Fan Club will contact
you with notification of acceptance or rejection.

I hereby acknowledge that the real "curse" is being a Yankees Fan. I hereby renounce the New York Yankees for
all eternity on this the

————————————— day of ——————————— , 200___

(Signed) _____
(Office Use Only)
[ ]   Approved
[ ]   Declined

_____

John W. Henry
Principal Owner
Boston Red Sox

Chapter 3
A Tale of Two Cities

"And Cain went out from the presence of the Lord, and dwelt in the land of Nod, on the east of Eden." —Genesis 4:16

"We wrestle not against flesh and blood, but against principalities, against powers . . . " —Ephesians 6:12

"I perceive that God shows no favoritism." —Acts 10:34

"God is a Yankee fan." —Mickey McDermott, former Red Sox and Yankees pitcher

" . . . the difference between a Bostonian's view of Dent's home run and a New Yorker's impression of the same event can be compared to another uneven rivalry in the literature of New England: to Ahab, the white whale was an obsession; to Moby Dick, the captain of the Pequod was an hors d'oeuvre." —Con Chapman

Is Boston really Eden and New York Nod? Or at its root, is it really just simple envy, that other Green Monster called jealousy? Is that why Boston fans have it in for New York, and for the Yankees in particular? Or are there grander issues involved—issues having to do with the very meaning and purpose of human existence?

How might the dynamics of the rivalry change, given the outcome of the 2004 season?

If it's just envy, nothing could be more understandable. After all, before 2004, the last time a Boston baseball team won the World Series was back in 1918, whereas the Yankees have won the Fall Classic 26 times since that year. The New York Giants won four times and the Brooklyn Dodgers won once. Even the Mets won a couple of times. While all this was happening, Boston fans waited, watched, and stewed, for a long, long time.

The Boston-New York rivalry is multi-dimensional. It even extends beyond baseball, if such a thing can be imagined.

Way back when the colonies were first established, Boston was the more pre-eminent city. Boston was established in 1630, ten years after the Pilgrims first landed in Plymouth, and the harbor city was the center for commerce in the colonies for most of the 1600s and 1700s. It was only around the time of the American Revolution that New York finally superseded Boston in importance and stature. Circumstances at the end of the War of 1812 gave New York a further boost and by the time the Civil War was over, the transition had become irreversible.

The crucible of the American Revolution was in Boston. New York was heavier with Tory sympathizers. Sam Adams, John Hancock and James Otis were among the leaders of the Revolution and most of the initial events—the Boston Massacre, the Boston Tea Party, the battles of Lexington & Concord and the battle of Bunker Hill—all took place in Boston. The British forces were driven out of the city entirely by March of 1776—more than three months before the Declaration of Independence. The successful expulsion of British authority in Boston provided a major impetus to the colonists to declare their independence from the Crown.

More of the leaders of the embryonic United States—Franklin, Hancock, and the Adamses—tended to come from Massachusetts (or Virginia—with Washington, Jefferson, Madison and Monroe) rather than New York, though let's give Alexander Hamilton a little credit, too. Hamilton definitely helped put the fledgling country on a more solid economic footing. Although Boston was the economic powerhouse during the colonial period, New Yorkers excelled at business and the center of commerce for the new country became based in New York.

Social and even ideological factors helped facilitate this change. The Massachusetts Bay Colony was created by religious pilgrims and was, in effect, a theocracy. New York was first settled by Dutch traders and, from the start, was less encumbered by religious strictures. Whereas an early merchant in Boston could be roundly condemned for extracting "excess profit"—a sin in the eyes of the more ascetic Puritans and Calvinists—such opprobrium would be hard to find in New York colonial history.

It is perhaps of significance that the first notable event in Massachusetts was the celebration of Thanksgiving, an act of appreciation and sharing, where that of New York was one of sharp trading (one could almost say theft)—Peter Minuit's purchase of Manhattan for 60 guilders, some $24 worth of beads and trinkets. Or was it 26 dollars, as in 26 world championships? Perhaps it is ironic that the Yankees baseball team and its fans have had more to be thankful for. Even though it was the early settlers of Massachusetts who created Thanksgiving, the Yankees traditionally got the bounty and the Red Sox got stuffed. Yankees dollars now buy up ballplayers left and right, although it would be disingenuous to pretend that the Red Sox aren't near the very top in payroll terms, too.

From the very beginning of American settlement, there were distinct differences of purpose. Those who settled in New Amsterdam—later, New York—were primarily looking to build livelihood and fortunes through commerce and trade. The Puritans, however, were engaged in another sort of mission—to create a glorious New World. Leaders such as John Winthrop saw themselves as more than refugees or exiles. They envisioned themselves as "engaged in a permanent and long-range mission of cosmic proportions, offering to lead the whole world to the new freedom and fulfillment of the Reformation. Every moment of their lives, they were conscious of building their tiny outpost . . . into the 'City upon a Hill' that would become the veritable hub of the universe and the inspiration for all mankind." [Thomas H. O'Connor, *The Hub*, Northeastern University Press, 2001]

That's a hard row to hoe—and a hard role to shake off, too.

The Puritans approached life with an unforgiving certitude; this sometimes led to excess. Those who were not devout in the same way were often driven out, or worse. Dissenters such as Roger Williams were forced to strike out for Rhode Island. Anne Hutchinson was one of those banished from the colony; she was later killed along with most of her family in Hell Gate, Rhode Island, in an attack deemed an Indian massacre. New York honors Anne Hutchinson today, with the Hutchinson River Parkway. The persecutions in Salem, known as the Witch Trials, were another manifestation of Puritanism gone awry. There was a shameful century of narrow-minded holier-than-thou presumption and, truth be told, pomposity. Allowing our minds to wander back momentarily to baseball, this reminds us of the needling anti-Sox T-shirts of the last few years: "Hey, any team can have a bad century."

The Puritan legacy still may affect self-perception amongst many New Englanders. Some could argue that it has bred a distorted sense of self-importance that too often betrays itself in arrogance—and a disapproving, even disparaging view of those who live their lives in the pursuit of monetary reward. Without a doubt, there are those Red Sox fans who find a greater purity in striving and falling short than wallowing in the wash of 26 World Series victories. To be a resolute rooter for Red Sox Nation is a far nobler calling than to be a minion of Mammon.

After independence, in the nineteenth century, a sense of enlightenment began to pervade New England. There was still a sense of mission, but it was a far more tolerant one.

Certainly, the Commonwealth of Massachusetts has long been known for its role as a center of learning. Harvard College was founded in 1636, where the first college in New York was not created until over a century later—Kings College (now Columbia), established in 1754. Even today, Boston remains much more of an academic center than New York, with thousands of New York youths coming to Massachusetts for their higher education. Some even see the light and convert to the Red Sox cause. The first public schools were established in Boston, and a couple of centuries later took on new life under Horace Mann.

As New York became more and more a center of commerce, Boston became more of a "culture city"—fashioning itself as the "Athens of America." Why stop there? Oliver Wendell Holmes saw Boston as "the hub"—and he didn't just mean a locale where roadways radiated into the central city. He literally viewed Boston as the hub of the universe. The "flowering of New England" manifested itself in the Transcendentalists and other writers of the early 19th century—Emerson, the Alcotts, Hawthorne, Longfellow, Thoreau.

The sense of *noblesse oblige* has always been strong in Boston. It is perhaps no accident that Boston has long been a leader in the field of medicine, with the Massachusetts General Hospital often in the forefront. More recently, much of the pioneering work in cancer treatment emanated from

Dr. Sidney Farber (the "father of chemotherapy") and the work in fighting and treating cancer which he pioneered, with crucial backing from the Boston Braves, Ted Williams, and the Boston Red Sox.

Other movements for human benefit have centered in Boston as well—William Lloyd Garrison's anti-slavery publication *The Liberator* was based in Boston, and a strong case can be made that Margaret Fuller gave first voice in word and life to the movement for women's equality. It is ironic, and disgraceful, that the Red Sox were the last team in baseball to integrate. The Yankees were the next-to-last. Will Boston field the first female player? It may be a long time in the future, but perhaps lessons have been learned that will allow for the possibility.

Generations of Bostonians probably do continue to see Boston as not just "another city" but as one perhaps anointed—"a city set apart by its origins, its history and its dedication to excellence, destined to accomplish great and unusual things for the glory of God and the benefit of the community." There remains a strain of intellectual superiority in Boston, whereby a segment of the citizenry hold themselves above the crass commercialism of New York. (Funny how once you lose commercial dominance, it becomes a little something to turn your nose up at.) New Yorkers may not be oblivious to this. It is perhaps noteworthy that the first entries in the T-shirt wars pitted "Boston Sucks" against "Yankees Suck"—two quite different targets.

Is there a sense of Athens versus Sparta? Did the ancient Athenians sport anti-Spartan togas, with "Sparta Sucks" emblazoned in Greek across the front? Was there a small band of even more offensive Athenians who wore "Leonidas Swallows" on theirs?

It would trivialize the differences between the New York and Massachusetts colonies to pit writers Thomas Wolfe and Norman Mailer against John Updike and Stephen King in a mud-wrestling competition. Likewise, to argue that the shrine which is Fenway Park is today's equivalent of the "City upon a hill" while Yankee Stadium is an anteroom to Hell would doubtless be going a little far. In their weaker moments, one or other of this book's authors has even argued that the rivalry between these two teams may not entirely be that of Might versus Right, Good versus Evil. Such heresies are rare, however, and when one occurs, the other author usually schedules an intervention featuring filmed highlights of the 1978 playoff game, commentary by Bill Lee.

Whatever the root causes, somehow over the last hundred years, there has developed a rivalry between these two proximate cities that has blossomed not only into baseball's greatest rivalry, but into the greatest rivalry in American sports. That the two urban centers are just a few hours from each other by car, bus, train, or plane is an enabling element. It's not hard to find the familiar "NY" ballcap on the sidewalks of Boston, and several New York pubs offer islands in the storm to dedicated Bosox fans.

Maybe it really comes down to baseball, though, and not a lot more. There were a couple of different kinds of baseball played in the early nineteenth century. The kind of "town ball" played on the commons and in the fields of New England was sometimes called "the Massachusetts game." There was another variant of early baseball played around metropolitan New York, be it by Alexander Cartwright or Abner Doubleday or their ilk. It became known in time as "the New York game." The style of play favored by the New Yorkers prevailed. The "New York game" beat out the "Massachusetts game"—and maybe the people of New England have never forgiven them.

It took a while to dawn on observers that a rivalry in which one team always comes out of top is, in some regards, not that much of a rivalry. Tell that to the more devout fans in either camp, though! Now that the Red Sox routed the Yankees in 2004, is the rivalry going to end? No more talk of the Curse. No more "19-18" chants. Will everyone just get on to other things? Doubtful. The Yankees have something more to prove. After all, they haven't won a single World Series at any time in the New Millennium. And the Red Sox want to repeat. One trophy is a statistical anomaly. Even going back to the start of each franchise, it's still 26-6. There's a little room for improvement there. If anything, the actual rivalry on the field of play should become more intense, not less so. Each game won't be fraught with such momentous psychodrama, but each game will likely be fought with passion from both sides. Perhaps a little more self-respect on the part of the fans, a little more generosity of spirit, and a little more appreciation of the play of the game itself. Baseball for baseball's sake.

"As much as the people in the stands dislike each other in both cities, they're exactly alike. They have a rival chant that is meaningless to both clubs. In Boston, it's 'Yankees Suck.' In New York, it's '1918.' Neither means anything to the players, but the fans seem to think that's the winning chant every night somewhere. There's so much history, you can make a name for yourself in one inning, one play, one pitch that you can't make in another series with any other team." —Curt Schilling, 2004

Periods when the Yankees Lay Dormant

Beginning with their re-birth as a New York franchise in 1903, here is how the Yankees have finished over the years. An asterisk indicates a pennant. A number indicates how many games behind the pennant or (beginning in 1969) division winner the Yankees ranked. As one can see, there are certain periods when the Yankees lay dormant like a hibernating grizzly. The late 1980s, the middle to late 1960s—those were good years for Yankees haters.

Sometimes we forget how recently the Yankees have suffered. Mike Lupica reminded us in late 2003: "There now is this idea that the Yankees have always won with Steinbrenner, that the Yankees mystique is some kind of constant in our lives. Forget that . . . they won twice in the 70s and then went nearly two decades without winning again. The 1980s were the first decade since Ruth that the New York Yankees did not win the World Series. And for most of the 80s, it was Steinbrenner calling the shots, Steinbrenner hiring and firing people, Steinbrenner acting exactly the way he is acting now. Which means loopy, and that's on his good days."

In the 21st century, the team has been very competitive, but they've also been eliminated four years in a row.

Here are the years the Yankees finished first with the Red Sox right behind them, in second place. It's happened thirteen times, and seven years in a row: 1938, 1939, 1941, 1942, 1949, 1978, 1998, 1999, 2000, 2001, 2002, 2003, and 2004.

What was great about 1901 and 1902?
There was no New York team in the American League.

What was great about 1903, 1904, 1905, 1908, 1909, 1911, 1912, 1913, 1914, 1915, 1916, 1917, 1918, 1946, 1948, 1966, 1967, 1968, 1969, 1971, 1972, 1973, 1975, 1979, 1982, 1986, 1988, 1989, 1990, 1991, and 1995?
Boston finished ahead of New York in the standings in every one of those years.

1903	17 games behind (4th place)	1955	* LOST World Series
1904	1.5 (2nd place)	1956	* WON World Series
1905	21.5 (6th place)	1957	* LOST World Series
1906	3 (2nd place)	1958	* WON World Series
1907	21 (5th place)	1959	15 (3rd place)
1908	39.5 (last place—8th place)	1960	* LOST World Series
1909	23.5 (5th place)	1961	* WON World Series
1910	14.5 (2nd place)	1962	* WON World Series
1911	25.5 (6th place)	1963	* LOST World Series—swept
1912	55 (last place—8th place)	1964	* LOST World Series
1913	38 (7th place)	1965	25 (6th place)
1914	30 (6th place)	1966	26.5 (last place—10th place)
1915	32.5 (5th place)	1967	20 (9th place)
1916	11 (4th place)	1968	20 (5th place)
1917	28.5 (6th place)	1969	28.5 (5th place)
1918	13.5 (4th place)	1970	15 (2nd place)
1919	7.5 (4th place)	1971	21 (4th place)
1920	3 (3rd place)	1972	6.5 (4th place)
1921	* LOST World Series	1973	17 (4th place)
1922	* LOST World Series	1974	2 (2nd place)
1923	* WON World Series	1975	12 (3rd place)
1924	2 (2nd place)	1976	* LOST World Series—swept
1925	28.5 (7th place)	1977	* WON World Series
1926	* LOST World Series	1978	* WON World Series
1927	* WON World Series—sweep	1979	13.5 (4th place)
1928	* WON World Series—sweep	1980	* LOST the ALCS—swept
1929	18 (2nd place)	1981	2 (3rd place)
1930	16 (3rd place)	1982	16 (5th place)
1931	13.5 (2nd place)	1983	7 (3rd place)
1932	* WON World Series—sweep	1984	17 (3rd place)
1933	7 (2nd place)	1985	2 (2nd place)
1934	7 (2nd place)	1986	5.5 (2nd place)
1935	3 (2nd place)	1987	9 (4th place)
1936	* WON World Series	1988	3.5 (5th place)
1937	* WON World Series	1989	14.5 (5th place)
1938	* WON World Series—sweep	1990	21 (last place—7th place)
1939	* WON World Series—sweep	1991	20 (5th place)
1940	2 (3rd place)	1992	20 (4th place)
1941	* WON World Series	1993	7 (2nd place)
1942	* LOST World Series	1994	* There were no MLB playoffs in 1994
1943	* WON World Series	1995	7 (2nd place)
1944	6 (3rd place)	1996	* WON World Series
1945	6.5 (4th place)	1997	2 (2nd place) advanced to
1946	17 (3rd place)		playoffs, but lost the ALDS
1947	* WON World Series	1998	* WON World Series—swept
1948	2.5 (3rd place)	1999	* WON World Series—swept
1949	* WON World Series	2000	* WON World Series
1950	* WON World Series—sweep	2001	* LOST World Series
1951	* WON World Series	2002	* LOST the ALDS
1952	* WON World Series	2003	* LOST World Series
1953	* WON World Series	2004	* LOST the ALCS
1954	8 (2nd place)		

What was really great about 1908, 1912, 1966, and 1990?
New York finished in last place.

What was superb about 1912 and 1990?
Boston finished first and New York finished last.

Chapter 4
The Ballparks:
Friendly Fenway and
Cavernous Yankee Stadium

"Stand still and consider the wondrous works of God." —Job 37:14

"Fenway is a shrine. People come there to worship." —Bill Lee

"I don't subscribe to the conventional wisdom that says DiMaggio and I should have switched parks." —Ted Williams

"The atmosphere of the Red Sox in Yankee Stadium or the Yankees in Fenway Park just kind of picks everybody up and you just play at a different level. I don't know how many games people dive into the stands face-first in Yankee Stadium, but we had guys doing this, and that was July. It's just different. It's not like the other games. It just isn't." —Mike Mussina, 2004

The Boston American League team—they were known simply as the Boston Americans or the "Bostons"—first played in 1901 at the Huntington

Avenue Grounds. New York didn't field an American League team for the first two years of the league's existence. Boston did reasonably well in their initial two seasons, finishing in second place in 1901 and in third in '02. American League architect Ban Johnson wanted to place a team in the Big Apple, so he engineered the relocation of the Baltimore franchise—last-place finishers in 1902—to New York City in time for the 1903 season. A year later, he began to work to make the New York team more competitive. He was trying to build a business—the league—and had no compunction about using his considerable influence to move some of the players around, just as he tried his best to lure the best players from the rival National League.

The team that later became the Yankees first played in Hilltop Park, in the Washington Heights section of Manhattan (where Boston Red Sox 2004 World Series MVP Manny Ramirez grew up, as it happens). The park was built in a record six weeks, on land which formerly belonged to the New York Institute for the Blind (some wags of the day commented that the umpires had all been trained there). The New York A. L. team never did win a pennant while playing there. They weren't the Yankees then, of course; they were the New York Highlanders, and they played there from 1903 through 1912. They won their very first game 6-2, beating the Washington Senators behind Massachusetts native Happy Jack Chesbro.

Chesbro went 21-15 his first year with New York, but that was a come-down from the 28-6 season he'd enjoyed with the Pirates the year before. And didn't come close to Boston's ace Cy Young, who threw 34 complete games and won 28 of them against 9 defeats. Young had won 33 in 1901 and 32 in 1902. With 20 wins from Long Tom Hughes and 21 more from Big Bill Dineen, Boston won the pennant—and the very first World Series that year. Chesbro came back and won a staggering 41 games against just 9 losses in 1904, pitching 454 innings in 48 complete games! Chesbro set a record for victories which still stands today, and will probably never be matched—even with an asterisk for the 162-game season. New York came up just a game and a half short, though—the crucial loss to Boston coming in the ninth inning of a 2-2 tie on a Chesbro wild pitch. Here's a guy who won 41 games, but is remembered more for that one bad pitch—just as Bill Buckner, who banged in 102 RBIs to help lead the Red Sox to the 1986 pennant, is remembered more for a ball that he failed to field in the World Series against the Mets.

You'd get quite a laugh if you attempted to initiate this custom at Yankee Stadium today, but at Hilltop it was common for fans to pass the hat in an effort to raise a little extra money for the players. Chances are that the hat and all its contents would be stolen before it reached the end of the aisle in today's Yankee Stadium. At Fenway Park, though, you might even get a number of contributions. Sox fans have waited so long and wanted so desperately to win. They know that the deepest pockets are those of the Evil Empire.

When a fire burned down most of the wooden seating at the Polo Grounds—located not far away in northernmost Manhattan—a few days into the 1911 season, the Giants asked for permission to play at Hilltop and the two teams both shared the same facility until the Polo Grounds were readied for the Giants' return. The Highlanders' lease at Hilltop Park expired after the 1912 season and the Giants returned the favor, commencing a ten-year stretch of co-tenancy at the Polo Grounds. Over time, the Highlanders become known popularly (and then formally, beginning in 1913) as the Yankees.

The Red Sox were at first quite successful, winning the first World Series in 1903 and finishing first again in 1904—but dropping in the 1905 standings and plunging to last place in 1906, before beginning a bit of a climb back toward the top. It's said that every time the Red Sox build a new park, they win the World Series—and so they did in 1912. Fenway Park was built on land owned by the Fenway Realty Company. A major shareholder was General Charles Taylor, publisher of *The Boston Globe*, whose son John I. Taylor purchased the ballclub early in 1904. The *Globe* is now owned by the *New York Times*, which currently also holds a 17% stake in the Red Sox. In an early mark of respect for Red Sox tradition, the team actually transplanted the playing surface from their previous park. Ellery Clark explained why: "There appeared to be both a spiritual and a physical connection between the old and new parks. So good was the Huntington Avenue Grounds' turf that the Red Sox brought it with them to Jersey Street." [Clark, *Boston Red Sox*, p. 69] Little wonder that Fenway is considered by many to be hallowed ground.

The first official game was played at the original Fenway Park on Saturday, April 20, 1912 with the Red Sox defeating the New York Highlanders, in front of 27,000 fans, by a score of 7-6 in 11 innings. The Red Sox hero was future Hall of Famer Tris Speaker who drove in the winning run. In an ironic twist, the results of the inaugural game were forced from the Boston headlines by reports of the sinking of a transatlantic ship known as the Titanic. Boston bowed the next two years to the Philadelphia Athletics, but then re-claimed the pennant in 1915, 1916 and 1918. It was starting to feel like the beginnings of a dynasty. Meanwhile, the Yankees were sort of middle-of-the-pack, undistinguished throughout.

Despite the unheard-of 29 home runs swatted by a young pitcher named Ruth (9-5 in 1919), Boston slipped badly in 1919, as the Chicago White Sox won the pennant—only to lose the World Series. Deliberately.

The next year, 1920, baseball was to change forever, thanks to a cast of characters who in Boston at least will go down in infamy. Baseball had suffered its worst scandal ever in 1919, as the "Black Sox" threw the series (the plot was supposedly hatched by Boston and New York gamblers—though not affiliated with either team). But for Bostonians, this was not nearly as scandalous as the legitimate sale of one player. Babe Ruth's sale to the Yankees and the 54 home runs he slammed out of the park in 1920 began a whole new era of baseball, but the dynasty which the Red Sox had begun to create was decimated—and worse—through the sale of Ruth and a host of others, most all of whom were sent on to New York in a dispiriting series of sales over the years.

Red Sox owner Harry Frazee, a New Yorker, even took out a mortgage on Fenway Park itself—to the tune of $300,000, the mortgage extended by Yankees owner Jacob Ruppert. Years later, after Tom Yawkey had purchased the Red Sox, Ruppert became angered when the Sox swept a series from the Yankees—and called the mortgage note in full. Yawkey was so wealthy that he was able to pay off the mortgage with an indulgent chuckle.

The Yankees played for years—including Ruth's first three years with the team—in the Polo Grounds (years later, during renovations of the Stadium, they would also be forced to play regular season games at Shea Stadium). By 1923, though, they had a new park of their own: Yankee Stadium (designed by Osborn Engineering Company of Cleveland—the same firm which had designed Boston's Fenway Park. The first game played at Yankee Stadium featured the visiting Boston Red Sox). The home team won the April 18, 1923 game; the score was Yankees 4, Red Sox 1— the margin of difference was, predictably, Babe Ruth's three-run third-inning homer.

The two parks could hardly have been more different. Fenway Park was considered a large park when first built, but nonetheless even then a "lyric little bandbox" compared to the later grand structure that was Yankee Stadium. Geographical considerations—such as the railroad line which ran behind Fenway's left-field wall—dictated the configuration of Fenway far more than that of Yankee Stadium, which was built on more than ten acres of trashed-out wasteland in the Bronx. Fenway was built on landfill, designed to improve a smelly swamp. Both graced the land on which they were situated, Fenway taking on an odder footprint with its famous left-field wall—later dubbed the "Green Monster." An imposing 37-foot high structure, in that deadball era it was thought that no one would ever hit a home run over it. Six days after the park's opening, though, Hugh "Corns" Bradley did just that, one of only two home runs he ever hit.

One could argue that each ballpark represented not only the different character of the two cities that hosted them, but also the separate eras in which they were designed. Fenway was built in an era that had just begun

The All-Star Games

There is one occasion each year when some of the Yankees and some of the Red Sox join forces on the same team—the annual All-Star Game. Several times, the Midsummer Classic has been played at one of their two ballparks.

The first time the All-Star Game was played at Yankee Stadium was July 11, 1939. Joe DiMaggio hit a home run for the third run in a 3-1 victory for the American League.

Fenway Park hosted its first All-Star Game on July 9, 1946. The American League's Feller, Newhouser, and Kramer pitched a shutout, allowing just three hits. It was returning war hero Ted Williams, however, who owned the day—he was on base five times with one walk, two singles, and two home runs. He scored four times and drove in five.

In 1960, Yankee Stadium was the All-Star venue for the second time, on June 13. The Nationals shut out the Americans, with five pitchers sharing the honors.

The next year, baseball's showcase event returned to Fenway. After nine full innings, the game ended in a 1-1 tie, but not because the Commissioner arbitrarily called off the game. Heavy rains arrived, preventing play from continuing.

July 19, 1977 saw the NL beat the AL 7-5 at Yankee Stadium, when junior circuit starter and future Hall of Famer Jim Palmer gave up four runs in the top of the first.

The return of Ted Williams to Fenway stole the show. He threw out the first pitch, and was immediately surrounded by a *Who's Who* of old-time and current greats who broke ranks and left their positions on the field to greet the aging Kid. Pedro Martinez started for the AL and struck out the first four batters, possibly injuring his arm in the process. AL 4, NL 1.

to accept the motor car as more than a passing fad; right up until 2002, the park lacked a loading dock. This wasn't a problem when, in fact, the "equipment truck" was the horse-drawn wagon run by a man named Pat Daley. Fenway was completed well before America entered into the First World War. The single-deck park suited the smaller city, and felt comfortable. Pat Daley and Son is still today, in the 21st century, the firm that transports team equipment to and from the airport.

Yankee Stadium isn't even a ballpark; it's a stadium, like the ones the Romans used with the Christians and the lions, but without the ambience. With its three decks, the Stadium's original 60,000 capacity is almost exactly the same seating capacity as the Roman Coliseum. It was built amidst the ebullience which characterized the end of the "war to end all wars." Knowing that the world was now "safe for democracy," Americans kicked into full swing with the self-confident Roaring Twenties, and the size and grandeur of Yankee Stadium suited the larger scale of the day.

Fenway fits snugly into the urban landscape, so much so that several players have been dropped by cabs right outside and didn't believe they were there. Roger Clemens took a taxi from the airport. Delivered to the ballpark, the cabbie said, "Here you go." Clemens told Dan Shaughnessy, "I looked out and there was this warehouse. I said to the driver, 'No, Fenway Park. It's a baseball stadium. It's a stadium.' And he said, 'Yeah, this is it.' And I said, 'No, this is a warehouse.' He told me to look up, so I stuck my head out the window and looked up and saw the lights."

Yankee Stadium is BIG. To get to its upper deck, you have to walk up and up—and up. Fenway has no upper deck, save for a relatively small—but growing—number of roof box seats. The first thing many visitors remark about Fenway Park is how small the place is; no one ever says that about the Stadium. You almost feel you could put Fenway Park in Yankee Stadium and still have room for Ebbets Field. That's clearly not true in terms of the field of play. But it was true in terms of capacity:

YANKEE STADIUM—largest paid crowd: 83,533 (May 30, 1938, versus. . . . the Red Sox!)

FENWAY PARK—largest paid crowd: 41,766 (Aug 21, 1934, versus. . . . the Yankees!)

EBBETS FIELD—largest paid crowd: 41,209 (May 30, 1934, Dodgers versus the Giants)

Add FENWAY and EBBETS = 82,975, and the difference between the total and the Yankee Stadium figure is 558 paying customers.

Fenway did best Yankee Stadium with one attendance figure—though by a razor-thin margin. The smallest Fenway Park crowd on record was comprised of 409 souls on September 29, 1965 in a game where the Red Sox hosted the California Angels. At least it was a decent game, a 2-1 victory over the Angels featuring an Earl Wilson win, a Radatz save, and a Tony Conigliaro home run that gave Boston the lead in the fourth inning. The Red Sox finished that season 40 games out of first place and even though Dave Morehead had pitched a no-hitter just 13 games earlier (before just 1,247 fans—one of whom has co-authored this book), there was clearly no subsequent bump in ticket sales. The Red Sox lost their 100th game of the season before just 487 fans. After the game, everyone went out for dinner together. (The last sentence isn't true. We made that one up.)

A year later, Yankee Stadium made a run at the Red Sox record but fortunately—or not—four more fans showed up. Yankee Stadium's smallest attendance mark was 413 paying customers for the September 22, 1966 game against the White Sox. Chicago won easily, 4-1, as the Yankees avoided the shutout only in the bottom of the ninth inning. By then, some of the 413 may have made for the exits. Yankees radio and TV broadcaster Red Barber was fired for accurately announcing the attendance figures that day. The Yankees finished dead last in the standings that year, sparing the Red Sox the embarrassment—but just by a half-game.

In 1974 and 1975, the Yankees played at Shea Stadium, while their own ballpark was being renovated. The Stadium is owned by the City of New York. Fenway Park, on the other hand, is owned by the Red Sox. The Boston Braves played at Fenway Park in the 1914 World Series, because it held more people than their own South End Grounds. The following year, 1915, when Braves Field had been built, they returned the favor and in turn loaned their now-larger park to the Red Sox. The Red Sox again used Braves Field in 1916—and one of the umpires was Bill Dineen, who had been their hero in the 1903 World Series.

After being sold to New York, Babe Ruth hit 148 homers for the Yankees during the three years they played at the Polo Grounds. As the 5'9" Mel Ott proved, that could be a homer-friendly ballpark for a left-handed pull hitter, with its right-field foul pole standing just 256 or 257 feet from home plate.

"The House That Ruth Built" was in part a house built for Ruth. The Stadium, with its relatively close right-field bleachers just 281 feet away (and only 296 feet down the line in left) was built to help pull hitters. Note to Red Sox owners: Bring Fenway's bullpens in to 290 feet or so, and you can not only squeeze in a couple of thousand more fans, but David Ortiz might hit 60 home runs, not counting the games on the road!

In the very first game he played at Yankee Stadium, the Babe homered into what quickly became dubbed "Ruthville" off Boston's Howard Ehmke. Ruth was, of course, the first player to hit 30 home runs in a season. And the first to hit 40. And 50. And 60. In Boston, he'd hit 29, in 1919.

The same day that Ruth hit that Opening Day homer, across town, Columbia University pitching star Lou Gehrig struck out 17 batters in the game he was playing. Like Ruth (and Williams), Gehrig excelled early on as a pitcher.

Not to be outdone, Fenway later developed its own parallel architectural change—Williamsburg. After Ted Williams' rookie year, Tom Yawkey installed bullpens on the field in right to shorten the distance required for a Ted Williams pulled home run. Even then, though, it took more of a blast to drive the ball out of Fenway than Yankee Stadium, and in later years there was a lot of speculation as to how well Williams would have done had he played his full career in Ruth's ballpark. How well would Joe DiMaggio done at Fenway? It can be nothing but conjecture, of course, but most fans have heard of the evening that Tom Yawkey and Yankees owner Dan Topping reportedly traded Joe and Ted over late night drinks—but thought better of it in the sobering light of morning.

Both parks were relatively homer-friendly—and both teams excelled in acquiring marquee sluggers. There were eight teams in the league until the 1961 expansion, and either the Yankees or the Red Sox fielded the home run leader in 32 of the first 58 seasons (granted, many times his name was Ruth). From 1903 through 1992, the home run champion in 40 of those years came from one of the two feuding franchises.

Both parks are readily accessible by subway. ("The Yankees fan is a carnivorous creature that slinks out of the subway," impartial observer Bill Lee once said.) Neither offer much more of a challenge in the way of automobile parking, though Stadium prices are less than half the cost of parking around Fenway. Both ballparks are surrounded before games by an array of urban hustlers, scalping tickets or hawking peanuts and T-shirts, often rather uncomplimentary ones about their respective rivals.

Both facilities also feature a number of incredibly long-serving employees. Despite the number of times George Steinbrenner replaced field managers (Billy Martin alone was hired and fired on five occasions), Eddie Layton played the organ in Yankee Stadium from 1968 to 2004. Pete Sheehy was the team's equipment manager from 1927 through 1985. Public address announcer Bob Sheppard continues to serve today more than fifty years after taking the job. He also has handled the p.a. work at the Polo Grounds, at Ebbets Field, and for the New York Giants football team at the Meadowlands in New Jersey. Fenway Park has many long-time employees with three, four, and five or more decades under their belts.

Baseball purists may cringe, but Fenway boasts one creature the Stadium lacks—its own mascot. Wally the Green Monster—so the newly-created legend goes—actually lives inside the left field Wall. It only took him something like 80 years to finally emerge from behind the old manual scoreboard, when he first appeared in 1997. As mascots go, he's relatively inoffensive. The Yankees tried a mascot once—Dandy (Yankee-doodle dandy, get it?)—but he only lasted two years and was soon dispensed with. Sparky Lyle described Dandy's 1980 debut: "He looked like he had escaped from a comic strip: he had a huge belly, a large round nose, a mustache that unfurled, and a hat that spun around, and he wore a Yankees uniform. A lot of people thought he looked a little like me." [Lyle, *The Year I Owned the Yankees*, p. 56]

Fenway Park has been used for other non-baseball purposes—football, the occasional political event such as a Eugene McCarthy for President rally in 1968, and the even more infrequent concert—but for many years it had been reserved for baseball alone until new ownership invited The Boss (Springsteen, not Steinbrenner) to perform for two nights there in September 2003. Jimmy Buffett did a show in 2004, and the park has been featured in many movies (e.g., *Field of Dreams*) and television shows.

Yankee Stadium could be rented out for almost anything, it seemed. From 1925-46 the Army vs. Notre Dame football games were hosted there. In 1928, the Yankee Stadium locker room is where Knute Rockne successfully inspired the Fighting Irish to "Win one for the Gipper." From 1956-73 the New York Giants played at the Stadium. Thirty world championship boxing matches were held at Yankee Stadium. Pele played there often in the 60s and 70s. Circuses and rodeos were held in the 50s, and rockers U2,

Billy Joel and Pink Floyd followed in the 90s. Pope Paul VI said mass in October 1965 and Pope John Paul II did the same in October 1979. Papal visits require a lot of advance planning. Did they get The Word that the Yankees would not be in the playoffs either year? The facility is ecumenical, however: Billy Graham preached in 1957 and the Jehovah's Witnesses often packed the place out in the 50s. Ethiopian Emperor Haile Selassie attended a game in 1954, and put on a glove when Casey Stengel gave him a baseball.

There have been moments of high culture at the New York ballpark. The Yankees had Robert Merrill of the Met as a frequent National Anthem singer. Poet Marianne Moore once threw out the first ball. The Red Sox have counted Robert Frost, Bart Giamatti, Doris Kearns Goodwin and Seiji Ozawa amongst their fans. Yankees owner George Steinbrenner studied Shakespeare at Williams College, but has yet to don tights and recite from *A Midsummer Night's Dream* for the faithful.

Perhaps not quite as high-brow, in late 2004, novelists Stewart O'Nan and Stephen King published *Faithful*, the dialogue of two devoted Sox fans that embraced the world championship season. The Yankees have a prolific author of their own in the erudite Lawrence Berra. To date, a half-dozen books of Mr. Berra's thoughts and sayings have been published to widespread acclaim and puzzlement.

Literary figures, though, have long tended to favor the Red Sox, perhaps in part due to the cluster of colleges and universities in the Boston area, or perhaps because tragedy tends to inspire more than habitual triumph. The 2004 World Series win is sure to unleash a deluge of new books on the greatest comeback in baseball history. Will future writers begin to migrate to Chicago now, where both the Cubs and White Sox thirst for the Trophy?

Though these two baseball shrines continue to attract patrons in large part due to their status as venerable venues and traditional ballparks, their continued existence can never be taken for granted. In the latter years of Yawkey ownership, the Boston ballclub was run by John Harrington, and his administration actively promoted a plan for a new Fenway Park to replace the existing one. They were even successful in obtaining government authorization of around $150 million for infrastructure improvements in the area. An advocacy group formed, dedicated to preserving Fenway Park. Save Fenway Park mobilized with passion and compelling preservation arguments, including a study which showed that as baseball's oldest ballpark, Fenway's biggest appeal lay in its very age and history. People liked that, particularly visitors to the region. It fit the New England character. The group showed that new ballparks initially drew large crowds, but once the bloom was off the rose, it was only the play of the team that could attract fans. Under-performing teams did not draw well; no one went to Three Rivers Stadium to soak up the atmosphere. Yet in Fenway, even when fielding mediocre teams, the Sox had an asset to fall back on—the tradition of the ballpark itself. Ted Williams played on that field. Babe Ruth played there. So had Ty Cobb and Shoeless Joe Jackson. A faux Fenway across the street would never be the same thing. The Red Sox couldn't find a bank or lending institution that believed the ballclub would prosper under the debt load that constructing a new park would require.

In New York, new ideas crop up from time to time for a new Yankees ballpark—in New Jersey's Meadowlands, on the West Side of Manhattan. Though it does not quite retain the character of the old Stadium, the renovated home of the Yankees nevertheless maintains and exudes a grandeur of its own.

Both ballparks are active, lively places to watch baseball. There is a magic that attaches to both parks. Both embody time-honored traditions and both house a fervid fan base. Through the 2004 season, Fenway Park has sold out nearly 150 consecutive games, and fans in tents and sleeping bags began camping out a full 72 hours before tickets for the 2005 season went on sale at the box office on December 11, 2004. Yankee Stadium is larger, but is usually well packed out and consistently boasts one of the best home attendance records in all of baseball. Both teams are fortunate to have such passionate followings, and because the two parks are only several hours apart, many fans of one team will bravely enter the other club's lair—though often electing not to display caps or insignia that betray their loyalty.

Quotes about Yankee Stadium:

"[The Yankees are] a moneyed industry bloated with pride, ego, nasty innuendo, fans who have properly been called animals in a park appropriately called a zoo." —Raymond Mungo, author

"To me the glacial territory of Yankee Stadium is a Siberia for the novelistic soul. Though championship flags abound, the place is desolate and icy. The armies of Russia rumble through its winter midnights. The stadium is witless, vulgar, and ugly. To watch it demolished would be like seeing Marxism die, but replaced, no doubt, by the granite of poverty, its neighborhood overflowing onto its empty space searching helplessly for home." —Jonathan Schwartz

"There's the bigness of it. There are those high stands and all the people smoking—and, of course, the shadows. It takes at least one series to get accustomed to the stadium and even then you're not sure." —Ted Williams, in Life magazine, shortly after his retirement.

"I grew up loving Southern League baseball. When I was four my daddy took me to the old Rickwood Field in Birmingham. Then, coming to Yankee Stadium in 1937 for the first time—where the greats like the Babe, Lou, and DiMaggio played—was just beyond my dreams. Suddenly, here I was, a guy supposed to practice law, broadcasting Yankees home games on radio from this Mecca of baseball. This was THE place, the number-one place in baseball. The Stadium was like the Empire State Building or The Grand Canyon of baseball, and every time I stepped inside of it I had to pinch myself!" —Mel Allen

"I'll have great memories of this place. Obviously, it hurts losing, but the atmosphere here is matched nowhere. It's exciting to be out there on that mound in front of people going freaky. It's wild. Even though we lost, in a while we're going to appreciate being in this place." —Greg Maddux, after losing Game Six, 1996 WS

"When I came up to the Yanks from Newark at the end of the 1946 season, I took one look at the stadium and thought, 'Geez, whatta big place!' " —Yogi Berra

"There was a great, dark mystery about it when I first came here from Oklahoma. I still get goose pimples just walking inside it. Now I think this is about the prettiest ball park I ever saw." —Mickey Mantle, 1976

"You can talk until you're blue in the face about what it's like here and it doesn't matter until you experience it. The electricity that goes through here is unlike any other stadium. When Yankee Stadium is packed, the place is bigger than life." —Willie Randolph

Quotes about Fenway Park:

"We used to take a blanket and spread it out in the outfield. We had a radio and listened to the game, in the sun, looking for four-leaf clovers too, to try to win the game." —Jean Yawkey, about her and husband Tom

"If someone was trying to drive a left fielder nuts, this [The Wall] was just the way to do it." —Carl Yastrzemski

"The lack of foul territory at Fenway Park was even more important than The Wall. There's nothing much down the left-field line, as a matter of fact there's nothing at all hardly, other than about three feet. Down in right field, your line doesn't run all the way down to the very end. It cuts off fairly short and that leaves very little foul territory there. And there isn't much depth behind home plate and the back screen. Any foul ball has a good chance of going into the seats, so you lose a lot of outs. You would get outs in other ballparks, where the hitter is going to get another swing of the bat at you in Fenway." —Mel Parnell

"A left-hander's first look at the left-field Wall, the Green Monster in Fenway, is an automatic reason for depression. And that's when viewed from the dugout. From the vantage point of the mound it looms even closer. I felt like I was scraping my knuckles against it every time I went into motion, and I was always afraid that it would fall down and kill Rico Petrocelli at short." —Bill Lee

"I seldom pitched well at Fenway Park. I think I had a complex about it going back to that first game there when I was 17. I looked at that left-field Wall and felt hemmed in. I knew Cronin and Foxx could pop it over with half a swing." —Bob Feller

Chapter 5
Border Wars:
The Geo-Politics of Rivalry

"... brother will fight against brother, neighbor against neighbor, city against city, kingdom against kingdom." —Isaiah 19:2

"My father was a Yankees fan. My brothers were Yankee fans. Me? I like to be different. I just liked the Red Sox." —Harry Burke

"While it's not entirely true that my move from New York to New England was to be closer to the Red Sox, it's not entirely false either." —John Updike

The Boston-New York rivalry is multi-dimensional. It even extends beyond baseball, if such a thing can be imagined.

Unlike stolen automobiles, Red Sox-Yankees loyalties can legally be transported across state lines. Because of the particular geography involved, with New York and Boston just 200 miles and roughly four hours apart from each other, both teams have overlapping spheres of influence. Both have fan bases that butt up against each other. There's no Berlin Wall, but there is a perceptible borderline between Red Sox Nation and the dark realm that is home to the Evil Empire of the Yankees.

Boundaries can be reasonably well delineated between the two, with a northern line for Yankees fandom stretching through southern Connecticut and maybe a bit of southern Rhode Island. The Yankees claim pretty much all of New York State and even a sliver of western Vermont, up along the Hudson River valley to the Canadian border. The Red Sox have staked a solid claim to the rest of the six New England states. They also hold sway in Canada's Maritime Provinces, the domain of United Empire Loyalists who abandoned New England for a less-rebellious northern home. Ironically, Maritimers are now united in their loyalty to the Boston Red Sox.

And, as we know, Red Sox Nation is well entrenched throughout the rest of the country. There's no team that people love to hate more than the New York Yankees. The Sox have been the lovable losers, the perennial underdogs. Nevertheless, there are Yankees fans everywhere as well, as *Sports Illustrated's* 50-state survey of fandom clearly showed. They just aren't as demonstrative at ballgames; you don't find several thousand Yankees fans cheering loudly at a game in, say, Anaheim or even Baltimore. Thousands of Sox fans turn out, though, when the Red Sox play away games.

Roger Angell asked Red Sox manager Jimy Williams if he noticed all the Red Sox fans that chant "Yankees suck" even when Boston is playing another team. Jimy answered Angell, "Yeah. It's a contagious disease. It's around the country. If we play an exhibition game in spring training in Houston, there's people chanting 'Yankees suck.' It's like there's some type of audio system around the country. You really understand what they are saying. There's no Boston accent. I don't know what it means, but that's OK. I've heard my name in the same sentence."

Geography is a good indicator of fandom. If you're born in New York, you can be a Mets fan or a Yankees fan or, if you like nostalgia, even a Dodgers fan. If you're born in New York, rooting for the Yankees is acceptable. You couldn't help it; you were born there. You've got a valid excuse. If you're from the Midwest, though, or the South or West, and you're a Yankees fan with no family back in the Big Apple, then what's that all about? You're a front-runner? You just want to be with a winner? Do you root for Microsoft against the software startups?

Seriously, there are as many stories as there are individuals. Like the

Civil War, it has divided communities and even siblings into warring camps. There are towns split down the middle; there are families divided down the middle. There are even small enclaves of Sox fans ensconced behind enemy lines, right in the heart of Manhattan. They know where to meet on game nights to be among like souls. We'll visit some of those places, and we'll hear from some of the fans on the front lines of the border wars between Red Sox Nation and the Yankees Empire.

Connecticut

Where is the borderline? How precise is it? Does it run right through Chippy's Bar in Bristol, Connecticut? There seems to be general agreement that the line bisects New Haven at one point. Frank Sauer says, "I've lived in the Naugatuck Valley Region of Connecticut, my entire life. Grew up in the Lower Valley, hung out at times in New Haven, Bridgeport and Waterbury . . . Bridgeport is really more Yankee-Mets territory. New Haven is a bit of a mixture it seems. The Valley, though, is pretty well a melting pot, though as you move up toward Waterbury away from Ansonia/Derby/Shelton there is a stronger Sox following. If I were to draw a line it would be a dotted line through the Valley Region angled down through New Haven and skewed across from Waterbury to Danbury. That bloc would most likely be the stronger Yankees following and all to the East and North would be Sox Nation."

Josh Mamis reports: "It is conventional wisdom around here that the Q-Bridge, that funky bottleneck in New Haven where I-95 meets I-91 divides Yankees and Red Sox fans. I'm not sure it's that simple anymore, but it's a great device."

Ted Fischer adds from experience, "New Haven County is definitely divided (at least when I was growing up); however, I suspect Red Sox fans have the edge."

David Miner agrees: "I lived for some time in the Waterbury/Watertown area of Connecticut. It seemed to be fairly equally divided between Sox and Yankees fans. This seemed to be the true DMZ." Miner now lives in Brattleboro, in southeastern Vermont. "Here it is largely Red Sox country. The cable system added NESN [New England Sports Network, which carries Red Sox telecasts] to its package, much to my delight, and both radio and newspaper coverage is largely tilted in favor of the Sox—which is a good thing."

The largest station in Hartford is WTIC, a long-standing Red Sox Radio Network affiliate. Mike Koblish grew up in Meriden, Connecticut at about the mid-point between Hartford and New Haven. "Every grade there was some obnoxious kid who'd wear his full Yankees uni to school. I've always disliked Yankees fans much more than the Yankees team. From newspaper coverage I always assumed Hartford to be part of Boston territory and New Haven part of Yankees territory. My town was pretty mixed. Heck, my own household was mixed. My dad is a lifelong Yankees fan. The Sox AA team was close by—first in Bristol and then in New Britain. I'd get my dad to take me there. My older brother was a big Red Sox fan. I simply followed my brother instead of my dad. I do think my brother went to the Sox in some ways to rebel against the old man—that was his way—but since he blazed the path there wasn't any friction for me. My dad certainly finds my Sox obsession strange, but he's always been supportive."

Bill Lee (no, not *that* Bill Lee) grew up in Bristol, which hosted the double A team in the early '70s. Bill graduated in 1976, and recalls strong feelings on both sides. "At the time, it was a solid blue collar town where local sports ruled. I'm not really sure why there were so many Yankees fans even though we had a Boston affiliate. The fan base was solidly New York or solidly Boston. I'm not sure why there was such a split in team loyalty. Bristol is too far to commute to NYC but I wouldn't describe it as Rockwell New England either."

Lee has a very distinct memory of where the borderline ran. "The line must have run through Chippy's Bar across from Muzzy Field in Bristol. Even though the BriSox were playing during my youth, I have vivid memories of a 50-50 split among the town. The arguments at Chippy's when the TV was on and the Sox-New York game was playing were classic. Highly emotional. I do remember one fist fight over a Red Sox-Yankees game." Did it make a difference when the BriSox moved to New Britain and became the BritSox? "No one would have switched loyalties because the farm club moved. As everywhere else, I'd guess, the love of the BoSox or the Yankees is too deeply ingrained."

Robert Van Der Maelen has lived in Pittsburgh for thirty years. He wrote *Blood Feud*: "I grew up in New Haven, and in my experience, the dividing line went right through my family: my mother's side of the family were rabid (!) Yankees fans; I wouldn't have been surprised had they had pinstriped diapers. My father's family were Sox. The tension must have been too much for my psyche, 'cause I ended up in Pittsburgh." It was actually marriage that brought Bob to the other side of the Allegheny Mountains, but he says he still feels connected to New England as home. "You don't follow the Sox because it's the cool thing, or because it's the latest bandwagon you jump on. You're almost fated to have a connection to the team. At least, that's how it seems out here in Western Pennsylvania."

Bob's sister lives north of New Haven. She tells the story of her husband and her taking the kids up to Fenway for a game. Mo Vaughn was still with the Sox at the time, and their kids adored him; they were all wearing Red Sox shirts with 42 on them. "At one point in the game, Mo came through with a clutch hit. As everyone went crazy, my sister turned to an elderly woman to her right and yelled, 'Don't you just LOVE HIM?' The woman replied, 'Yes, I do. He's my boy!' "

Former Yankees fan Bob Rigby now works at Fenway Park; he's in charge of some of the suites on the left-field roof. "I grew up in Connecticut, right on the line there in Wallingford. I went to the University of Connecticut. Down there, you're either Red Sox or Yankees fans. I was a Yankees fan growing up and Mickey Mantle was my idol. But when I moved to Boston, I had to root for the home team! It's good for the game. When the Yankees come to town, I feel a little tug, but I hate those Yankees! They're a totally different team. You know, they're so successful. I'd rather be an underdog at this point."

Jeff Greenberg is an attorney who works in New York City, a dedicated Yankees fan and season ticket holder. He was raised in north-central Connecticut, in Manchester, about eight miles east of Hartford. He told *Blood Feud*: "In that area, as a kid, you have no local team of your own and you have to decide whether to be a Yankees or Red Sox fan. I first became a Yankees fan around age 7 or 8. I had a white Zenith transistor radio that I took to bed every night, and in the nights I could pick up WABC, and I often went to sleep hearing Phil Rizzuto broadcast the Yanks. I couldn't get any Boston stations. I was torn. There were fans of each team in my neighborhood, but more favored the Red Sox. I think there was a big Boston-leaning and New York-hating Irish Catholic contingent there. My dad was born and raised in Brooklyn—a Dodgers fan, and Dodgers fans certainly had no great love for the Yankees! But he liked being out of Brooklyn. His folks moved to Boston and my grandfather took me to my first major league game at Fenway. I always had a fascination with New York, though. My mother and her friends often took me into the city to see shows."

Joe Ulam is a Sox fan who also now works in New York, as Director of Annual Giving for Columbia University. His Brazilian girlfriend couldn't understand why he kept watching Red Sox games—games that they so often lost. Why not root for a team that wins more often? "Like most Brazilians, she is a huge soccer fan. I asked her why she continues to root for Brazil, instead of France after the last World Cup. She looked shocked I could even consider such a thing. I think now she understands my passion."

Then there's Mike Bloomberg. He was born in Medford, Massachusetts, but made his fortune in New York. When he began his campaign for Mayor of New York, he made an appearance at a Rotary luncheon on Staten Island and dodged one question deftly. Asked if he were a Mets fan or a Yankees fan, he replied, "Just to show you that while I am not a professional politician, I am slowly learning something. My answer to that is: I grew up in Boston, sir." Laughter and hisses were the response. Campaign spokesman Ed Skyler later explained, "He grew up with Ted Williams and Carl Yastrzemski. Mike's not the type to give up on his heroes." Just like Hillary Clinton, though, it didn't take too long. After becoming Mayor, Bloomberg began wearing a Yankees cap and announced his conversion. Clinton, another carpetbagger who matriculated in Massachusetts, started wearing the cap in 1999 after the Yankees won the World Series that year. It sure is easier that way. Could a political hopeful be elected in New York wearing a Red Sox cap? Not likely.

Vermont

In September 2003, as the primary season was beginning to heat up, and the baseball season was coming to a climax, Massachusetts Senator John Kerry accused former Vermont governor Howard Dean of being a Yankees fan. Dean had been born in New York. Dean said the accusation was insulting. He was a Red Sox fan.

"Howard Dean has a relationship with the Yankees that goes way back so we hope he is willing to put some chowder behind his childhood team,"

Kerry spokeswoman Kelley Benander said. Dean told reporters that he was rooting for the Red Sox and the Cubs. "I always root for the underdog," he explained. "Those are the two biggest underdogs."

So, the line runs through Chippy's, does it? Cliff Otto writes to *Blood Feud*: "Team loyalties had to do with newspaper, radio, and television coverage (as well as commuting destinations in western Connecticut). If your local newspaper assigned its beat writers to the Yankees, chances are you became a Yankees fan, unless there was a previous family loyalty to another team. If your local radio and television broadcasts were of Red Sox games, you became a Red Sox fan. If your father commuted to New York, you'd go to ball games in that city."

Cliff, though, had no such issue in the small Red Sox town where he grew up. "I can't speak to the divided cities issue, but I grew up in New Hampshire and I consider anyone living south of Maine, New Hampshire, and Vermont to be southerners (well, I do allow a little latitude for northern parts of Massachusetts)."

Vermont does present an interesting case, because the New York influence seeps in from New York State to the west. In earlier days, that Yankees influence even crept as far east as Springfield, as mystery author Robert B. Parker once explained: "I grew up, the early years of my life, in Springfield, in western Mass. At the time I was a very young boy, the 'blue laws' were still in effect, and they could neither broadcast nor play baseball on Sundays in Boston. My father, being a baseball fan, would listen to the Dodger and Yankees games that we'd pick over what was at that time WHN in New York and WPRS in New York.

"It was 1941 and I remember when he was listening, and I would have been 9 years old at that time, and the Dodgers were after a pennant. My baseball reckonings actually woke up with the Dodgers more than they did with the Boston team because it was a hot year for the Dodgers and my father took to listening to them on days other than Sundays. So I grew up more of a Dodger fan than a Boston baseball fan, really."

Being a real Yankees partisan, though, sometimes means you have to work at it. The Red Sox do have a stronger presence throughout New England because of the entrenched Red Sox Radio Network. Some of the Yankees radio affiliates aren't as strong. Yankees fan Will Forest lives in the Burlington area. "I don't think I've been in a location in Northern New England where I can't get the games. I know almost as much about the Sox as I do the Yankees. Most times that's all we can get, and hey, in business as in baseball, you always have to stay on top of the competition. The one thing all Vermont Yankees fans share is how to get the games on the radio. The Burlington station has only a daytime range, so we can BARELY get the afternoon games. We have to drive west toward Burlington. South of Montpelier and you're out of range. However, at night, the signal dies, but we can tune into 770 WABC in New York after sundown. So to hear the games we have to tune into a station 300 miles away and can't get reception from one that is 30 miles away."

Was there a bit of a change going on before the 2004 season? A Red Sox fan to the core, Ron Jacobs also reports from Burlington. Native Vermonters are far less likely to be Yankees fans than Sox fans, but "in recent years, fair weather Yankees fans seem to be showing their colors more. More Yankees hats, jerseys, t-shirts—and definitely more gloating in September and October. The *Burlington Free Press* sports section is predominantly Sox turf, although I am told by staffers it depends on which sports editor is working as to which team gets the front page. When I work with Little Leaguers, Red Sox fans are definitely in the clear majority." Jacobs was an immigrant himself, what native Vermonters call a "flat-lander." He became a Sox fan despite growing up in Laurel, Maryland. The 1967 "Impossible Dream" team captivated his 12-year-old imagination. "It just gave me the hope that underdogs can win."

Does it take a little more bravery to be a Yankees fan in some regards, in Burlington? "In the bars, it certainly does."

Now, as it happens, the Yankees do have some radio affiliates—even on Massachusetts soil. For the last few years, WNNZ has broadcast Yankees games from its station in Springfield. "We've had great success with the Yankees," Promotions Director Scott Harris wrote to *Blood Feud*. "Admittedly some sports fans would like to hear the Sox on the ZONE." One envisions Mr. Harris writing this from behind concrete barriers, from a secure bunker safe from Sox fans with firebombs. It might not have been the station's first choice but WHYN already carried the Sox so perhaps WNNZ had to settle for second best—the Yankees.

If pure geography did not always dictate loyalty, sometimes ethnic background might. Beginning in the 1930s and 1940s—the era of DiMaggio, Crosetti, Lazzeri, Rizzuto, et. al.—a lot of Italians (even in Massachusetts) followed the Yanks. There were enclaves of Italian-

Americans in Worcester who followed the Yankees. Barry Crimmins remembers hearing his dad talk about the Italians in Worcester, and Barry himself came to know another similar cluster in Providence.

Paul Penta found the phenomenon right inside Boston city limits: "I don't know about the Italians in Worcester, but I do know about some in my home town of East Boston. They were older, first and second generation Italians who couldn't find any Sox stars, other than brother Dominic, whose names ended in vowels and who had such an impact on the game.

"Joe DiMaggio was the very first baseball player's name I ever heard. I'll never forget being in my uncle Angelo's living room, as he bounced me on his knee one day singing the praises of Joe D. I could not have been more than 3 or 4, but it sure made an impression on me. I'm sure that's why my favorite Sox players have been guys like Malzone, Pagliaroni, Petrocelli, Jerry Casale, the Conigliaro brothers, Merloni and Mirabelli."

Rhode Island

James Bomba of North Smithfield, Rhode Island, was raised in North Providence. That's solidly Red Sox Nation. "Massachusetts is in my back-yard, but I've always been a Yankees fan. I was born and brought up in North Providence. I became a Yankees fan back when I was a kid. My father liked the Yankees and his father liked the Yankees. They were from Massachusetts. I guess I started following them back then—Mickey Mantle and Roger Maris. We're Italian. I think that's what really did it for my grandfather."

It wasn't a matter of being frontrunners. "Back when I was a kid, the Yankees used to lose. If you look from the middle 60s on up, they were ter-rible. As a kid growing up, there were mostly Red Sox fans in my neigh-borhood. All the kids were basically Red Sox fans. There were maybe one or two kids who were Yankees fans. That was a real strong Red Sox area. There was a lot of teasing back and forth. They knew I was a Yankees fan. I always had a Yankees cap on. When they lose, you'd really take a ribbing. When they win, they'd get very, very silent. They don't say anything. Down close to Narragansett, there are more Yankees fans. Our offices now are in Johnston, Rhode Island. We have maybe seven offices in the building and the whole section is Yankees fans.

"I played a lot of baseball growing up, and I went to Fenway all the time. When the Red Sox won, I rooted for them. But my heart was with the Yankees. Always for the Yankees. I like to see the Red Sox win! I'd like to see them come out tied at the end of the year—so the Yankees could beat them in the last game! I always had a Yankees cap on. Just like my son. He doesn't like to wear it to Fenway Park, though."

Why do Red Sox fans get down on Jeter so much? "I think it's the Garciaparra/Jeter thing. If the Red Sox had Jeter, then Nomar would suck. But they better watch out, because we're going to wind up picking up Nomar and we're going to make him a second baseman, and we'll give him a ring, because Boston's never going to have one. We get all your great players, we put them on our team, we give them a ring and then they retire."

Josh Lott spent his formative years (from 1969-1983) in Kingston, Rhode Island, maybe 15 miles from the Connecticut border. "Rhode Island, as you know, is tiny. There's only one statewide newspaper, the *Providence Journal*, and it was and continues to be Red Sox only. Same for the local network affiliates—there's only one of each in the state and they're pro Sox. Growing up in southern RI, however, my family read the *ProJo* every day and *New York Times* on Sunday, never the *Boston Globe*. Yet, we were firmly a Red Sox household (partly, I'm sure, because my mother grew up a Brooklyn Dodgers fan and antipathy to the Yanks runs deep).

"We got the Providence network affiliates, and could tune into the Boston affiliates with some difficulty. New York TV stations were impossible, and who really cares about Connecticut? The Sox radio network had stations throughout New England. I'm sure I could have heard the Yanks, but never wanted to.

"I always thought my town was very Red Sox-centric until October 1978 when all the Yankees fans in my Junior High loudly and cruelly came out of the woodwork."

Asked if there was a borderline that ran through Rhode Island, Josh replied, "Newport and Block Island, and other beach areas, have lots of summer residents. They come from all over, a lot from the NY/NJ area, and I don't consider them Rhode Islanders. The year-round residents are mostly Red Sox fans throughout the state."

Moving back a little bit more to the west, Emily Alling talked about life in southeastern Connecticut. "I grew up in New London County. I would say that Sox fans are a fairly comfortable majority. However, the Yankees fans are particularly obnoxious—what they lack in numbers, they make up for in sheer despicable-ness. And Mets fans came crawling out of the woodwork in 1986! Going to junior high school and sitting next to them on the bus, in class, etc. was not pleasant.

"There was a common perception that there were a lot of Yankees fans in Rhode Island because of the large Italian population in Providence. I guess the thinking was that they were fans of Joe D., Phil Rizzuto, et al., although we had Dom . . . 'better than his brother Joe.' New London has a pretty big Italian population too, so maybe that contributed. The rivalry in southeastern Connecticut is very bitter. I'm glad to be safe in western Mass now."

"The Yankees . . . are a family. A family like the Macbeths, the Borgias, and the Bordens of Fall River, Massachusetts." —Ron Fimrite, Sports Illustrated

Divided Families

There are any number of stories of families divided. And then there are those where marriage even overcomes the rivalry.

Dorian Massella, a state probation officer in Connecticut, has an unusual situation within her family—twin boys, one a diehard Sox fan and the other a stalwart Yankees fan. The whole family comes from New Haven originally, and both Dorian and her former husband are Yankees fans. She wasn't raised that way.

Dorian's father Harry Burke said, "My father was a Yankees fan. My brothers were Yankees fans. Me? I like to be different. I just liked the Red Sox. I liked Ted Williams. I liked Bobby Doerr. Everything around here was Joe DiMaggio. I said, 'In my opinion, I think Dom DiMaggio's a better ballplayer. He may not be the hitter, but I think he's a better ballplayer.' I used to take a lot of kidding. The Red Sox were losers and the Yankees were winners. I'd say, Well, wait 'til next year. Then they'd come around, 'Is this next year, Har?' But I stayed with them. I just went with the Red Sox all my whole life. My family was always Yankees fans. Even my wife, when we got married, she was a Yankees fan. Finally I converted her over to the Red Sox.

"When I grew up, in the city of New Haven, there was no television. When it first came in, it was strictly the Yankees and the Dodgers. The *New Haven Register* writes up the Yankees. They write only very small stories on the Red Sox. It was that way then; it's that way now. If the Yankees win, it's on the front page of the sports page. If the Yankees lose, it's on about page four of the sports section.

"I think as you get further up to Hartford, it's more for Boston. You get to the southern part of Connecticut, it's mostly Yankees. They're closer to New York. Most of your television . . . in New Haven, they don't telecast NESN and they don't telecast Fox 25. But I live in Branford now, which is a little further north from New Haven—and they get both."

When his daughter married Jimmy Massella, a Yankees fan, did Harry object during the church ceremony? "No, we're fans—but not to that extreme!"

His grandsons Lucas and Zachary, though, are twins. They share a room, but not team loyalties. The boys had never seen major league baseball until Harry was able to get them tickets to Fenway. "Since he saw them in person, Lucas is strictly all Red Sox. And the brother, Zach, is strictly Yankees. They razz each other. Both their parents are Yankees fans."

Dorian explains: "They share a room and half of the room is the Yankees and half of the room is the Red Sox. My father is a huge Red Sox fan, and Jim's father is a huge Yankees fan. So the boys would go with their grandfathers and they just ended up liking the different teams. Zachary likes baseball—he enjoys baseball—but Lucas, it has been his salvation. [Lucas was born with a serious spinal cord condition.] He cannot play any contact sports, so he plays baseball. He does research, and he can cite all the different statistics about the Red Sox and what year *this* happened and what year *that* happened. I think it's pretty funny that a little kid has taken such an interest. Usually kids just like whoever the famous player is.

"Derek and Nomar. That's their bedroom. Half Yankees. Half Red Sox.

"We had never been to Yankee Stadium, but my father got them a four-pack of tickets for Christmas. So they've been to four Red Sox games, and one of them was a Yankees-Red Sox game. It was a game that Pedro and Clemens pitched against each other. The boys thought that was great. Unfortunately for Lucas, the Yankees won that game. I think the Red Sox won every other game but that one, but that was a killer for Lucas, that the Red Sox got beat by the Yankees."

After the 2003 season, Lucas was devastated but he showed the kind of resilience and loyalty that is typical of Red Sox fans. When the Red Sox won the World Series in 2004, Lucas finally felt the joy of victory.

Friends Nevertheless

In August 2001, the two authors of *Blood Feud* visited Montreal where the Expos hosted the Red Sox in interleague play. Watching batting practice before the game, we struck up a conversation with two other visitors to Quebec, one wearing a Red Sox cap and the other sporting a Yankees cap. They seemed to be on speaking terms.

Mark Pogact was the Yankees fan. He said, sure they rooted for opposite teams but he had no problem cheering for the Red Sox in Montreal because they were a good team and—as long as they weren't playing against the Yankees—he was glad to root for them. All in all, what I like, he said, is just to see good baseball. New York Yankees fans can perhaps afford to be a little more magnanimous on occasion. Garret MacCurtain was not quite as generous.

"I grew up in Baldwinsville NY, a suburb of Syracuse," Mark explained. "I watched a lot of baseball with my father. He was born in the Bronx and grew up in Demerest, NJ. He went to a lot of Yankees games as a kid, and even saw Bob Turley's no-hitter. When my father's parents came to visit, they would both always watch the Yankees on TV every night they stayed. My grandfather would always bring me Yankees stuff whenever they visited. I had a lot of yearbooks, hats, coats, etc. from him. That pretty much established me as a Yankees fan." Mark lost interest in baseball at college, but after he took a teaching job near Barre, he met Garret and found they had a mutual love of baseball. "You don't get a chance to see the Yankees much here, so to watch baseball, I watch the Sox. He was a very biased Red Sox fan. To try to stay in the conversation, I just kind of listened.

"We would argue about the Sox and Yankees, and then we began building a mutual respect for each team. Slowly I got an appreciation for the Red Sox, mostly because of our interaction. You can really appreciate a team that works so hard, does pretty well, but hasn't won it all in a lot of years. That David and Goliath theme. Anyone can relate to that. Garret still dislikes the Yankees, but not as much, while I began loving the Red Sox too.

"It's like a big soap opera with them. It's really interesting, and sometimes sad. When the Yankees and the Red Sox aren't playing each other, I've got the Red Sox on and I'm rooting for the Red Sox.

"Garret is a lot more passionate. He gets a little more frustrated when the Red Sox don't do as well, and he shuts them off."

Garret MacCurtain, for his part, sees things just a bit differently: "I still highly despise the Yankees. So he's got false information there. I grew up in Braintree. I've always been a Red Sox fan. Just like other Bostonians, I'm waiting like my father and grandfather did—for a World Series championship. I went to college in Vermont. I think most native Vermonters are Red Sox fans. There's a lot of Yankees fans in Vermont—I'd say 65/35—35% Yankees. I think a lot of the people who are Yankees fans are fairweather fans, too, because the Yankees have been on top for so long. Red Sox fans are just generally more passionate.

"The Yankees are winning now and he's, like, so into it. Part of me thinks that I have to congratulate him or give him support. I can't tell him that I hope the Yankees get slaughtered tonight. That would hurt our friendship. I'll tell everyone else that I hope the Yankees get slaughtered and I hope Clemens breaks his arm. I wouldn't tell Mark that."

There's friendship and then there's marriage. Some people fall so hopelessly in love that they forget to ask the important questions. When Kerry Carle moved in with her boyfriend Mark Crough, it turned out she'd been harboring a dark secret. "Upon arriving in their new home, Carle opened her suitcase to unpack. Suddenly, before her swain's astonished eyes, out tumbled a . . . Yankees hat. 'I didn't know, recalls Crough, 35." Carle and Crough married nonetheless, in 2003. [Dan Aucoin, "Irreconcilable differences," *Boston Globe*, October 9, 2003]

Some relationships struggle with an in-house Sox-Yankees rivalry. When couples marry outside the faith, family tensions can boil over. Michael Rodman of Lincoln told the *Boston Herald*, "We have different religions and political views, and we can live with that. But this Yankees thing is a very difficult situation. I mean, she leaves their hat and T-shirts lying around our house." His fiancée knew where to draw the line. Passing a tattoo parlor one day, she talked about getting a "NY" logo tattoo. "She doesn't seem to realize the Yankees are evil," Rodman sighed, further explaining that he'll "really have to try to rein my brothers in."

When the two teams meet, Alyssa Toro sits in one room and her husband Matt, the Sox fan in the family, sits in another. "We have to," she said. "It gets too intense." Many other families report separate viewing as a prerequisite to togetherness. Can the children make the difference? Maybe. Suzie Byers grew up a Yankees fan in New Jersey, but then moved to Lexington, Massachusetts. Her husband Carl said he tried to "get her to come over from the dark side" but she remained steadfast. When their five-year-old son Jake started rooting for the Red Sox, Suzie realized she had to mute it a bit. "I cannot be a full-fledged Yankees fan anymore, because my son adores the Red Sox so much. But every time the Yankees win, I'm happy for my father. I'm secretly on the fence." [*Boston Globe*, ibidem]

Islands on the Island

There are outposts behind enemy lines. Oases offering succor to Sox fans stuck in Manhattan. Islands on the Island. The most famous of these is the Riviera Café in the West Village. Being a diehard Bosox fan in New York, with no cable channel carrying the Sox, can leave you wanting to watch ballgames with other fans of a Boston bent. The Riviera usually draws 30 to 50 Sox fans for each game, but during the 2003 playoffs, Vern Trotter wrote in an e-mail, "the place was full with about 20 standing outside for the weekend games watching through the window. The big attraction there is Jim, the bartender. Gets so crowded it is not always comfortable." Tanya Laplante said, "It's like an embassy in a foreign country. You're surrounded by your countrymen."

Riviera GM Steve Sertell said the place can get raucous when the Red Sox win. The Riviera offers 28 television screens. They even show the NESN pre-game and the post-game wrap-up. "There's pandemonium," he told a *Globe* correspondent. "So maybe they knock over a dozen glasses—so what? I can't remember having to throw somebody out." Sertell himself is a Yankees fan, but respects the Red Sox rooters. "Of all the sports teams that have had fan bases in this place, there are no better supportive fans. They are the most enthusiastic. You'll be downstairs and hear the place go wild, and you come upstairs—and somebody got a walk."

After Game Seven of the 2004 ALCS, the New York Police Department urged the Riviera to close early. There were just too many people outside on the sidewalk and street.

Trotter's father Bill pitched for seven seasons for the St. Louis Browns and Cardinals. Vern lived in Boston for about 20 years, and was imbued with Red Sox fever early on. "When you live in Boston, it's like being bit by Dracula," he said.

Seamus Flynn owns the Hairy Monk on Third Avenue at 25th Street. The bar has 8 or 9 television screens and draws Sox fans in the summer and Patriots fans in the fall and winter. So if it's Guinness you want with your gopher balls and grounders, the Monk could be the place.

Pino's is closed now. Owned by former Red Sox pitcher Jerry Casale, the 34th Street eatery served hearty, old-fashioned Italian food within rooms whose walls were covered with Red Sox photos, pennants, and paraphernalia. There weren't any TV screens, but it was an oasis that drew Sox fans over the years, and more than a few players. Even Ted Williams ate there in years gone by. Sadly, Pino's closed at the end of 2003, when the landlord declined to renew Casale's lease.

On the Upper West Side, there is Harrison's Tavern. It's a new place. These Red Sox outposts seem to be prospering. They're spreading.

It is almost inconceivable to imagine a similar center in Boston. A Yankees pub in Beantown? Who would underwrite insurance coverage on that? Perhaps a Prohibition-era speakeasy would be the way to go. Knock four times on the door and a peephole opens. You murmur the secret watchword—maybe "Cashman"—and the door is cracked so you can sneak in.

In years past, some Sox fans in New York chose not to mourn but to organize. The BLOHARDS are the Benevolent and Loyal Order of the Honorable Ancient Red Sox Diehard Sufferers. They typically meet twice each year, 100 or more fanatics, and for years they've chartered a bus from the City to come to Fenway's Opening Day. The BLOHARDS go way back. Jim Powers, originally from Cambridge and Uxbridge, Massachusetts, even saw Ted Williams play his first game in New England—the 1939 exhibition game Ted played in at Worcester's Fitton Field. Working in New York as an advertising executive, he founded the BLOHARDS with some friends— some forty years ago. It's even an older organization than the venerable Bosox Club in the Boston area. Sixteen days after the Sox won the Series in 2004, the BLOHARDS convened a special luncheon and Dr. Charles Steinberg of the Red Sox brought down the trophy so the loyal rooters could have it all to themselves for a couple of hours, midday in midtown Manhattan.

BLOHARDS member Howie Singer, who sends occasional bulletins from behind enemy lines to TheRemyReport.com, enjoyed Game Seven in person at the House that Ruth Built. He is relieved that he can now return to ballgames in the Bronx in a wholly different frame of mind. "I can now go back to watch baseball games at Yankee Stadium, and never hear or see '1918' again. Ever. I can't overstate how big that is for me and every other New York dwelling Red Sox fan. Particularly all the members of the BLOHARDS. Maybe we can actually just watch the game without the morons who turn their backs on the field, preferring to yell at us. As I said earlier, nothing bothers me now. Not work, not crowded subways, not city traffic, and not the lousy weather. Not even Yankees fans, who I must say, have been more congratulatory than expected. Most of them have said, 'You guys deserved to win', and some seem to think that maybe some of the bandwagon Yankees fans of the past few years will fall off. Others repeat the inane headline from the *Daily News* that appeared the day after the series ended, saying, 'maybe you'll win again in 2090.' Whatever. They don't affect me anymore."

Multitudes of Red Sox rooters can breathe freer now, stand up a little straighter, feel a little inner peace. The Boston Red Sox have caused a kind of group therapy for Red Sox Nation, a unique kind of faith healing. We kept the faith and now it's a whole new ballgame.

Outposts of Red Sox Nation are springing up in other cities, too. Walk into Sonny McLean's on Wilshire Boulevard in Santa Monica, and you might think a teleportation device has whisked you into a comfortable sports bar in an unassuming neighborhood somewhere in Greater Boston. Jim Conners has created an oasis for Boston sports aficionados and developed a devoted following. In 2004, Conners and customers chartered seven busloads of Sox fans to make the trek to Orange County and catch a Sox/Angels game. In 2005, the Angels aren't making it easy on them, claiming they don't have tickets to accommodate these loyal Red Sox rooters. Tom Werner lives not far from Sonny McLean's, and on the day after Thanksgiving 2004, the World Series trophy even paid a transcontinental visit to Sonny's.

Chapter 6
Color of the Curse

"The person who turns after mediums and familiar spirits, God says He would set His face against that person and cut him off from his people." —Leviticus 20:6

"I don't think God is a Yankee fan. I think that that organization is run by a more malevolent type of deity. I think there are more witches and warlocks in New York than there are in Massachusetts. We've gotten rid of ours." —Bill Lee

"Without the curse to fall back on (or the Curse, if you prefer), they might have to actually write about the games." —Stephen King.

A lot of people in New England have come to curse the accursed idea of the Curse. Dan Shaughnessy can take credit for popularizing the notion, in an entertaining book entitled *The Curse of the Bambino*. After that, all heck broke loose. HBO has subsequently done a special on it and any number of clever articles by any number of clever writers have been crafted over the years. But for some it just got to be too much. The whole thing ballooned and became overwhelming, and ridiculous. Sure it was fun at first, like a fresh new joke. Everyone had his or her own ideas of how to break the Curse. Father Guido Sarducci sprinkled his own particular sort of holy water onto Fenway Park—from a rented cherry picker because the un-amused Red Sox establishment of the day didn't actually welcome him inside. Laurie Cabot, a witch from Salem, tried her best to remove the Curse. Veteran mountain climber Paul Giorgio placed a Sox cap on top of Mount Everest in 2001, and burned a Yankees cap, hoping his hats would do the trick.

Other people tried to find and salvage a piano that a partying Babe Ruth supposedly pushed out on the frozen surface of a pond in Sudbury, Massachusetts, and let sink through the ice. Surely, they thought—for no logical or apparent reason—raising a musical instrument would be the key to satisfying the Babe. Maybe a hot air balloon would somehow lift the Curse, others decided; and another group attempted that. Speaking of hot air, a Massachusetts legislator introduced a resolution to break the Curse, by honoring Babe Ruth. Companies baked "Break the Curse Cookies" and the venerable Brigham's created special "Reverse the Curse" ice cream. Everybody and his uncle had an idea, and often a headline ensued.

No less an authority than Stephen King denied there was such a Curse, and that ought to have been good enough for all of us. It was not.

The whole idea of a Curse fed into what one Toronto writer termed the "New England whine industry"—but it just became too, too much. It became overbearing and overdone. The whole thing escalated to such a point that everyone in the region simply got sick of it. And still it wouldn't stop. Every time the Red Sox were thrust into the national spotlight the story was regurgitated once more for anyone in South Dakota or Albuquerque who may have missed it. There was only one way to make it go away. The Red Sox just had to win in order to reverse the curse of the Curse!

New York never really needed to cast a spell on the Red Sox—or did it? Once or twice, the Yankees may have resorted to delving and dabbling in the black arts. They're not telling. Certainly Yankees manager Joe Torre believed there were ghosts in Yankee Stadium. "There are ghosts here and a rich tradition," he said. "You can sense it all around you. It's not just an invention of the press. When I was a youngster I rooted for the National League teams and I sat in the stadium grandstand to watch Don Larsen's perfect World Series game in 1956. By the end of the sixth inning, I was rooting for Don to do it, even though I wasn't a Yankee fan. When I became manager here, the first time I walked down the runway leading to the dugout from the clubhouse I thought of Ruth and Gehrig and DiMaggio and all the others taking the same path. In my office there's a photo of Gehrig behind my desk. I inherited it, but I wouldn't think of removing it. That's what the stadium is all about."

For New Englanders, at least those who lived outside the Yankees sphere of influence which steals into southern New England, watching the New York team accumulate its 26—count 'em, 26—world championships, all since the sale of Babe Ruth, was a lot more haunting than any mild notion of Joe Torre's. In case you didn't get that, 26. It is not surprising that Bostonians and Red Sox rooters everywhere sometimes desperately sought to invoke any powers they could to counter the juggernaut.

For the record, here are the details of some of the ingenious cures for the Curse. Of course, the problem is, when the symptoms of the Curse disappear now that the Red Sox finally won the World Championship, which act of Curse-breaking gets the credit? Was it a group effort?

Laurie Cabot, the "official witch of Salem," was one of the first to attempt something supernatural. She didn't take on the entire Curse at one time, that might have been too daunting for even her. She came in with a specific task in mind. This was in 1976. Bernie Carbo had been slumping and the Red Sox were on a losing streak. Cabot says, "I unhexed Bernie Carbo's bat to end a ten-game losing streak." It may have worked in the short run, but it didn't last. And Carbo was traded to Milwaukee a few weeks later.

Bill "Spaceman" Lee, who admits to once being Cabot's accomplice, thinks that the evocation of spirits works both ways:

"The fatalism of Red Sox fans has been bred into them since the times of the Salem witch trials. It is why we maintain a tiny green ballpark, and a wall just beyond third base that makes every right-handed hitter pull the ball whether he should or not. That's the Curse of the Bambino. The witches aren't always on our side. In the '86 World Series, the New York Mets fans who were spinning their hands behind home plate in Shea Stadium in New York were witches! That's exactly what that symbol is! They were succubi from New York who were trying to suck the power out of Calvin Schiraldi and Bob Stanley. That's why it's so true when they say that New York sucks! That's my theory; Ruth was pulling for the Mets. It all fits in with the Curse. I see that stuff all the time."

It was good publicity, though, and for nearly the last thirty years, Cabot has often been asked to opine on matters concerning the Curse. Finally, maybe a little fed up, she just quit the whole thing in 2004. She told the *Boston Herald*'s Jules Crittenden, in mid-October 2004, "Last year I did a spell bottle to break the curse of the Bambino, if there is one," Cabot said. The Sox lost anyway. "Of course it did nothing," Cabot said. "There is no curse," Cabot said. "I have another theory. They are who they are. I think they should play as the players they are and not use my magic to do what they are supposed to do," Cabot said. "I'm hoping they do their best. I'm hoping they win, because it will prove what I said is true. There is not a curse." A few days later, she said the curse of the Bambino was a bunch of bunk. "They don't really need it," she said of special spells. "I'm a Red Sox fan and I think they can do it on their own steam. Fans should realize that. Look how far they've come. It's just a matter of time. They are going to win."

Red Sox pitcher Curt Schilling agreed, from a quite different perspective. "As a Christian, I know for a fact that the Curse doesn't exist. Boston hasn't won a World Series not because of a curse but because the teams they played have been better than them." Three years earlier, Pedro Martinez had given his full agreement: "[All the talk] was just curse, curse, curse, curse," said Martinez. "It's not baseball. I believe in God, not curses." Another victory for Good over Evil!

All the talk of curses, of course, became tiresome. But it couldn't help but have a negative impact. The Amazing Kreskin told Bob Ivry of NorthJersey.com that curses were silly—except when they seem to be working. He explained, "Teams are highly suggestible. Even if they don't talk about it, they have to be affected. It's reinforced each year that it's not broken. It makes it worse. The curse affects them on an unconscious level. They've been handicapped by the past. No team should have arrayed against them so many negative factors."

Although a Yankees fan, The Amazing Kreskin told Ivry early in the 2004 season that he would be willing to meet with the Red Sox for 20 or 25 minutes alone in the clubhouse. Using the power of suggestion, he would plant a seed in their minds "so they'd be influenced to have a greater belief in themselves."

"If Kreskin's power of suggestion doesn't work, then a natural healer who calls himself Monche, of Botanica Santa Ana in Passaic, has an Rx,"

Ivry continued. "In order to lift the curse, Red Sox manager Terry Francona would have to undertake three cleansings involving sponge baths with infusions of natural healing plants, prepared in a secret method. Then, at every stadium at which the team played, the Red Sox would have to sprinkle a special potion. 'In four days,' Monche said, 'the Curse of the Bambino would be lifted.' " Right. One can just imagine Francona having his sponge baths during those first three games of the ALCS, desperately dosing himself with natural healing plants. Try dipping your head in Rogaine while you're at it Terry, just so it's not a complete waste of time.

In the early 1990s, Father Guido Sarducci, a Saturday Night Live regular, was brought to Boston to perform an exorcism. The Red Sox did really well for about a week afterward. The exorcism worked, but it didn't last. Taken to task, and asked to comment for *Blood Feud*, Father Guido was defensive. We asked the good father, "Maybe the Sox hadn't done enough penance for the pennant?" "Hey, it's not my fault how the season ended," the padre replied. "It worked—but why didn't it keep working? 'Cause I didn't get a thing! No lobster in the mail from the mayor. No clams on ice. Not even a hot dog! Not even one baked bean on my porch. No thank you, even! One hand has to wash the other one. It's kind of their fault.

"The other thing is, they wouldn't let me into the park. They made me do it outside. What do they want? They want the curse to go away but they won't do what what they need to do. They had us go up on a cherrypicker outside. It was a little dangerous. They had us standing in like a plastic garbage thing, you know, on the crane. It could have given way. It was really dangerous. We were outside looking in and I couldn't get a lot of holy water in there. You know what I mean? Just on the side of the park. You have to go in! I should have been inside."

"I asked them for ten gallons of Perrier. They got me regular water. Tap water! I asked them for fourteen pounds of incense. They got me NO incense! The only thing they did right was to get me that assistant! A really pretty girl! She had on this little Catholic plaid skirt."

Perhaps someone in the Vatican finally made a sacrifice on behalf of the good father Guido and his Red Sox. After all, this year it was the Cardinals who watched their Series hopes go up in smoke.

Paul Giorgio from Auburn, Massachusetts climbed Mount Everest on May 23, 2001. Covering all his spiritual bases, he sought salvation for the Sox not from the Holy Father but from a Tibetan lama. Smoke played a part here, too. He'd explained his mission to a lama beforehand, and was advised to place his Red Sox cap atop the world's highest peak. He told *Blood Feud*: "I left the cap at the summit with the American flag. I pinned it through the adjustment strap on the back. Two days later, as soon as I got back down to base camp, I took a Yankees cap and burned it on the puja as an offering to the gods to complete the entire cycle." It wasn't easy to try to burn a cap in the thin air on Everest. It finally took, but didn't seem to help in the seasons that immediately followed.

Playright David Kruh and composer Stephen Bergman created a musical entitled *Curse of the Bambino*. The 2001 production enjoyed a six-week run in downtown Boston.

That fall, Massachusetts State Representative Angelo Scaccia introduced a resolution to honor Babe Ruth for his service in Boston, feeling that perhaps it was that we never said "thanks" which resulted in the Curse. Canton resident Harvey Robbins joined Scaccia in an attempt to lift the Curse—with the help of a hot air balloon. Robbins outlined the plan in an interview. "Yes, we hear about the Curse and all that. Truly Babe Ruth had never been honored here. He was a great athlete who had never been given his due in Boston, and I wanted to address that.

"I invited Babe Ruth's daughter from Conway. I wrote a long letter through her publisher. She thought it was an honor she would appreciate and she agreed to come. We had a limo service—a friend—bring her down. She spent the day, signed 189 copies of her book. We had a number of activities—an oxen pull and all that.

"We decided to do a hot balloon lift—to lift the Curse. We had this huge banner made up—'BABE RUTH, BOSTON RED SOX, 1914-1918'. I had all the TV crews—4, 5, 38, 25, 56. There were all there." The lift, though, was delayed. The excuse was the weather; it was a little windy. When he finally owned up to it, however, Robbins' assistant confessed that he forgot to bring the banner and had left it on his kitchen table all the way back in Worcester.

"Meanwhile, we lose an hour and a half and the TV crews, one by one, are leaving. This is terrible. Finally it does arrive and we got some good coverage on Fox 25. One of the other stations left too early and they showed the balloon deflated and lying on the ground. They were saying the Babe Ruth thing fell flat on its face—because they didn't stay around long enough. It did go up. The people hung around and it was a great event.

"We affixed the banner to the balloon. Babe Ruth's daughter walked out to the site and cut the red ribbon on the bottom as we launched. It was too turbulent to go up fully, but we went up about 100 feet and the symbolic lift did occur. The balloon was filled with people wearing the retired numbers of the Red Sox players—Bobby Doerr, Joe Cronin, Yaz, Fisk and Teddy. We carried the Babe Ruth uniform with us—he didn't wear a number with the Red Sox—and the symbolic lift took place. It was a great event. Now the Red Sox can feel free to win, as long as they clean up their real act."

The lift didn't work, either. Once again, the Sox finished second to the Yankees, and didn't even win the wild card.

Paul Giorgio decided to try again. On a second climb of Everest, in the spring of 2003, the mountaineer said, "The lama said I didn't explain myself thoroughly. What I needed to do was bring the Babe himself. I got a picture of Babe Ruth from 1918 and took that with me." Well, we all know how the 2003 season turned out. Perhaps the speed of prayer can be slow, and it took a full year to work its way from Everest's summit to St. Louis. Giorgio plans a third summit in 2005, but with the Red Sox triumph in 2004, Paul can simply continue to enjoy the feeling of being on top of the world.

In 2002, the Restoration Project of Sudbury, Massachusetts sponsored a search of the town's mile-wide Willis Pond. Ruth had a home on the shore back in 1920, and during a party had reportedly pushed his piano out on the ice while continuing to play. The party eventually veered off in another direction. The piano remained and eventually sank. The notion was to recover the piano, restore it, and the Curse would be lifted. Divers dove, others searched, all in vain. Finally, the Restoration Project turned to John Fish of American Underwater Search and Survey. Fish had a pedigree; he'd been involved in the 1996 search for TWA flight 800 fragments. After the World Trade Center attack, he helped search Ground Zero for the black box recorders of the two airplanes used in the attack. At Willis Pond, he searched with an advanced magnetometer but, in the end, turned up nothing.

The town of Salem got involved again when Mark Hillner, a teacher at Salem High, asked his class to construct a shrine in the classroom. There were rituals involving sticking a pin in a Yankees teddy bear. Todd Hart of the *Salem Observer* explained that "one peculiar item in the shrine is a squash brought in by another teacher. Using a Global Positioning System the students and Hillner pinpointed the direction of Fenway Park from SHS and pointed the oversized vegetable straight at it." Squash the Yankees?

This was, admittedly, getting a little weird and far-fetched even by supernatural standards. Years from now, historians will not grasp how strained some of the attempts at exorcism had become. Points were stretched, metaphors multiplied, and at times it was as painful to endure as a trip to the dentist. In fact, now that we mention it, a teenaged boy was hit in the teeth by a ball during a game at Fenway. Maybe that could that end the Curse? "Why?," you could reasonably ask. Yes, there was a twist here, too. Turns out the boy lived in a house that Babe Ruth used to occupy back when he lived in the Boston area.

The boy was Lee Gavin and he was 16. He lived in Sudbury on Dutton Road in Ruth's old house. On August 31, 2004, he was hit in the teeth by a slicing Manny Ramirez foul ball. Gavin was in section 9, box 95, row AA and that's where the ball landed, knocking out his two front teeth. An ambulance took him for treatment. Fortunately, he got to keep the ball. He noted that it was a full moon. Manny was his favorite player. "I'm not sure why he didn't catch it," said his mother Julie. "He's a good player. But look at how bad the Yankees lost that night." *The Boston Globe*'s Brian McGrory column a couple of days later was headlined, "Taking Teeth Out of Curse." He wrote, "Lee's father, Dennis, said he doesn't believe in the curse, but did note that Lee attended Tuesday's game with a friend named Jarrett Lowe, who has a brother named Derrick. Coincidence? Is it also a coincidence that Lee wasn't sitting in the seats down the left-field line, where his father has season tickets, but instead down the right-field line where the ball landed?"

Doctors were able to reinsert his teeth. Gavin told McGrory he believed in the Curse. "So does he also believe his spilled blood has helped to lift it? At this, he smiled and said, 'I hope so.' "After the World Series victory, the story surfaced again. Had this event been the one that broke the Curse?

". . . curse, curse, curse, curse. It's not baseball. I believe in God, not curses . . . .Babe Ruth was one of the greatest men in the community. I don't think he would curse anybody. I don't get into all that." —Pedro Martinez, 2002

Lastly, there was "Tessie." During the 1903 World Series, the very first Fall Classic between the pennant winners in the National League and the American League, the Boston Americans were down. The first three games were in Boston, but they'd lost two games and won just one. A loyal group of Boston fanatics—the Royal Rooters—had traveled to Pittsburg. (The city name had no "h" in 1903.) The Rooters, led by " 'Nuf Ced" McGreevey, created a parody of a popular song of the day named "Tessie." They changed the words to heap insults on Pittsburg's stars, and seemed to spark a Game Four ninth-inning rally. The team appeared to revive its sense of self-confidence, and the Bostons turned the tide in the Series; "Tessie" became a Rooters' favorite for years—despite driving even many Boston partisans to distraction. Deliberately meant to annoy the opposition, it was sung repeatedly, sometimes ten or more times in a row.

"Tessie" was invoked as late as the middle teens. It was played during the 1915 World Series, and some think it might have led Nap Lajoie to commit five errors all by himself. In a game that had come down to two outs in the ninth, Boston had runners on second and third. Third baseman Eddie Murphy's failure to catch a "comparatively easy fly" by Heinie Wagner allowed two runs to score. Might it have been due to the Royal Rooters band and the old warhorse "Tessie" which they "tooted incessantly"?

Historian John Holway wrote that the "Curse of the Bambino" was nonsense. But he said he knew what it would take for the Red Sox to resume their role as champions of the world: "When the Fenway organist strikes up a happy, lilting rendition of 'Tessie' again, I believe, the Red Sox will return to the glory days of old." [John B. Holway, *The Baseball Astrologer: And Other Weird Tales*, p. 167]

The Red Sox organization decided to try just that in 2004. A band named the Dropkick Murphys recorded a version of "Tessie" and shot a video featuring Colleen Reilly as "Tessie." The first time the Dropkick Murphys played the new "Tessie" at Fenway Park was before the famous July 24 game where Varitek and A-Rod fought, Mariano Rivera blew a save, and the Sox won on a Bill Mueller extra-inning homer. It maybe took about a week to get fully up to speed, but in August the Sox went 21-7 and lost only one game from August 16 through September 3. They were on a roll. "Tessie" had now joined "Dirty Water" as part of the Red Sox repertoire of Fenway hits. They went on to win the Wild Card and, of course, the rest has been recorded as glorious history.

Going through the Yankees to get to the Series, winning four in a row from their most fearsome foe, routing their historic rival, toppling the titans—after all that, the Red Sox ride through the Series was like a heated knife cutting through soft butter. If there ever had been a Curse, the Curse was reversed. The Curse was in a hearse. The Curse was dead.

Chapter 7
The Grady Bunch: 2003 Season and Playoffs

"Boast not of tomorrow, for you know not what a day may bring forth." —Proverbs 27:1

"Who can understand his own errors?" —Psalm 19:12

"The more self-centered and egotistical a guy is, the better ballplayer he's going to be. You take a team with twenty-five assholes and I'll show you a pennant. I'll show you the New York Yankees." —Bill Lee

"It would be hard to find a New Englander this morning who would doubt the veracity of the story Joe Torre told on the cusp of last night's rubber game between the Red Sox and Yankees. The Yankees manager described an encounter he had yesterday with a couple while riding the elevator at the Ritz-Carlton, where the team spent the weekend. 'They were kidding, but you could still see an edge to it,' Torre said. 'They told me, "If it came to a choice

between getting Saddam Hussein or beating the Yankees, we'd take
beating the Yankees." I think they were kidding.' " —Gordon Edes,
Boston Globe, July 28, 2003

"The New Englanders who follow the Red Sox are as deeply scarred
by loss, particularly loss to the Yankees, as they are loyal to their
club. But it's more specific than that. They are especially scarred—
traumatized would not be too strong a word—by loss to the
Yankees in the late innings . . . ."—Stephen King, Faithful

For Red Sox fans, winter is invariably the longest season. In springtime
hope springs eternal; in summer the hopes grow and often prosper; in the
fall, instead of ripening and bearing fruit, they shrivel and fall with the
leaves and are dragged to the curb for disposal. And in the winter we are
left to contemplate what might have been.

Figuratively speaking, the New England winter of 2003/2004 was long
enough and cold enough to cause Dr. Zhivago to abandon Lara and flee to
southern climes. Climatologists would probably tell you that it was a normal northeastern winter, with its share of snowstorms and sunshine. Don't
believe it. It was a nuclear winter for Red Sox Nation.

The 2003 Red Sox were a colorful lot, with a team spirit and a non-con-
formity that was both refreshing and endearing. This spirit was epitomized
and to a large extent inspired by Kevin Millar, the free spirit DH/first
baseman/utilityman whose "Cowboy Up" attitude infected the Red Sox
clubhouse and eventually spread throughout New England. The team iden-
tity seemed to coalesce around this journeyman eccentric who had signed
to play for the Chunichi Dragons in Japan before the Red Sox practically
shanghaied him and pressed him into service at Fenway, compensating the
distressed Dragons in due course.

Millar was a perfect fit for the Red Sox. He immediately befriended
Manny Ramirez and David Ortiz and brought an intangible element of
cohesiveness that had often been missing on talent-laden teams of the '70s,
'80s and '90s. He kept the team loose and attracted some of the constant
media glare that is both the blessing and curse of playing baseball in
Boston. Millar's school days video of "Born in the USA" was played on the
scoreboard to try and incite a few late-inning rallies. And who could resist
the "Cowboy Up" T-shirt depicting David Ortiz in a cowboy hat? Millar's

impact may not have been fully evident in his statistics, but it was significant nonetheless.

The 2003 Red Sox won 95 regular season games and lost 67, finishing second in the American League East by six games to the 101-61 Yankees. The two teams had played to a virtual dead heat in the 19-game season series, the Yankees winning 9 and the Red Sox 9 until the final game of the year tipped the balance ever so slightly in New York's favor.

In the A.L. Division series, the wild card Red Sox were pitted against the formidable Oakland Athletics, winners of the A.L. West crown. The always-tough Minnesota Twins, survivors in the A.L. Central, blocked the Yankees' path to the World Series.

After losing the first game in the Twin Cities, the Yankees disposed of the Twins in three straight games and lay waiting in the reeds for the winner of the Red Sox-A's series.

It took the Red Sox all five games to beat out the "moneyball" squad assembled by Billy Beane. The Red Sox lost their first two games in California and traveled back to Boston on the verge of a three-game sweep. The restorative powers of home cooking are amazing, however, and the Red Sox rallied to win the next three games, earning their trip to the ALCS and yet another showdown with the Yankees.

The Red Sox captured Game One at Yankee Stadium as Tim Wakefield out-dueled Mike Mussina in a 5-2 series opener. David Ortiz was the offensive hero for Boston, launching an upper deck home run.

The Yankees came back in Game Two to beat the Red Sox 6-2 behind starter and winner Andy Pettitte, a Red Sox nemesis. With the Red Sox leading 1-0, Nick Johnson homered with a man on to give the Yankees the lead.

Back in Boston, with the Series tied 1-1, the Yankees hoped to continue their roll in a dramatic clash between Boston's reigning ace Pedro Martinez and their former ace turned Yankee Roger Clemens. This was Roger's return to the home park that had first made him a household name. Once loved throughout Red Sox Nation, he was now greeted with all the affection accorded Michael Moore at the 2004 GOP convention.

This game had all the elements for an instant classic. The two right-handers seemed safely ensconced in the pitching pantheon of Boston baseball, right up there with the Babe and old Cy Young.

The Red Sox scored first when Manny Ramirez singled in two runs. The

Yankees fought back and drew even on a Derek Jeter third-inning homer. The boys from the Bronx followed with another run in the fourth to take the lead, and Pedro was in trouble. With runners on second and third and no one out, Martinez glared in at Karim Garcia and threw the next pitch, a fastball, high and inside. Garcia was able to react quickly enough to have the ball deflect off his back, but the atmosphere at Fenway immediately ratcheted up in intensity. Minutes later, Garcia took his anger and frustration out on second baseman Todd Walker, sliding hard and late into second.

The Yankees bench began shouting at Pedro, and Martinez responded by pointing to his head and mouthing something at Jorge Posada, the most vocal of the Yankees shouters. What Pedro's message was is open to conjecture. Many interpreted it as an outright threat to bean Posada next time up. Broadcasters claimed to read Pedro's lips, declaring he'd said, "I'll hit you in the head." Perhaps in their haste, they'd forgotten that the Dominican Martinez would likely be speaking Spanish to the Puerto Rican Posada. Some who watch Pedro on a regular basis contend that he was only saying "Use your head, why would I want to intentionally hit him?"

Whatever the case, the exchange infuriated Yankees bench coach Don Zimmer, who has four tantalum buttons inserted in his head thanks to a near-fatal beaning experienced during his playing days.

In the bottom of the fourth, with tensions so strong you could feel them through a TV screen, Clemens threw a high fastball to Manny Ramirez. Ordinarily, it would have been just another pitch, but in the context of what had preceded it, and in light of Clemens' reputation as a headhunter, it became a trigger for another nasty scene. Manny cursed the pitcher, who returned the sentiments in kind. Players from both teams charged onto the field and began pairing off in various combinations. It looked like the action would be contained before any serious damage was done. And then out of nowhere came the portly Don Zimmer, Yankees bench coach and sometime hemorrhoid pitchman, charging like a mad bull toward Pedro Martinez. Martinez was forced to either take evasive action or engage in fisticuffs with a senior citizen. He chose the former alternative and sidestepped the onrushing Zimmer while pulling him head-first to the ground. It was an ugly episode for the two teams and for baseball.

New York's Boston-born Mayor Michael Bloomberg said later that Pedro would have been charged by the police if the same thing had happened in his town. Apparently, the mayor's conversion from Sox fan to

Yankees yahoo was complete. He didn't pass judgment on Zimmer's inno-
cence or guilt.

The game resumed and seemed destined to end peacefully until an
unexpected fight suddenly broke out in the Yankees bullpen. Now, who was
fighting, and about what? Apparently, a number of Yankees players had
jumped one member of the Boston ground crew. The participants in the
incident would eventually end up in the courts, with two of the Yankees
found guilty and sentenced to community service.

After the dust had settled, the game that looked to be Roger's curtain
call at Fenway was a triumphant one, as Clemens exited the game in the
seventh with a 4-3 lead. The lead held, and the Yankees claimed a 2-1
advantage in the best-of-seven clash.

In Game Four, Tim Wakefield, whose signature knuckleball suggests
anything but consistency, was as steady as a rock as he once again out-shone
the Yankees' Mike Mussina. The veteran Red Sox pitcher allowed just one
run before giving way to reliever Mike Timlin in the eighth inning. Trot
Nixon and Todd Walker each homered to give the Red Sox the 3-2 win.

With the teams scheduled to return to New York for the final two
games of the ALCS, Game Five in Boston seemed to be a must win for the
Red Sox. What team would want to head into Yankee Stadium for the final
two games, needing to win both? The card for the scheduled nine-round
bout pitted Yankee pitcher David Wells, a wily veteran who worshipped
Babe Ruth (and whose stomach was of Ruthian proportions), against Derek
Lowe, a brilliant, but often erratic, sinkerball artist for Boston. The Yankees
scored three runs in the second inning and hung on to defeat the Olde
Towne Team 4-2. Karim Garcia exacted a measure of revenge by driving in
two Yankees runs on a bases-loaded single.

As Game Six got underway, the Stadium was poised for a post-game
celebration. The glitterati of the city were present to see and be seen in the
heart of the media Mecca. But there would be no final hometown hurrahs
this day. Boston's pitching staff was depleted, so Grady Little started his
fifth man, John Burkett, winless against the Yankees and sporting an ERA
approaching 9.00. The Red Sox rose to the occasion—thanks in part to a
Varitek home run, and posted a 9-6 win over the AL East champs thereby
forcing a final, deciding Game Seven between the two bitterest rivals in all
of baseball. On the mound: Roger Clemens for the Yankees and Pedro
Martinez for the Red Sox.

The final icy blast before the winter of our discontent began on the evening of October 16, 2003. The two teams were now meeting for the 26th time since moving north from spring training.

Sox fans were pumped as the Cowboy Up boys racked up a 4-0 lead off the Rocket. Yankees- and Clemens-killer Trot Nixon homered in the second for the first two. Varitek doubled. Enrique Wilson threw wild to first on a routine Johnny Damon grounder and Varitek scored. Leading off the fourth, Kevin Millar hit the first pitch for a home run to left field.

Pulling out all the stops, Joe Torre then brought in Mike Mussina, who threw three full innings of two-hit ball. The Yankees first scored on a solo home run off Pedro by Jason Giambi in the fifth. Before you could say BALCO, Giambi took Pedro deep again the next time up, making the score 4-2. Only a year later did the federal grand jury testimony come out; Giambi admitted taking illegal steroids and performance-enhancing human growth hormone in 2003. His testimony came on December 11, 2003, just eight weeks to the day after Game Seven.

In the top of the eighth inning, David Ortiz answered Giambi's second homer with a solo shot of his own, to boost Boston's lead to three runs, 5-2.

The Red Sox cold snap began in the form of a brain freeze by an otherwise competent manager named Grady Little.

At precisely 16 minutes after midnight on Friday morning, October 17, if you listened carefully, you could hear the tragic sound of hearts and hopes breaking across New England. It was not unlike the sound made by an iceberg being hit by a large ocean liner. The good ship Red Sox had sunk with all hands on board. There were no survivors. As soon as Aaron Boone swung the bat at the very first pitch served up to him in the 11th inning, it signaled the start of a long, cold winter. Every Sox fan knew that when the ball landed, their baseball season would be over. At that point, Grady Little surely became the most productive goat in history because the Boston talk shows milked him every day, all winter long and into the springtime.

Little had made a fatal, glaring mistake. Despite cruising with a four-run lead, and a fully-rested, battle-tested bullpen at the ready, Little left a clearly-tired Pedro Martinez in the game too long. Sighs of relief ushered out of living rooms across Red Sox Nation when Martinez made it through the seventh, only giving up one run. The Sox had a three-run lead with just six outs to go, and Sox fans smiled as Pedro left the mound, pointing heaven-ward as he headed for the showers; a moment later, the exhausted ace accepted the embraces of his teammates and congratulations for a job well done. The Boston bullpen had been brilliant in the post-season so far. Barring unforeseen circumstances, Pedro Martinez was the winning pitcher and the Red Sox were going to the World Series.

Jaws dropped around the country when the Boston pitcher took the mound in the bottom of the eighth. It was, of all people, Pedro Martinez. The appearance of Lazarus himself would not have been much more surprising to anyone watching. Boston fans were screaming at their TV screens for Grady Little to take him out and put in Alan Embree or Mike Timlin, all warmed and ready to go. It didn't happen.

Pedro quickly retired Nick Johnson on a pop-up. One out. The score was 5-2 for Boston, and the Red Sox were now just five outs from a trip to the World Series. Martinez suddenly couldn't get anyone out. With his pitch count over 100—the pitch count is baseball's breathalyzer, and Pedro was over his personal limit—he allowed four straight hits in the eighth inning as the Yankees scored three times to tie the game.

Jeter lined a double down the right field line that rattled off the fence. Bernie Williams followed with an RBI single over the shortstop, making the score 5-3. That's when Little emerged from his burrow and strode purposefully to the mound. Red Sox Nation heaved a great—but premature— sigh of relief. With Hideki Matsui on deck, there could now be no doubt Pedro would at last be allowed some relief. Matsui had doubled twice off Martinez in the series, once earlier in this same game. It was a no-brainer.

But not for Little, who later offered weakly that "Pedro wanted to stay in there. He's the one we want on the mound over anybody we can bring in out of that bullpen." And indeed, it looked briefly as if Martinez may have summoned the strength to finish the inning. He got two quick strikes on Matsui, but then the Japanese slugger pulled the next pitch down the right field line and into the stands for a ground-rule double. Yankee Stadium was fired-up. With Embree and Timlin still looking on from the bullpen, Martinez faced Posada. With the count 2 and 2, the catcher fisted an inside pitch just out of reach of the Red Sox infielders, scoring two runs and knotting the game.

As Jim Caple aptly put it, "That's when Little finally took the ball from Pedro, and by that point, the only surprising thing was he didn't immediately hand it to Denny Galehouse."

The game wasn't officially over at that point, of course. The score was tied and it was, the announcers told us, a brand new game. Red Sox fans knew better. Actually it was the same old story, same as '78, same as '86, same as '67. Different no-name Yankees hero, same result. Final score: Yankees 6, Red Sox 5. The actual blow came off Tim Wakefield, which was perhaps the unkindest cut of all. Wakefield did not deserve this. The noble knight of the knuckler had beaten the Yankees twice already in the ALCS. He was the quiet hero, the Gary Cooper of the Red Sox staff. Boone on the other hand was the Gary Coleman of the Yankees offense. No, we don't mean Jerry Coleman, we mean Gary "What you talkin' about, Willis?" Coleman. Wakefield pitched through the tenth and was brought back again in the fateful 11th. Boone had not started Game Seven and his Series had been very forgettable to this point.

The ball arrived low and inside and departed high before landing beyond the left field fence. Home run.

And the rest is Red Sox history, and even though we have paid heed all too expertly to the old admonition to learn from our history, we were still condemned to see it repeated. "Ah, well. There's always next season." The words sounded especially hollow this time

"I was touched by the Lord," said Rivera, the MVP of the ALCS who ran to the mound and collapsed after Aaron Boone's 11th-inning homer in Game 7. "I had a big conversation with the man, and He came through. I just ran to the mound and hugged the mound." Asked if Boston received similar divine help, Rivera said, "No, He's not a Red Sox fan." —reported by John Shea, San Francisco Chronicle

The 2003 / 2004 off-season

Determined to position the team for another shot at the pennant, it didn't take GM Theo Epstein long to begin making off-season moves. Anyone could see that Manny Ramirez wasn't that comfortable as a member of the Red Sox, and the long-term contract that Epstein's predecessor Dan Duquette had signed with Ramirez still had $104 million to run. That was a lot of money that could be put to other use, if Manny wasn't happy in Boston anyway. Maybe another team would take on the remaining Ramirez salary and free up some major payroll for the Red Sox. Just four days after the Marlins beat the Yankees in the 2003 World Series, on October 29, the Red Sox put Manny Ramirez on irrevocable waivers. For the negligible waiver price, any team in baseball could claim one of the game's most productive batters, though they'd have to take on his salary as well. No team made a move.

Another baseball star might have felt offended and shamed by being left dangling out there that way, and the media waited for the outburst from Manny's camp. Instead, Manny's agent said he appreciated the willingness of the Red Sox to let him leave. Ramirez himself seemed to take it in stride, perhaps realizing, "OK, I guess Boston's where I'm going to be. I might as well make the most of it." The 2004 edition of Manny Ramirez played in 152 games, more than any other member of the team. And he enjoyed himself as never before, talking with fans and the media but, more importantly, excelling on offense while continuing to build on the improved defensive skills he'd begun to display in 2003.

The Red Sox then went hard after Alex Rodriguez. It had become routine for writers to call A-Rod "the best player in baseball." He had the numbers to back it up. He was still young, certainly a solid shortstop, and a personable and willing figure, ready to appear at corporate and sponsor events as the "face" of the team. It was a role Nomar Garciaparra had eschewed; a little shy, he just wasn't that comfortable in the spotlight. Nomar mostly just wanted to play ball.

And Nomar's future was at issue here anyway, with just one year remaining before free agency. The fan favorite was no longer putting up the offensive numbers he once did. He was still an excellent hitter; it just wasn't clear that he was ever going to be able to fully come back from a wrist injury that had cost him so much playing time in recent years and may never have fully healed. There was talk of moving him in a trade to the White Sox, if the Sox could get themselves a new shortstop in Rodriguez. Had it all worked out as Epstein had envisioned, the Red Sox would have A-Rod at short and Magglio Ordonez in the outfield, Ramirez would be with the Rangers, and Garciaparra with the White Sox. Rodriguez really wanted out of Texas. He had family in Boston and found the idea of playing for a contending club—in particular, the Red Sox—so appealing that he was willing to accept a massive $28 million reduction in his contract to enable the deal to fit the parameters of what the Sox felt they could afford.

The Players' Association nixed the deal. They didn't like the concept of players negotiating to *lower* their salaries. They would, under duress, have allowed A-Rod to take a $14 million cut, but not one double that amount. The Sox were not prepared to come up with an additional $14 million, so the deal was scotched—and on February 16, George Steinbrenner entered the picture in dramatic fashion. It cost him Alfonso Soriano and a lot of money, but A-Rod agreed to play baseball for the New York Yankees. In deference to Derek Jeter, the Yankees captain and shortstop, he also agreed to a move to third base. For the second off-season in a row, the Yankees had scooped up a major acquisition when the Sox seemingly had the inside track. The year before, it had been in the mutual pursuit of Cuban pitcher Jose Contreras. Once again, the Sox felt wronged by the Evil Empire, the team with the really big bucks and the uncanny ability to entice players into pinstripes. Of course, the big bucks might have had something to do with that ability. Writing in the *Guardian*, George Kimball averred that the Yankees were "a team whose $194 million payroll dwarfs the gross national product of many small nations."

In the end, the whole A-Rod hoopla turned out to be a sideshow. Shortstop was not the biggest need for the Red Sox, anyway. The Sox needed a new manager, another strong starter to complement Pedro Martinez, and a solid closer. There was no way that Grady Little could ever come back after the debacle in Game Seven of the 2003 ALCS. Rather rapidly, the Red Sox interviewed several candidates and settled on Terry Francona for the job.

The Red Sox then turned their attention to the mound market and focused on two prime pitchers in Curt Schilling and Keith Foulke. With Francona on board, with prospects to deal, and with the stats at hand to convince Schilling that Fenway need not be a right-hander's graveyard, the Diamondback ace signed on—appropriately for a grateful Red Sox Nation—just after Thanksgiving. Schilling served as his own agent, saving himself the agent's commission, and he even negotiated for himself a bonus clause which would pay him $2 million every year the Red Sox won the World Series. The Sox sent four prospects to the Diamondbacks. In one of those small baseball ironies, the savvy starter had first been drafted by the Red Sox in 1986. He recognized that he could make a real difference in Boston—maybe help the Sox go all the way. "Yes, that's enticing," he admitted. He soon was featured in a Ford truck commercial which depicted him hitching his way to Boston, intent on beating a curse.

The Sox had really coveted Montreal's young starter Javier Vazquez, but couldn't work out a deal with the team that had all but served as their farm team in recent years. The Yankees snapped up Vazquez, but not before Boston had added 2003 Fireman of the Year, Oakland's Keith Foulke, now a free agent. This time it wasn't Francona that made the difference, perhaps so much as an assist from Bobby Orr of the Boston Bruins; Foulke was a real hockey nut and Orr gave him a call as part of the pitch to come to Boston. Foulke signed on December 14. Vazquez signed with New York on December 16. It was classic rivalry fodder. Also on the 16th, the Red Sox signed Mark Bellhorn, courtesy of the Colorado Rockies. Bellhorn was being asked to take the place of Todd Walker, the surprising hero of so many late season and post-season games for the 2003 Sox. Walker was up for arbitration and Epstein and Company thought they could probably replace him for far less money. They were right. Walker had made $3,450,000 with Boston in 2003. Bellhorn's 2004 salary was $490,000. With some of the money they saved, the Sox also signed infielder Pokey Reese just one week later, on December 23, for an even $1 million.

2004 was shaping up to be the year. Several major stars in the Red Sox galaxy were due to become free agents at year's end—Garciaparra, Lowe, Martinez, and Varitek among them. It was now or never. 2004 would provide another shot for the team that took the Yankees into extra innings in 2003's Game Seven. Of course, fans were wary of the Yankees, and with good cause. The Red Sox had a history of dashed hopes, and more than any other team it was the New York Yankees who figured in the dashing of those dreams. But this really could be the year. The Yankees were older. They'd lost Clemens, they'd lost Pettitte, they'd lost David Wells. They'd almost lost the ALCS the year before—probably had lost it, until they got a Little reprieve. It looked like the Sox had made all the right moves, though there was some worry that Nomar was offended at being so publicly packaged in the A-Rod deal that never came to pass.

As spring training got underway, bad news came quickly. The Sox had only suffered one serious injury in 2003. In 2004, Trot Nixon showed up for spring training unable to play; he'd somehow strained his back driving south to Florida. Garciaparra was hurt; apparently a ball hit his Achilles' heel in the very first warmup. Much was made of the fact that no one actually witnessed the injury, but that seems unfair to such a competitive man as Nomar. He did brood, though, and distanced himself from the media.

He was seen as a sullen presence in the clubhouse. Here were two of the team's stalwarts out of action before spring training got underway. Each injury seemed to take forever to heal, and neither Nixon nor Nomar rejoined the club until into the month of June.

These disturbing facts were set aside as the Sox got themselves off to a terrific start. At the end of April, they were 15-6 and had already taken 3 out of 4 from the Yankees; they were 4½ games ahead of the Yankees in the standings. Fans were pumped: "when we get Nomar back, when we get Trot back . . . "

But May proved lackluster. Pedro Martinez kicked off the month by announcing on May 1 that he was no longer going to negotiate during the season. Fair enough. No one would blame him for that, but he then went on and made very critical, personal comments about Principal Owner John Henry and President Larry Lucchino, in both cases suggesting that they had proven losers with previous teams. The point of this was unclear, but it added a very sour note at precisely the wrong time. The team lost its next five games and played 16-14 ball for the month of May. Mid-month, reigning AL batting champion Bill Mueller went down with a knee injury that required surgery. Kevin Youkilis came up, hit a home run in his first game, and played capably, but now the Sox lacked three of their nine regulars in the lineup.

Nevertheless, there was still a sense that this could be the year. So even in May, Boston fans were watching the standings (and fans at Fenway were watching the scoreboard), not just to see what the Yankees were doing but where the Sox would stand in the Wild Card. History taught Sox fans that they might come in second in the AL East, but second could be sufficient to get them into the playoffs.

June was not a good month. Neither was July. Even though Nomar returned, and Nixon came back, the team was just not firing on all cylinders. These were the doldrums. June saw the Sox go just 11-14, and July wasn't a whole lot better (14-12.) Meanwhile, the Yankees were making hay and picking up ground.

What was the turning point? How did the Red Sox turn it around? Was it the Varitek/A-Rod fight? The trade of Nomar? Or were there just 162 games, with the usual ups and downs? No one can say for sure, but the season was marked by a strong surge out of the gates, and then three months of treading water, followed by a frenzied, free-style race to the finish. From

August 16 through September 3, the Sox won 16 of the 17 games they played. That became 20 of 22. Something was happening. Momentum was building. Why? That may be the subject of study in a number of other books, but is not our brief here. We're just thankful that the team came together, it all jelled, and the Sox earned the Wild Card for the second year in a row.

Chapter 8
19 Games:
The 2004 Regular Season
Series and the Division Series

"To everything there is a season, a time for every purpose under the sun . . . a time to lose and a time to seek." —Ecclesiastes 3:1-8

"This has to be the year, because there won't be anybody left." — Manny Ramirez, spring 2004

"I wish I'd never see them again. I wish they'd disappear from the league." —Pedro Martinez

The American League schedule demanded that the Red Sox and Yankees meet a total of 19 times during the 2004 regular season. Some people said that it was too much, that the novelty and urgency of the feud could not be maintained over the course of so many face-to-face confrontations. Those people did not know the depth and breadth of the animosity between the two franchises. Familiarity might breed contempt, but it also breeds excitement and passion. Every game between these two teams in 2004 was significant, each one was fresh, and each one had a playoff atmosphere.

After taking the 2003 ALCS to the eleventh inning of the seventh game, only to fall short once more, the Red Sox were ready for revenge. The two teams played two exhibition games during Grapefruit League spring training; tickets for the meaningless March 7 match-up in Ft. Myers were reportedly being scalped for $500 or more a pair. Red Sox Nation was thirsty for another shot. Theo Epstein and his baseball operations staff had worked hard during the off-season, securing some players he sought while coming up empty with others.

They lost the chance to add Alex Rodriguez to the roster, even though his first choice was to come to Boston and he was willing to take a hefty pay cut to make the move. Most Sox followers are predisposed to finding fault with anyone in NY wearing pinstripes, whether they be Yankees owners or Yankees players. Despite what many fans think, the villain in this particular act of the ongoing melodrama was not the Yankees organization. It was the Players Association, who didn't want their best-paid player to trim salary as much as he was willing to do. The Yankees simply took advantage of an opportunity that presented itself; the Red Sox did not. Sox fans nonetheless felt aggrieved because Boston didn't get him, and New York did. Irrational? You bet!

Theo and company did win over Curt Schilling, who had already represented two other teams in the World Series. "I guess I hate the Yankees now," he said on signing with the Sox. "If Red Sox fans weren't passionate and [bleeped] off and angry and bitter and hated the Yankees, they wouldn't be who they are." New York GM Brian Cashman admitted he had been caught off-guard. Schilling had stated that he would like to play in New York or Philadelphia, and would not play in Boston. "When a player publicly says he won't go somewhere, I never expected Boston to try to make a play to convince him otherwise," Cashman acknowledged.

The Red Sox also added ace closer Keith Foulke, a move that proved to be a masterstroke by the youthful GM.

The Red Sox lost both spring training games to the Yankees, but everyone knows those tune-up games don't really count. There was anticipation as the Bronx Bombers pulled into Boston for a four-game set in mid-April. Dan Shaughnessy called it possibly "the most hyped April series in baseball history."

First Season Series (Fenway Park, 4 games)
April 16

In their first meeting since Aaron Boone became a new member of the Bucky Dent Unlikely Hero Club, the Red Sox and Yankees picked up where they left off in October, 2003, in a nationally televised game in Boston. The Red Sox sent Tim Wakefield to the mound. The same Tim Wakefield who had trudged off the mound after Boone hit the walk-off home run to win Game Seven of the ALCS, some 182 days, 19 hours and 51 minutes earlier. Wakefield was the longest-serving Sox staffer, a veteran of nine years with the Bosox. And virtually no one in Red Sox Nation blamed him for being touched up for Boone's blast; the game never should have gone into extra innings. Wake had thrown the last pitch of Game Seven; now he threw the first pitch of the 2004 season to the Yankees. It only took him eight pitches to dispose of the Yankees in the top of the first, and he threw seven strong innings, allowing just four hits and two runs (one earned).

The Yankees starter was newly-acquired Javier Vazquez, who looked to be a star in the making if he could handle pitching in the pressure-packed atmosphere of New York. Johnny Damon led off and reached first base on Jason Giambi's error; this was not to be Giambi's year. Next up was reigning A.L. batting champion Bill Mueller. Home run. After Vazquez got Ortiz on strikes, Manny Ramirez hit a home run of his own. Another error led to yet another run, and it was a four-run first.

New Sox skipper Terry Francona had tried to downplay the game as just another mile marker along the marathon route that constitutes the baseball season. "I still woke up in the morning and looked in the mirror and had no hair. Some things don't change." No one was fooled by the folliclely-challenged manager. Everyone, from A-Rod to Pokey Reese, knew this was a passionate rivalry. The Fenway faithful were out for blood.

With chants of "Yankees Suck" filling the 41-degree Fenway air, the Red Sox exacted a small measure of revenge with a 6-2 victory in the first of a four-game set. The contest was the first chance that Sox supporters had to vent their feelings about Alex Rodriguez' signing with the Yankees after almost becoming a member of the Red Sox. The fans were vocal and merciless, in their contempt for A-Rod. They cheered his every futile at-bat as the "best player in baseball" went 0-4 in his debut against the Sox. An unsuccessful steal attempt ignited another round of derision toward the newest Yankee. "The fans here are always intense and rabid. Tonight was as loud as I've heard it," he said after the game.

Boston's new closer Keith Foulke pitched the ninth. Doug Mirabelli, who always caught when Wakefield pitched, was pleased with his man's effort. The best back-up catcher in baseball hit a homer, too, off Vazquez in the fourth. "Regardless of when you play the Yankees, you get excited to play. There's no downplaying it. It was a playoff atmosphere . . . no doubt about it." The Fenway faithful went home with a small but satisfying taste of redemption.

In a side note that reflects just how intense and how tight the two-team rivalry has been in recent times, New York's loss enabled the Baltimore Orioles to slip briefly into first place in the A.L. East. For every one of the preceding 50 head-to-head battles between Boston and New York, the two teams were first and second in the division; it was the longest such stretch in baseball history and dated back to 2001.

Final score: Boston 6, New York 2

April 17

The following day, the Fenway faithful had a chance to see two aces. Mike Mussina of the Yankees had inherited the role after the departure of Andy Pettitte and Roger Clemens, while in Boston Curt Schilling was vying with Pedro Martinez for the distinction. This was the same Curt Schilling who, in 2001, had been asked about the Yankees' mystique and aura. Sounds like a couple of nightclub dancers, he sniffed. The last time Schilling had faced the Yankees was as an Arizona Diamondback in Game Seven of the 2001 World Series. He went 1-0 and had a 1.69 ERA against New York, and was co-MVP of the Series with Randy Johnson.

Schilling was in no doubt about the import of any matchup between the Red Sox and the Yankees. The opportunity to pitch for the underdog in baseball's biggest rivalry played a major part in his decision to sign with the Sox. For him, putting on the Sox home uniform was like coming full circle. He'd been a prospect in the Red Sox minor league system, but traded away before he could secure his first starting assignment. Now, at last, he had himself a start as a big league Boston Red Sox.

The newly-minted Red Sox starter mixed a fastball in the mid-nineties with a devastating splitter to befuddle the vaunted Yankees lineup time and again. The final score of the Red Sox 5-2 win did not begin reflect the ineptitude of the New York contingent. Derek Jeter struck out three times while committing an error. The team average was a bottom feeding .206. Boston got their first run when Mussina walked Johnny Damon with the bases loaded. After three innings, it was 3-0 in Boston's favor. Schilling threw 6⅓ innings; like Wakefield the day before, he gave up just one earned run.

Final score: Boston 5, New York 2

April 18

The Yankees finally awoke from their hitting coma in the third game of the set as they got to Sox starter Derek Lowe by plating six runs in the third inning. Lowe was pitching on 10 days' rest, and that's too much rest for any pitcher, let alone a sinkerball specialist. He didn't finish out the third, and Boston bats never overcame the 7-1 Yankees lead. Lowe said he'd stuck around until the Yankees "kicked their extra point." Yankees starter Jose Contreras seemed determined to let the Red Sox back into the contest in the bottom of the third, and Joe Torre pulled him, too, after Manny knocked in a pair with a double. A stellar relief stint from Paul Quantrill slammed the door on the Sox. Neither team scored in the final six innings, but that left the Yankees with a win. You win some, you lose some.

Final score: New York 7, Boston 3

April 19

In the final game of the series, the traditional 11 A.M. game on Marathon Monday, the Red Sox rolled out Bronson Arroyo to start, against New York's veteran Kevin Brown, another of the off-season acquisitions. In Arroyo's previous start, he was rocked for five runs in just one-third of an inning. Only two of those runs were earned, but he was still looking for a chance to redeem himself. "I'm jacked up," he said pre-game. "It adds something, not just the rivalry, but knowing the lineup they've got over there. Any time you're going in to face a lineup that's got probably eight of the nine guys as All-Stars, it definitely adds something to the mix."

Boston bumbled a bit in the second and the Yankees scored three times on three hits and one error. It doesn't show up in any boxscore, but twice in the bottom of the second inning baserunner Gabe Kapler lost track of the number of outs and may have cost Boston a chance to put up more than the one run they did.

Kevin Brown was staked to a 4-1 lead after three, but Bill Mueller doubled in the fifth and Ortiz singled him home. Jason Varitek led off the sixth with a home run to make it a one-run game. Three singles in the seventh gave the Sox another run, to tie it up.

Boston was the beneficiary of some bad Yankees luck as leftfielder Hideki Matsui lost sight of David McCarty's eighth-inning drive off Tom Gordon. The Sox bench saw Matsui's uncertainty in lining up for the ball and were screaming to McCarty to run hard; it dropped in just out of Godzilla's lunge and McCarty's effort earned him a double. Gabe Kapler singled hard to center, and McCarty scored the go-ahead run. With single runs in four straight innings, the Sox had taken the lead and didn't have to bat in the bottom of the ninth as Keith Foulke closed it out for his third save of the young season.

Foulke had taken over for Mike Timlin, whose eighth-inning sprint helped keep the Yankees off the board, while outside the park Dawn Timlin was running in the Boston Marathon.

The ninth was dramatic, the top of the order up for New York. Derek Jeter struck out—always a sure way to rev up a Red Sox crowd. Then Bernie Williams hit a hard line drive to left field, and Manny Ramirez speared it while slamming hard into the scoreboard.

After going 16 at-bats without a hit, Alex Rodriguez came up to bat in the ninth, with two outs in a one-run game. He'd not had a good four days, striking out six times, and only getting the ball out of the infield four times in the entire series.

Behind the right field grandstand, heavy smoke poured into the sky from a fire outside the park. Those of the 20,404 registered runners in the Boston Marathon still in the race were pounding their way along the pavement just a couple of blocks away, as they ran through Kenmore Square to the downtown finish line.

Sox GM Theo Epstein admitted after the game, "I turned to the guy next to me and said, 'The apocalypse is upon us. The tying run is coming to the plate in the form of A-Rod, who hasn't had a hit all series. Foulke's facing him. Right field's on fire. Apparently, we're all going to die. This is the end of the world.' "

A-Rod singled, but Foulke struck out the hapless cleanup hitter, Giambi, on a called third strike. The world did not end, though Giambi's baseball career would be in jeopardy before the year was out.

Final score: Boston 5, New York 4

Second Season Series (Yankee Stadium, 3 games) April 23

The next meeting between the two rivals took place in Yankee Stadium four days later. The Yanks had brought their team batting average up to .229, and were 8-8 on the season. The Sox were 9-6, but the Blue Jays had hit a grand slam off Curt Schilling in the eighth to win a 7-3 game, and the Red Sox weren't feeling too pleased as they left Canadian air space. They were looking forward to the series in the Bronx, though. In particular, Derek Lowe wanted a win. "It's going to be electric from the time our bus rolls up to Yankee Stadium," he predicted. "I imagine it's going to be as close to a playoff atmosphere as we're going to see all year." Games against the Yankees were different: "You have a little extra adrenaline."

This was the first visit back to the Stadium since the 2003 season had ended so abruptly for the Red Sox, with the Yankees going on to the World Series. Jason Varitek denied that the team would be "spooked" to be back in the Bronx after the loss in the ALCS. He told Jack Curry of the *New York Times*, "Why should we be? Because we got beat on one hit? Some things went well. Some things didn't go well. We were one step closer than we've been in a long time. We look forward to the games and winning them."

Boston scored first, in the top of the second, but it was the fourth inning that made all the difference. With one out, Millar and Bellhorn hit back-to-back home runs. Reese singled. Damon walked. Joe Torre had seen enough and sent Contreras to take an early shower. He brought in Donovan Osborne, but Bill Mueller welcomed him with a three-run home run.

Home cooking hadn't revived either the Yankees or their bats. By the seventh inning stretch, it was Boston 10, New York 0. Yankees fans were booing their high-priced lineup, with special scorn heaped on Jeter, Giambi, and A-Rod when they were retired quietly in the eighth.

Bill Lee (glove on right hand), New York's Elliott Maddox, and a horizontal Rooster (#7) on top of Yankee Lou Piniella (#14) in the May 20, 1976 brawl at Fenway. Possible peacemaker Don Zimmer approaches from the right. (Photo by Neil Leifer)

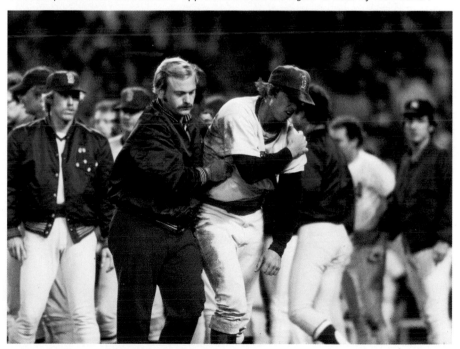

A farewell to arm: Red Sox trainer Charlie Moss leads an injured Bill Lee away from the brawl. (Photo by Neil Leifer)

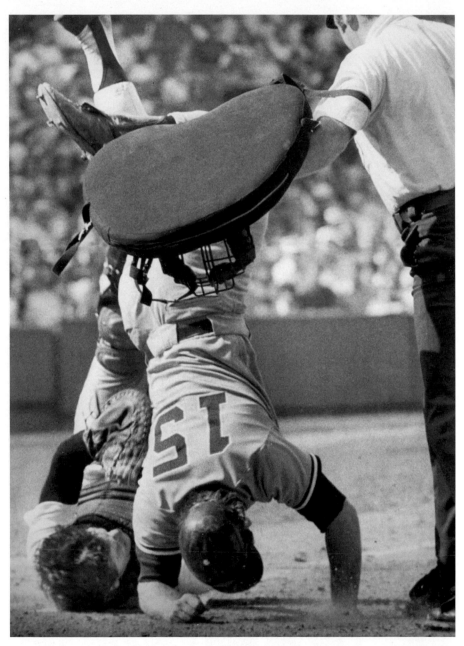

Home plate umpire Joe Brinkman observes Carlton Fisk and Thurman Munson employ an experimental Blood Feud anti-gravity exercise routine, August 1, 1973. (Photo by Mike Andersen / From the collection of Richard Johnson)

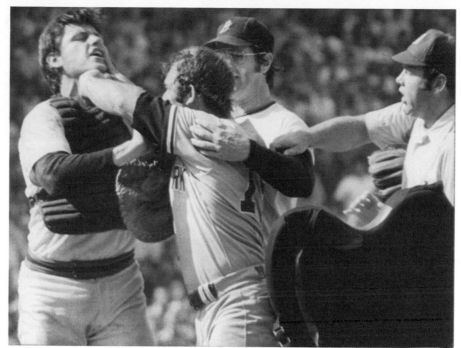

Thurman Munson offers Carlton FIsk a facial massage during a home plate get-together on August 1, 1973. Red Sox won the ballgame, 3-2. (Photo by Mike Andersen / From the collection of Richard Johnson)

Jason Varitek's glove greets Alex Rodriguez's face, returning the favor by proxy in a July 24, 2004 re-enactment of the classic Munson / Fisk confrontation. (Courtesy of Wireimage)

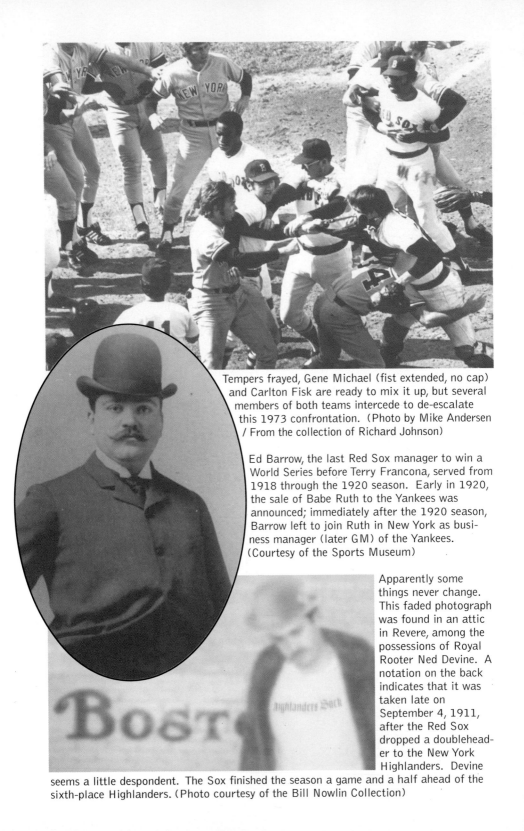

Tempers frayed, Gene Michael (fist extended, no cap) and Carlton Fisk are ready to mix it up, but several members of both teams intercede to de-escalate this 1973 confrontation. (Photo by Mike Andersen / From the collection of Richard Johnson)

Ed Barrow, the last Red Sox manager to win a World Series before Terry Francona, served from 1918 through the 1920 season. Early in 1920, the sale of Babe Ruth to the Yankees was announced; immediately after the 1920 season, Barrow left to join Ruth in New York as business manager (later GM) of the Yankees. (Courtesy of the Sports Museum)

Apparently some things never change. This faded photograph was found in an attic in Revere, among the possessions of Royal Rooter Ned Devine. A notation on the back indicates that it was taken late on September 4, 1911, after the Red Sox dropped a doubleheader to the New York Highlanders. Devine seems a little despondent. The Sox finished the season a game and a half ahead of the sixth-place Highlanders. (Photo courtesy of the Bill Nowlin Collection)

Four twenty-first century scenes from Yankee Stadium depicting condescending Yankees fans at their arrogant worst.

Several scenes showing kind Sox fans gently chiding the rival Yankees.

A Hallowe'en effigy in Fenway's visitors' dugout.

Paul Giorgio plants a Sox cap atop Mount Everest.

Giorgio performs purification burning of Yankees
cap at Everest base camp.
(Everest photographs courtesy of Paul Giorgio)

Waiting on Yawkey Way for an early 2004 match
between the Yankees and Red Sox.

Improved road sign on Storrow Drive, Boston.

Dazed and confused. This young lady can't decide whether to follow her heart or her head. Perhaps she has since completed her Yankees-to-Red Sox Fan Conversion Form.

Hear No Evil Empire, Speak No Evil Empire, See No Evil Empire! Author Jim Prime flanked by the enemy outside Yankee Stadium, 2001.

A desperate mother seeking seats for Game One of the 2004 World Series. Perhaps Ford pitchman Curt Schilling was able to assist.

Banner in stands during Game One. Score tied 9-9.

Pedro Martinez aboard a Duck Tours boat during Red Sox celebration parade following World Series victory, October 2004.

Author Bill Nowlin and son Emmet (with Dave Godowsky in background, left) on the field at Fenway before the victory parade.

All across New England, Sox fans visited the graves of dearly departed devotees of the Olde Town Team to share their joy in the Red Sox triumph.

For many fans, the win over the Evil Empire ranks almost as high as the ultimate World Championship.

(All photos by Bill Nowlin, except as noted.)

The final score of 11-2 accurately reflected the futility of the game for the Yanks and their fans, as the season record against their archrival Red Sox dipped to a pathetic 1-4. Every facet of the game was lacking for the New Yorkers, who committed laughable errors and misplays, and displayed batting-practice pitching, while Jeter remained in a monumental slump (1 for his last 21, and that an infield single). Even Old Faithful Bernie Williams was batting an anemic .196.

Lowe pitched well, as did Timlin and Lenny DiNardo in his major league debut. "It's fantasy camp for me being with these guys," DiNardo said. "It's a dream come true."

Contreras, on the other hand, was living out a nightmare. Pursued so strongly by the Sox after the 2002 season, he'd proved a dud so far. In eight appearances against the Red Sox, he was now 0-3 and had given up 20 runs in 10 innings of work. Dan Shaughnessy suggested that "any Red Sox rout of Contreras is like watching a giant Cuban cigar explode in the Boss's face."

Final score: Boston 11, New York 2

April 24

The second game of the series brought no relief for Steinbrenner's troops. This time the Red Sox used pitching and defense to emerge victorious 3-2 in 12 innings. Jeter's hitting woes continued. The Yankees captain, frustrated by his inability to drive in the winning run in the bottom of the tenth, flung his batting helmet at a nearby TV camera. Derek went 0-5 in the game, bringing his futility index to a 1-for-26. The Red Sox starter Bronson Arroyo limited the Yankees to a single hit before giving way to a strong Bosox bullpen after the sixth.

Meanwhile the Red Sox were hardly an offensive juggernaut, going a startling 0-for-19 with runners in scoring position. Still, there is bad and there is *bad*, and the Yankees were *bad* on this day. The Red Sox relief corps took over in the seventh inning, shutting off the dripping tap that was the Yankees offense and allowing no further hits.

It did take 12 innings to win, though. Ramirez doubled off Quantrill to lead off the twelfth. He moved to third base on Varitek's ground ball to second base and (after Millar was hit by a pitch) scored on Mark Bellhorn's sac fly to center. Foulke had already thrown the tenth and eleventh, so Mike

Timlin closed out the game. Four Red Sox relievers threw five innings of no-hit ball.

Final score: Boston 3, New York 2

April 25

In the final game of the three-game set, the brooms were out for the Yankees and for good reason as the Sox completed the sweep with a 2-0 win over New York. The only good news for the home team was that they didn't have to face the boys from Boston again until the end of June. Jeter's falling fortunes at the plate continued as he went 0-4, wearing the collar as often as Lassie, striking out three of the four times.

New York's least favorite visitor, Pedro Martinez, was the author of this win. A decent pitching performance by Vazquez was squandered by the dearth of hitting. The two-run Ramirez homer in the top of the fourth was enough to win the game as Pedro pitched seven innings, scattering four hits, and Scott Williamson retired all six batters he faced.

George Vecsey of the *Times* wrote a column decrying the "surly locals" who were booing Derek Jeter. This was "the personification of this wonderful Yankees era, the player who took over at shortstop in 1996 and has helped win four World Series." Jeter, for his part, said, "I'd boo myself."

Willie Randolph was asked about the Yankees losing six out of the first seven games. "We'll beat the Red Sox," he said. "We always do."

Final score: Boston 2, New York 0

Third Season Series (Yankee Stadium, 3 games)
June 29

When the two teams faced off once again in New York, the American League East landscape had changed considerably. The Red Sox had been playing .500 baseball (27-27) since the end of April. The Yankees had been going in the other direction, putting together an impressive 40-15 streak since they were swept in New York in late April. Their pitching was, indeed, weaker than 2003, but with the Yankees scoring runs in football-like numbers, it seemed to matter little.

The Red Sox struck first, with leadoff man Johnny Damon launching a home run off Vazquez to begin the evening. After the Yankees evened it up in the second, the pesky Damon came through again with another home run to right field in the third, staking the Red Sox to a 2-1 lead. Then the floodgates opened for the Yankees offense as they used timely hitting and poor Red Sox defensive play—three errors in all—to take a 4-2 lead in the third, which they ratcheted up to 7-2 after four, and 9-2 after five.

Red Sox starter Derek Lowe struggled and the sinkerball specialist was not helped by sloppy infield play by Garciaparra. The confident Yankees, with George Steinbrenner holding court with Republican bigwigs Cheney, Pataki, and Giuliani, won, 11-3. The Boston players were philosophical after the blowout—they'd won six of eight from the Yankees this year, after all—but it felt like a harbinger of doom to some stunned Sox fans. "Toto, we're not in April anymore," wrote the *Globe*'s Mr. Shaughnessy.

Final score: New York 11, Boston 3

June 30

The second game was closer, but Boston basically blew it. The Red Sox had a 2-0 lead after six. Wakefield got into trouble in the seventh, hitting Sheffield, walking Matsui (after a K for A-Rod), then leaving the game after a passed ball charged to Mirabelli. Both baserunners scored when a ball which rightfully should have been the third out of the inning tore right through the webbing of Ortiz's glove. Two runs on no hits. Score, 2-2.

Nomar erred again in the eighth, and the Yankees broke the tie with two runs on three hits. Red Sox principal owner John W. Henry was moved to say he still had faith in his team and that talk of any trade for trade's sake was off-base. Of Sox icon Nomar Garciaparra, subject of a lot of speculation, Henry wrote in an e-mail, "Sorry, I'm not going to answer any questions or comment on his demeanor or his future." That was not exactly a ringing endorsement.

Final score: New York 4, Boston 2

July 1

The brooms were out again for game three of the set and not since Harry Potter entered Hogwarts were brooms put to better use. In a game that was to become an instant classic, New York newcomer Alex Rodriguez, accustomed to playing in more pastoral and less combative settings, later called it "the greatest game I've ever watched, played or been in the ballpark for. It was an unbelievable war." Welcome to Red Sox-Yankees baseball, A-Rod, where there is never a war that ends all wars.

The game was a battle from the first pitch. Pedro Martinez, on the mound for the Red Sox, plunked Gary Sheffield in the back in the first inning after the Yankee outfielder showed disrespect by stepping out of the batter's box twice. Tony Clark's two-run homer in the second inning gave New York an early lead. They added another run in the fifth.

Yankee rookie starter Brad Halsey, given a warning by the umpire after Sheffield's HBP, did not retaliate and pitched well into the sixth inning before giving up a two-run homer to Manny Ramirez. The Yankees were looking for the sweep; the Red Sox were trying to stop their momentum. The Red Sox tied it in the seventh, as David McCarty doubled to lead off. Youkilis singled to left and McCarty took third. He scored a moment later on Pokey Reese's double-play grounder, but the game was now 3-3. It stayed that way until the thirteenth inning.

This was a game that had everything: unbelievable, even courageous, fielding plays, dugout soap opera, fights, extra-inning dramatics.

Love him or hate him—and many Red Sox fans consider him the poster boy for Yankee arrogance and smugness - this was Derek Jeter's finest hour. He confirmed his status as the spirit of the New York Yankees. Jeter made a spectacular body-sacrificing, injury-defying dive into the left-field stands for a game-saving catch of Trot Nixon's twelfth inning pop-up. Two runs would have scored if Jeter had failed to make the sensational play. After the game, the Yankee captain looked like Captain Ahab after an encounter with Moby Dick. The usually dapper shortstop sported an enormous welt under his right eye and several stitches in his bandaged shin, along with other assorted cuts and bruises. A-Rod, in obvious awe of his friend and teammate said that he "looked like a 747," as he took off into the wild blue yonder prior to crash landing.

With blood staining his pinstriped shirt, Jeter received a standing ovation as the returned to the dugout after the play.

In contrast to Jeter's heroics was the absence of Nomar Garciaparra, who told his manager that he was unavailable to pinch-hit. The TV showed him in the dugout, looking "absent and withdrawn" in the words of Sean McAdam, while all his teammates were battling into extra innings. That didn't sit well with some, though only pure speculation could suggest he wasn't really hurting. Most likely he was, and most likely he wasn't going to be back with Boston after entering free agency in November.

Nevertheless, it looked like the Sox were going to avoid swapping sweeps with New York when Manny homered off Tanyon Sturtze to kick off the thirteenth. Curtis Leskanic, the fifth Sox pitcher of the day, struck out Posada and got Clark out on a ground ball hit right back to him. Then Ruben Sierra singled, and Miguel Cairo doubled him home to tie it up. John Flaherty came in as a pinch-hitter for Sturtze and singled to right field, knocking in Cairo and winning the game.

Jeter was being checked out, already in a hospital bed, when he learned that the Yanks had scored those two runs in the bottom of the thirteenth for a 5-4 Yankee win. Despite the result, even Red Sox fans had to tip their hat to the captain of the New York Yankees.

It was the kind of play on which an entire season can turn, the kind that can linger in the minds of teammates and opposing teams for entire seasons. This was the kind of play, and the kind of game, that can determine the outcome of a campaign. It was a rallying cry, an emphatic statement by the Yankees. It required an equally emphatic response from the Red Sox. And soon. The Sox had now fallen to 8½ games behind the Yankees in the standings, 9 back in the loss column. This was not the way it was supposed to be.

Final score: New York 5, Boston 4

Fourth Season Series (Fenway Park, 3 games)
July 23

The response did not come on this day. The Yankees played like the top dog and at the end, the Sox had to slink away like a whipped puppy with his tail between his legs. It wasn't that lopsided an affair, however, despite the plethora of injuries plaguing the Red Sox. David Ortiz was handed a five-game suspension for "inappropriate actions" (throwing bats toward a pair of umpires after being called out on a pitch he clearly didn't think was strike three). He appealed, so that he could play this set against the Yankees.

Curt Schilling got the start for Boston and the former Arizona ace coughed up a home run to Gary Sheffield in the first, but was pleased when his teammates scored three times in the bottom of the second off Jon Lieber. Nomar singled, Nixon doubled, and Mueller homered. The Red Sox added a run in the fourth, and it was 4-1 Boston. The Yankees got a run in the fifth, but in the sixth they really got to Schilling. A-Rod started it off with a single; the Yankees hit and then hit some more and took the lead on five runs and five hits. 7-4, Yankees. It was Schilling's worst outing—seven earned runs. Varitek doubled in Damon in the seventh, and Kevin Millar tied it up, hitting the first pitch in the bottom of the eighth for a home run off the Sports Authority sign over the Green Monster. That made it five home runs in his last three games. With one out in the ninth, Keith Foulke came on but Sheffield doubled high off the Wall and, to rub salt in a raw wound for Fenway fans, A-Rod clanged a ninth-inning single off the left-field scoreboard to give the Yankees a 8-7 lead. Mariano Rivera closed it out with his 35th save of the season.

The Sox had gone 15-6 in April, but since then were playing .500 ball. They'd been lackluster underachievers, very disappointing in a team from which so much was expected as the season got underway. It was approaching the point of embarrassment. Individual stats were pretty evenly matched with the Yankees; in fact, the Sox led the Yankees in team average, on-base percentage, slugging percentage, and even ERA. But the New Yorkers were winning the games they played and the Red Sox were finding new ways to lose theirs. The Sox had a huge payroll, topped only by the Yankees; the gap was still large, the Yankees spending about $185 million compared to the Sox' $130 million. The *Boston Herald* dubbed the midsummer Red Sox a "Fortune .500 company. They make a fortune and play .500." They hit, but they fell short of the fundamentals—fielding, baserunning, advancing the runner. It seemed like the Yankees just wanted it more.

Schilling shouldered sole blame for this one, a game he thought the Red Sox should have won. "I'm the only guy that came up short tonight . . . These guys did everything that everyone's been bitching about them not doing all year. For me to trip and fall down in a game like this, it's inexcusable, it's incredibly disappointing. This was a game where the box score tomorrow is going to show Keith Foulke with a loss. But this game falls right on me. This is a game we should have won."

Final score: New York 8, Boston 7

July 24

Finally, the next day, a statement from those underachieving Red Sox! In a game that was as much about respect as it was about baseball, the Red Sox finally broke through the culture of defeat and survived an 11-10 endurance test at the Fens. It was another of those Red Sox-Yankees match-ups that seem to defy logic.

With the field completely soaked from an overnight downpour, the Yankees left the field. ESPN broadcast that the game had been postponed and the New York players began packing up, ready to call it a day. The Red Sox wanted to play, though, and never officially posted a postponement. During the rain delay, the Dropkick Murphys played their new version of the old 1903 rally song, "Tessie," in hopes it would inspire the Red Sox today as it had inspired the old Boston Americans a century before.

Did you ever go to a heavyweight fight and a baseball game broke out? That's what happened in Boston on this afternoon. If Muhammad Ali had been the promoter of this dust-up he no doubt would have dubbed it the Fracas at Fenway. The super-heavyweight Yankees—their wallets alone put them in that category—and the slightly punch-drunk Bosox. . . . The Yankees were looking to deliver a knockout punch. When the game finally did get underway, the two teams locked in clinch after clinch.

The Yankees scored twice in the second but the match reached an early peak in the third round, er, inning when Red Sox starter Bronson Arroyo hit Alex Rodriguez with a pitch. A-Rod pointedly expressed his thoughts to Arroyo as he began to move down the line to first base, with Varitek escorting him. A-Rod challenged the Red Sox catcher. At that point, Varitek administered a brisk glove massage to the genteel face of the Yankee third baseman. Both dugouts emptied and several minor WWE-style clashes broke out.

When the dust had cleared, Rodriguez, Kapler, Lofton, and Varitek had been ejected for not complying strictly with the Marquis de Queensbury rules.

New York's starter was Sturtze. There's an interesting story. Tanyon

Sturtze was raised in Worcester, Massachusetts, the son of a Worcester policeman. It was his first start against the Red Sox, the team he'd loved as a kid. "I'm trying to treat it like any other start against any other team. But of course, it's different." It was, after all, the Yankees against the Red Sox, and Sturtze was on an emotionally unfamiliar side of the fence. His dad was a very big fan, who used to take his son to Fenway as a kid. They made 12 Opening Days in a row. Ken Sturtze taught his son about the things that really matter in New England. "You are brought up to hate the Yankees," he said. "As soon as you are born, they put you in a Red Sox outfit. Your baby pictures are of you in Red Sox stuff." Sturtze had hated the Yankees right up until just 70 days earlier; on May 15, the Dodgers traded him to New York. Yet here he found himself in the midst of a bench-clearing brawl and he was hitting the guys in white.

The Red Sox scored two times off Sturtze in the bottom of the third. He'd apparently injured his hand slightly in the fight, and so Padilla came on to pitch for the Yankees starting the fourth, and the Sox scored twice more, assuming a slim 4-3 lead. The Yankees seemed to put the game out of reach, though, scoring six runs in the top of the sixth. Arroyo was charged with eight runs and it was 9-4 Yankees by the time Leskanic and Mark Malaska worked their way out of the bloodbath. A few fans broke faith and slipped out the exits—just a little too early, though, since the Sox rebounded with four runs of their own in the bottom of the sixth. They'd cut New York's lead to one run, with three innings to play. New York grabbed another run on Sierra's homer leading off the seventh, and the Red Sox found themselves in the bottom of the ninth, losing the game 10-8.

Terry Francona had gotten himself ejected in the fifth for arguing a call; anything that might spark the Sox was worth trying. But it didn't look promising today. Mariano Rivera had come on and gotten the last two outs of the eighth and he took his warmup pitches in the bottom of the ninth. Varitek's teammates, though, were just not ready to give up and go home. Garciaparra doubled. Nixon flied to deep right, and Nomar tagged up and took third. The hot-hitting Kevin Millar (4-for-5 on the day) singled Nomar home. David McCarty came in as a pinch-runner—a sure sign that the Sox could use a little more speed on the basepaths. It was all academic a few moments later, though, when Bill Mueller hit a two-run blast off the usually-lights-out Rivera. Game won, 11-10! Varitek was in the clubhouse and when he saw the home run, he leapt up so high "my head almost hit the ceiling in the locker room." Francona was watching the game with Varitek and the similarly-KO'd Kapler. "I jumped right out of my seat and ran onto the field. I had no shoes on." All the way out the clubhouse door, down the steps, through the tunnel, up the dugout steps and out onto the field— barefoot. He joined the crowd of Sox players surrounding home plate as Mueller rounded third and headed home to touch the plate with the winning run.

It was one of those games that bring unity to a team. A perfect, if slightly delayed, response to Derek Jeter's heroics in the last series at the Stadium. A game of character building and camaraderie, thanks to Varitek, thanks to Bill Mueller, and thanks to a refusal to roll over and play dead after the Yanks had grabbed such a commanding lead.

This time, Nomar went 2-for-5 but an opportunity began to present itself to Theo Epstein to improve the ballclub. Though apprehensive of fan reaction, Epstein bit the bullet, and just a week later traded longtime Sox icon Garciaparra in a complex deal which brought in shortstop Orlando Cabrera, the speedy Dave Roberts, and historically solid-on-offense, solid-on-defense Doug Mientkiewicz.

Final score: Boston 11, New York 10

July 25

Still coursing with adrenaline from the previous night, the Red Sox rode their emotional high to a 9-6 victory over the suddenly mortal Yankees. Lowe vs. Contreras, and rumors were flying that D-Lowe was on the trading block and that this could be his last start for the Sox. He wasn't doing well, particularly against New York. He'd been 0-2 in the 2003 ALCS, and was 1-2 in the regular season so far, with a 9.22 ERA. He got off to a rough start on July 25, too, touched up for two in the very first frame. But so was Jose, who didn't do a thing for his own cause with a wild throw toward first base. The big blow, though, Kevin Millar's two-out, two-run single scoring Bellhorn and Ortiz. Contreras hit Mirabelli to start off the second, and Kapler singled. Then Johnny Damon hit a three-run homer to the Pesky Pole in right, and Bellhorn backed him up with a bomb of his own, right into the Yankees' bullpen. 6-2, Sox, after just two innings.

Millar hit yet another home run, into the Green Monster seats, to lead off inning number five. He contributed another RBI in the sixth, driving in David Ortiz, who had already doubled behind Bellhorn's double for an RBI of his own. It was 9-2 in favor of the hometown favorites, and when Lowe tired in the seventh and Timlin came on to walk Posada and give up a grand slam to Matsui, it still wasn't enough. In an interesting footnote that fore-shadowed an October event, Derek Jeter was called out for interference running to first base and blocking Mirabelli's throw by running on the inside of the baseline. 9-6 and Boston had a two-game winning streak.

Final score: Boston 9, New York 6

"The situation has got to get better between these two teams. This situation was created in what, 1820? We weren't even born when it started." —David Ortiz, July 31, 2004

Fifth Season Series (Yankee Stadium, 3 games)
September 17

The two teams had not met since the dog days of summer and much had happened during that period. The Yankees were now top dogs in the American League East by three and a half games over Boston, but the Red Sox, nipping at their tails, had closed considerably what was a ten-game gap as recently as August 9, and were now entertaining dreams of taking the division. The Sox had a healthy five-game lead over the Angels in wild card competition. Boston papers published the wild card standings every day.

This was their first series since the brawl game and its aftermath, and there was considerable anticipation for the rematch, particularly since it would be Arroyo again for the Red Sox. El Duque was slated for the Yankees.

Kevin Millar discounted speculation about physical confrontation. "We're not going there to fight. It's not rocket science. We're going there to play ball. Fights are just a part of baseball . . . There's no bitterness. It's real-ly not like we hate them and they hate us." He also downplayed the notion that the donnybrook had stimulated the Sox: "'We didn't go 10-0 after that happened. We went 5-5." Millar suggested that Bill Mueller get the credit for winning the July 24 game, not Varitek, and that even though it took a while to get going, once the team got into August, they started winning. "That game built a lot of momentum," he said.

Gary Sheffield remembered the fight, though. It galled some Yankees that Varitek kept his mask on when he shoved his glove in A-Rod's face, as though it were less manly of him to have done so. "If he wants to be a tough guy, we'll take that challenge," Sheffield said to the *New York Post*.

Schilling had just won his twentieth game on September 16 and he expressed disappointment that the rotation denied him the chance to pitch against the Yankees. He hadn't had the chance to pitch in Yankee Stadium all season long.

The *Herald*'s Steve Buckley suggested that there was a room in the psych ward at Bellevue for any player would utter the "just another game" line. And for those who said it wasn't really a rivalry, since New York always won—that it was like a rivalry between the hammer and the nail—Buckley wasn't buying that, either. "I still have memories," he wrote, "of Yankees grandpa Yogi Berra approaching current team captain Derek Jeter before the start of the 1999 ALCS and saying, 'Don't worry about them. They've been trying to beat us for 80 years.' " Yes, it's a rivalry. Why else would every paper in New York be sending staffers up to cover the games?

Yankees starter Hernandez and Sox starter Arroyo both suffered through two lengthy rain delays. El Duque's spirit and ERA were dampened by an upper deck home run to Johnny Damon in the third. Then the rains came, halting play for over twenty minutes. Hernandez finished the inning, but following a second delay in the bottom of the inning, he was sent from the outdoor showers to ones in the Yankees clubhouse, done for the day. Arroyo let one run in during the fourth, and an Olerud solo HR put New York up by one in the fifth. Miguel Cairo almost hit one out back-to-back, but Manny Ramirez leapt high enough to keep a sure home run out of the left-field seats. Cairo saw the ball going out. He didn't see Manny catch it, because he couldn't imagine Manny catching it. It was a highlight reel catch, juxtaposed by the oblivious Cairo, blissfully pre-occupied with his home run trot only to find out from home-plate umpire Hunter Wendelstedt that he wasn't safe at home, but rather was out. There was a certain symmetry at play. Back in the first inning, Manny hit a long foul ball down the left-field line. He watched it twist foul while still standing at home plate, but when third-base umpire Tim Timmons signaled it a home run, Manny starting circling the bases. He only got about as far as third base when it was clear there was going to be a conference to be sure the call was correct. The right call was finally made—foul ball.

Manny reveled in the catch as only Manny can. "When you make a catch like that, man, it's better than when you hit a grand slam. You get so excited, it's unbelievable." Manny might know. He's hit more grand slams than he's made catches like that. Credit where credit is due, Ramirez distinctly improved on defense in 2004.

Bronson threw six innings of four-hit ball, a quality start. After eight innings, it remained NY 3, Boston 2. And Torre called out Mo to close it. For the second time in a row, however, Rivera didn't get the job done. Yankees nemesis Trot Nixon worked a walk, and Francona put in Dave Roberts to run for him. Varitek struck out and Roberts stole second. Rivera hit Kevin Millar. Again, Francona put in a faster pinch-runner, in the person of Gabe Kapler. Orlando Cabrera singled in Roberts. Blown save number 2 for Rivera. Two of the players acquired in the Nomar trade played a role here, OC's single tying the game. Kapler was forced to hold at second base. Youkilis struck out. Two down. What would Johnny Damon do (WWJDD)? He blooped a broken bat single to center, scoring Kapler. It looked to many people—including a glaring Rivera—as if a little hustle by center fielder Kenny Lofton would have resulted in an out. A frustrated Rivera was seen on replays throwing up his hands and mouthing the words "Catch the ball!"

Rivera was still smarting from his last appearance against the Red Sox when he blew a save that resulted in a Red Sox win, an event about as likely as being struck by lighting. This night, lighting struck a second time. The final score was Boston 3, New York 2, and the Red Sox were now just two games behind the Yankees in the loss column.

Final score: Boston 3, New York 2

September 18

A victory by the Red Sox would put them just one game down, and another win the next day . . . .

It just wasn't to be. The Yankees scored early and often to expand their A.L. East lead. They banged out five runs in the first inning off struggling starter Derek Lowe. Lowe walked Jeter to open the second, and then took a hard-hit ball from A-Rod off the shin. He had to leave the game, charged with seven runs in all. Reliever Terry Adams didn't fare any better. It was the shortest outing of Lowe's career since mid-1997. On a scale of 1-to-10, with 10 being the ugliest, this was a 12 or a 13, suggested Doug Mientkiewicz. By the time the Red Sox came up in the third, they were already down 9-0.

Meanwhile Yankees starter Jon Lieber, laboring with an ERA of 11.07, pitched a true gem, keeping the Red Sox hitless for the first six and two-thirds innings. Riding a 13-0 offensive wave, the Yankees were going all out for their pitcher, while the Red Sox were playing their second string—except for Ortiz, who homered with two out in the seventh to ruin Lieber's no-no. Dave Roberts added a two-run homer in the ninth, but by then everyone was looking ahead to the third game of the series. The final score was a deflating 14-4. All the Red Sox could hope for is that the Pedro Martinez-Mike Mussina matchup the next day would go their way.

Final score: New York 14, Boston 4

September 19

Another day brought another crushing Red Sox loss at the hands of their hosts. Hopes of overtaking the Yankees faded with every out. With Pedro on the mound, Yankee Stadium took on the atmosphere of the old Roman coliseums. It was a universal thumbs-down on Pedro and somewhere you could imagine Emperor Steinbrenner leading the cry for his head. The chance to catch and pass New York was pretty much a dead issue, with the margin now at 4½ games.

Red Sox bats were as quiet as the grave. Jason Varitek, who attracted the wrath of New York rooters with his skirmish with Alex Rodriguez, went 0-for-10 in the three-game set and Manny Ramirez, playing almost within the shadow of the place where he grew up, was 0-for-8. Credit is due the outstanding outings of Yankees pitchers; in this game, the stylish Mike Mussina struck out eight and had the Red Sox off balance all game.

Martinez was unable to establish himself against the New York hitters, who came to the plate swinging. Sheffield went deep in the first to stake the home team to a two-run lead, and Jeter chipped in with another first-pitch shot in the third. Posada added another in the sixth and the rout was underway. The usually resilient Martinez was visibly shaken by the three-dinger barrage, and with the score 5-1 he seemed to lose his concentration, walking Olerud before Sierra doubled in advance of a two-run single off the bat of Cairo. He soon gave up another. In all, Pedro allowed eight runs, his worst outing ever against the Yankees—the one team Pedro consistently struggled with. Yankees fans love to hate Pedro, and they were on him good and loud. Final score 11-1, New York.

Sometimes things are not as they might appear. In the sixth inning, with the Yankees ahead 7-1, Derek Jeter bunted against Mike Timlin, who started jawing a bit, shouting over to Jeter. Was he calling Jeter for a chicken-shit move? Was another brawl brewing? Not at all. "He was joking that I bunted," Jeter said. "There was no barking. He was smiling." Timlin agreed. "It was pretty good-natured. Actually he made me look good by bunting the ball. He didn't want to swing the bat right there. I had to rag on him a little bit."

Despite being battered, Pedro hadn't given up the ship and he had a few words for the Yankees. "If we get to the playoffs, believe me, we're not going to be the ones that are scared." Remember those words, come Game Five of the ALCS.

Final score: New York 11, Boston 1

Sixth and Final Season Series (Fenway Park, 3 games) September 24

The Red Sox were pretty much assured of a playoff spot, but there was no lack of intensity. This was the Yankees, after all. Pedro was on the mound, but this was the mound at Fenway Park—for him a happier elevation from which to pitch. Some wondered if it would be his last regular season game as a member of the Red Sox, because Pedro could declare free agency after the season. Pedro hadn't beaten the Yankees in Boston since May 23, 2002. He wasn't having a vintage Pedro year. First innings now held some extra suspense; if he could get out of the first without difficulty it practically guaranteed a good outing. He had already allowed more home runs in 2004 than in 2001, 2002, and 2003 all wrapped together. By Pedro standards, he was also giving up an unusual number of walks.

He survived the first and the second this night, but a hit batsman, two stolen bases, an error, and a pair of singles added up to two New York runs in the third. Manny Ramirez struck right back, tagging Mussina for two runs with his 42nd home run of the year. When Nixon homered in the fourth, Boston took a 3-2 lead. The Yankees tied it in the sixth. The Sox regained a one-run lead in the bottom of the seventh on Damon's home run off Tom Gordon.

Was this the time to take out Pedro, after seven full innings and 101 pitches? Was this to become a case of déjà vu all over again, with Pedro left in one inning too long, just like a year earlier when Grady Little sent Pedro back out to open the eighth, ultimately allowing Aaron Boone his brief shining moment on the Yankee Stadium stage? Yes. Pitch #103 was propelled into the Red Sox bullpen by Hideki Matsui. Pitch #108 was converted into a double by Bernie Williams. And *still* Francona stuck with Pedro. He struck out Jorge Posada, but pitch #117 was his last as Ruben Sierra singled and scored Williams, staking the Yankees to a 5-4 lead. It was all the Yankees would need on this day, though they added one more run a bit later. To a loud chorus of boos, Francona came out to get Pedro. No Rich Little, his Grady Little impersonation had not gone over well with the crowd.

Mariano Rivera, who had blown his last two save chances when facing the Sox, didn't blow this one, though he was shaky—he walked Trot and Cabrera doubled, but not a run was scored and the Yankees went on to win, 6-4.

"It was all me, all me," said Pedro afterwards. "I wanted to bury myself on the mound." He was frustrated. This was the pitcher with the best won/lost ratio in Red Sox history, but the Red Sox were 11-19 in the 30 games he'd started against the Yankees. The frustrated future Hall of Famer also made another comment that would come back to haunt him: "I can't find a way to beat the Yankees. They beat me. They didn't beat my team. They beat me. I just wish they would [expletive deleted] disappear. Pardon me for using the F-word. I wish they would disappear and never come back. I would probably like to face any other team right now. I made some pretty good pitches, and they battled their butts off. What can I say? I just tip my hat to them and call the Yankees my daddy."

Pedro was now 16-8 on the season, but eight games were more than he'd ever lost in a year since joining the Boston Red Sox. The Yankees expressed nothing but respect for Pedro Martinez, though, and Joe Torre summed it up: "By no stretch of the imagination do we feel we have his number. I've said many times, we don't try to beat Pedro. We try to win the game he pitches, hopefully outlast him."

Final score: New York 6, Boston 4

September 25

The next day Pedro showed up with Nelson de la Rosa, a friend from the Dominican Republic who was short in stature, standing 28½ inches tall. Pedro carried Nelson in. It's easier that way. The game itself was 5-5 after 7½, but Boston erupted for 7 runs in the bottom of the eighth and that was the ballgame. Beating the Yankees for the tenth time in 2004, the most wins against the New Yorkers since 1978. But remember what happened in 1978.

Final score: Boston 12, New York 5

September 26

It was Kevin Brown's first start since breaking his (non-pitching) hand hitting a clubhouse wall back on September 3. He got hit hard, and after just two-thirds of an inning had allowed six hits and four runs. Esteban Loaiza gave up three more in the second, and the 7-0 Red Sox lead was going to be more than sufficient. A dispute broke out between Boston first baseman Doug Mientkiewicz and New York's Kenny Lofton, Minky saying that Lofton elbowed him while he was taking Bellhorn's throw at the bag. When pitcher Pedro Astacio subsequently threw behind Lofton's head, he was ejected. So was New York's Brad Halsey, who threw inside (and quite possibly on purpose at) Dave Roberts. Joe Torre was tossed, too. The dugouts and bullpens emptied, but no fisticuffs ensued. Neither team wanted to risk an injury this close to the playoffs. "I think we've played each other too many times," Damon said. "By the end of the season, both teams are pretty fried right now."

The Lofton/Mientkiewicz mini-feud wasn't a Yankees-Red Sox thing; it dated back to when Lofton was with the Indians and Minky with the Twins.

David Ortiz made light of it: "I guess they pretty much bump all the time. I guess they don't like each other from a long time . . . .I guess I'm going to have to tie them together someday and take them out for dinner, see if we can fix things up."

Schilling got the win, ending the season 12-1 in home games. Apparently Theo was right when he presented a set of stats to convince Schilling that it wouldn't be all that bad pitch in in Fenway Park. Although at one point, he threw 12 straight balls, walking the bases full, he only gave up one hit in seven innings.

Final score: Boston 11, New York 4

A summing-up of the season

These were two very different teams with very different styles. The Yankees have long had a tradition of businesslike professionalism and a certain staid dignity. They were invariably clean-shaven and adhered to a conservative dress code. They might have harbored substance abusers and other unsavory characters, but—hey—they dressed well. An argument can be advanced that the demeanor of the Yankees was that of a winner, and that looking the part helped fashion a winning attitude.

The 2004 Red Sox had a different kind of attitude. They'd been the "Cowboy Up" bunch the year before, but now they were self-professed "idiots." In '04, they were a wild and raucous bunch. They let their hair grow long, they sprouted beards and goatees, they tore their shirttails out at every opportunity. The contrast could hardly have been greater. Imagine Derek Jeter and Alex Rodriguez with hairdos like Manny and Pedro, rubbing locks with each other in the dugout after a big play. Imagine Johnny Damon and Bernie Williams both walking into George Steinbrenner's office to interview for a job as center fielder for the Yankees. 'Nuf ced.

This was a team that played loose, and maybe even had a few screws loose. But as Kevin Millar put it, at least they were "experienced idiots."

And though the Yankees payroll far exceeded the Red Sox payroll, the *Providence Journal*'s Bill Reynolds kept matters in perspective: the Sox were "not exactly the Little Sisters of the Poor here, as much as many Sox fans want to cling to the fiction that the Red Sox are the egalitarian underdogs, getting by with grit and heart, against the corporate Yankees."

Though the Red Sox only outscored the Yankees by one run (106-105), Boston's final season record vs. the Yankees was 11-8, something of a moral victory in light of the way the New Yorkers were burning up the league en route to 101 wins and the lead in the division. In each of their 19 regular season encounters in 2004, the rivals battled each other fiercely—so much so that 8 of the 19 games ended in one or the other team's final at-bat. Each team had one hurdle to jump—the American League Division Series—to make possible a rematch of the 2003 League Championship Series.

2004 American League Division Series

Red Sox fans were looking forward to going head-to-head with the Evil Empire, to the chance for a little payback, to taking on a foe they thought the Olde Towne Team could finally beat. To get to the Yankees, though, they would have to win the Division Series first. Who would they play? Oakland? Anaheim? Texas? Each potential opponent had its perceived strengths and its weaknesses. The Anaheim Angels were probably the team Sox fans feared the most—even though the Sox had swept the Angels in early September.

Vladimir Guerrero, Troy Glaus, Garret Anderson, Darin Erstad—this was a team with explosive power. The Red Sox acquitted themselves well enough against them; they'd won one more game during the regular season matchups, but in one of the losses, Guerrero had 9 RBIs. The Angels had some awesome sluggers, and every team that's ever made the playoffs fears a short five-game series. Anaheim was without one major threat; the team had disciplined Jose Guillen, even though he'd produced 104 RBIs, suspending him for the season. The Angels also had a very strong bullpen. And the Angels were, after all, only one year removed from being the 2002 World Champions.

Game One
Angel Stadium—October 5, 2004

Boston scored first. With two outs, on a 3-2 count, Manny Ramirez hit a hard shot that banged off Chone Figgins' glove. Manny ran hard, hustling into second for a double. David Ortiz swung at Jarrod Washburn's first pitch and drove Manny in on a broken-bat single of the seeing-eye variety. From early on, the breaks were going Boston's way.

Curt Schilling started for the Sox and got through the first three frames, yielding just a single in the first, a double in the second, and a single and a walk in the third. By the time the Angels came up in the bottom of the fourth, the game was for all practical purposes over because the Red Sox had scored seven times in the top of the third. Ortiz walked on four straight pitches to lead off the inning. Kevin Millar homered to make it 3-0. Two singles and a walk loaded the bases, with one out. Damon hit a grounder to third baseman Figgins, who fired home trying to force the lead runner (Varitek) at the plate and thereby prevent a run. His throw flew wildly astray, and Varitek scored, as did Cabrera behind him. Angels manager Mike Scioscia called on Scot Shields to relieve Washburn. Shields struck out Mark Bellhorn, but it wasn't so easy to get a ball by Manny Ramirez. He homered for three more Red Sox runs, making the score 8-0. The Angels had only allowed 36 unearned runs in the 162 games of the regular season. In this one inning, they allowed five. The seven runs the Red Sox scored were the most they'd ever scored in a post-season inning.

Troy Glaus homered to lead off the Angels' fourth. *Boston Herald* sportswriter Howard Bryant wrote, "Schilling clearly did not have his best stuff and the Angels knew it." They just couldn't cash in. Those watching closely worried as they saw Schilling clutch toward his ankle on a play in the fifth. It looked as though he'd tweaked a muscle, but Schilling stuck with it until the seventh, when Erstad homered with one out. Garret Anderson reached on Schilling's throwing error. Glaus doubled Anderson in with a line drive to center that drove Schilling from the game in favor of Alan Embree. Doug Mientkiewicz bunted for a hit in the top of the eighth, driving in Damon from third, but that was the last run scored. The bunt was the first post-season bunt-hit for any team since the Sox' Marty Barrett laid one down in Game Two of the 1986 World Series.

After the game, Scioscia talked about Washburn being knocked out early. "Wash will be back. He's got great makeup and he'll make better pitches next time." As events would play out, Wash did come back, but he only threw one more pitch.

Damon said post-game, "We know we have something to prove. We don't want to be remembered as a team that keeps making it to the playoffs, but keeps having tough losses. I mean, we want to be known as the team that rewrites the history books." The hardest chapters were still to be written.

Final score: Boston 9, Anaheim 3

Game Two
Angel Stadium—October 6, 2004

The Angels never got to a point where they could invoke the Rally Monkey in Game One. Their ThunderStix never got much of a workout either. The second game of the Division Series featured a matchup between Boston's Pedro Martinez and Anaheim's Bartolo Colon. Colon allowed two singles and a walk in the first, but escaped without allowing a run to cross the plate. After securing the first two outs in the second, the same situation presented itself—Mueller singled to right, Damon singled to right, and Bellhorn walked on five pitches. Manny Ramirez up, with the bases loaded. He took a walk, too, forcing in the first run of the game. David Ortiz was probably going to see some better pitches, despite the 139 RBIs he posted in the regular season, but Angels catcher Jose Molina caught Bellhorn drifting too far off second base and picked him off. Inning over.

A walk, a single that dropped in where it shouldn't have, and another single brought home a run for the Angels before Pedro got the first out in the bottom of the second, but he shut the door after that. Following four straight losses to finish out the season, Petey came out firing against the Angels, sustaining speeds in the mid-90s from the first pitch to the last. He set down the last seven batters he faced.

In the fifth, Pedro again worked himself into deep trouble; the first two Angels singled. Pedro retired a batter, but then hit Erstad to load the bases. Guerrero's single to right scored two and gave Anaheim a 3-1 lead in the game. Ortiz singled to lead off the sixth but was erased on Nixon's 4-6-3 double-play ball. Millar singled on a 3-2 count, and then Varitek homered on the first pitch he saw. Game tied. As it turned out, the only time the Angels ever led at any time in the Division Series was the time between Guerrero's single and Varitek's homer. Francisco (K-Rod) Rodriguez came in to start the seventh for the Angels and Bill Mueller singled. Francona began to work the sort of "National League ball" that he employed so successfully in the post-season, putting in Dave Roberts to run for Mueller. Unfortunately, Roberts was forced at second on Damon's grounder to short, but Damon stole second while Bellhorn was batting. Bellhorn drew a walk, and both runners moved up on a K-Rod wild pitch. Manny hit a sac fly to center and Damon scored to give the Sox a 4-3 lead. Pedro breezed through the seventh—and was not then asked to go back out again in the eighth.

In the bottom of the eighth, with the heart of the order coming up for Anaheim, Boston's bullpen came through big-time. Erstad singled off Mike Timlin, hoping to jump-start the offense but, after that, it was lights-out. Three pitchers, three strikeouts. Timlin got Guerrero, Myers got Garret Anderson, and Foulke got Glaus, and Boston held onto the slim one-run lead. The dominating Brendan Donnelly came on to throw the ninth inning for Anaheim. He got Bellhorn to fly out, but Ramirez doubled and Scioscia decided to walk Ortiz intentionally to get to Trot Nixon. Nixon had been pressing. He didn't play in the first game, and in Game Two had twice swung at first pitches and was already 0-for-4. Nixon came through, singling to center, plating Manny while Ortiz held at second base. On a wild pitch, the two runners moved up. Mientkiewicz grounded to second, but Ortiz had no chance to score. Varitek was walked intentionally to create a force at any base. Orlando Cabrera doubled to center field, clearing all the bases, and taking third on the throw to the plate. Foulke closed out the game and the Sox had taken both games in Anaheim. They were heading back home to friendly Fenway, where they always played well. Nevertheless, they remembered 2003 when it was the Red Sox down 0 games to 2 to the Oakland A's, and Boston came back and took three straight.

Final score: Boston 8, Anaheim 3

Game Three
Fenway Park—October 8, 2004

For the third game in a row, the Red Sox scored first, with two runs in the bottom of the third. The starters were Bronson Arroyo for the Red Sox and Kelvim Escobar for the Angels. It was Arroyo's first post-season start and he retired the Angels 1-2-3 in the first. After Anderson singled to lead off the second, he struck out the next three men he faced. For the Sox in the third inning, Bellhorn walked and then Ortiz doubled. Nixon singled in Bellhorn, and Ortiz scored on a grounder to second. 2-0, Red Sox. Glaus hit his second homer of the series, off Arroyo in the top of the fourth, a solo shot after two men were out. An error, a single, and a walk loaded the bases with nobody out for Manny Ramirez in the bottom of the fourth. He got an RBI with a sacrifice fly to left field. Scot Shields came on in relief. Ortiz doubled off him for another run. David Eckstein's error on a fielder's choice allowed Bellhorn to score, but Varitek hit into a double play and the Angels escaped further damage. They were losing the game, though, 5-1. Three singles in the fifth gave the Sox a 6-1 lead, and gave Manny another RBI.

It looked like the Red Sox could go on cruise control. Arroyo had only been touched for two hits and just one run, a true quality start. He walked the first batter of the seventh, though, and when the Angels sent up a left-handed pinch-hitter in Casey Kotchman, Francona decided it was time to turn things over to the bullpen. In hindsight, that might not have been the best move. Mike Myers walked the one batter he faced—right-handed Jose Molina, who subbed for Kotchman. Timlin was beckoned and got the next pinch-hitter, allowed a single which loaded the bases, then struck out Figgins. Erstad then walked, forcing in a run. Vladimir Guerrero was up with the bases loaded and the Angels now down by four. First pitch, grand slam. Game tied 6-6. The Red Sox had blown a five-run lead, the largest lead any home team had ever blown in post-season history. It had seemed too easy up to this point. Was this the turning point, the beginning of the end? Paranoia was beginning to creep into Fenway.

Both bullpens then buckled down and kept the game tied through nine, though the Red Sox had a scare in the ninth. After Eckstein flied out, Figgins singled. Then Erstad banged a ball off the Wall in left-center. Figgins was fast; he had 34 stolen bases, and he'd been off with the pitch, but he'd hesitated and held up at second, not scoring but only advancing as far as third. He later admitted that he hadn't played at Fenway enough to feel certain the ball was going to hit the wall. In any other park? "Then I score easily," he told Mike DiGiovanni of the *Los Angeles Times*. Second and third, one out, Foulke walked Guerrero intentionally to load the bases, but he still had to face Garret Anderson and Troy Glaus. He threw strikes. On a 1-2 count, he got Anderson to strike out swinging. On a 1-2 count, he got Glaus to go down swinging. Figgins was still stuck on third, and the score remained tied. In the bottom of the ninth, the Sox were scoreless.

Derek Lowe came in and pitched the tenth inning for the Red Sox. A walk, a sacrifice bunt, and a single still couldn't quite get a run across and Lowe was a little lucky to get out of the tenth. Damon singled to kick off the bottom of the inning, but was thrown out at second when Bellhorn's sacrifice bunt was hit a little too hard to third base. Manny Ramirez struck out for the second out. David Ortiz was headed for the batter's box. Rodriguez had already thrown 2⅔ innings and was pitching on fumes. Troy Percival could have been tapped. Ortiz was only 1-for-10 against him, and despite being right-handed, he'd held left-handed hitters to just .218 on the year. He had 316 saves in his career. Instead, Scioscia went with the sole southpaw on the staff—Jarrod Washburn. On Washburn's very first pitch, Ortiz went the other way and lofted a home run into the Monster seats in left field.

Ortiz's walk-off homer was the third in Red Sox playoff history, the first being Fisk's in 1975 and the second being Trot Nixon's in the 2003 ALDS. Of course, there would never have been any late-inning heroics had not the bullpen let the Angels score five times in the top of the seventh. "We don't do anything easy," said Theo Epstein. But no one was going to worry about the bullpen in the midst of the celebrations that ensued, as Fenway rocked out.

Lowe got the win. This was the man that Steve Buckley described as "jettisoned from the starting rotation and sentenced to the rock pile of long relief in the bullpen." But it was David Ortiz who was the real closer tonight. "David as Goliath" was the headline in more than one publication. It was hard to remember, Howard Bryant reminded us, that when Ortiz first came to the Red Sox, he was expected to be the backup for Jeremy Giambi.

It took the Red Sox ten innings to take Game Three, but the Sox had swept the Angels and were ready to take on the winner of the Yankees-Twins series. The Sox said it didn't matter which team won. "I don't care about facing the Yankees," said Mike Timlin. "The only team I want to be facing is the last team in the National League."

There's no question who most of America wanted. They longed for a rematch, to see the two northeastern franchises go head-to-head in the American League Championship Series. When New York clinched their third game the next night, it was with a little more of that Yankees magic; they roared back from a 5-1 deficit in the eighth inning, winning the game in the eleventh. The stage was set for the showdown Sox fans had dreamed of since the 2003 season came to a crashing end just a year before. And the Sox couldn't have been in better shape in terms of the rotation: Curt Schilling was due to start Game One and Pedro Martinez to start Game Two. If the series went the full seven games, they'd both be pitching again on five days' rest.

The sweep was just the second post-season sweep in Red Sox history, the first since the 1975 playoffs. "Now we have two more celebrations to go," said a drenched-in-champagne Epstein in the Red Sox clubhouse.

Outside, the stands were still filled with fans who were ready for more. There was no doubt who these fans hoped they'd see in the League Championship Series. Adrian Wojnarowski of the *Bergen Record* noted, "The voices started screaming into the cool October chill on Friday night, a chorus growing louder and louder inside Fenway Park. 'We want the Yankees . . . We want the Yankees . . . We want the Yankees.' The Red Sox hadn't thundered back down the dugout steps, through the tunnel and into the champagne-soaked clubhouse celebrating that two-run, two-out shot for an 8-6 victory in the 10th inning before they could hear the words ringing in their ears, too."

Final score: Boston 8, Anaheim 6

The Sox out-hit the Angels, with a team average .302 to Anaheim's .226. Sox pitching posted a 3.86 staff ERA; Anaheim's was a horrible 8.13. Boston batters knocked in 23 runs; Angels hitters just 12.

Chapter 9
The 2004 ALCS and the
World Series

Sometimes one word is sufficiently eloquent. "After the NLDS series between the St. Louis Cardinals and Los Angeles Dodgers ended, the clubs shook hands. Red Sox first baseman Kevin Millar was asked prior to last night's game whether Boston and New York would do the same, and he said 'No.' " —reported by Joe McDonald, Providence Journal

"O thou of little faith, wherefore didst thou doubt?" —Matthew 13:31

"I thought I had an idea of what it was going to be like when I signed last winter . . . but I had no idea that it was going to be at the level it was right from the get-go, from spring training through April . . . all the way through the season." —Curt Schilling.

"If the good guy dies in every production since 1918, you might get a little fatalistic, don't you think?" —Leigh Montville

"The fact that Theo Epstein's grandfather co-wrote Casablanca led all Red Sox fans to believe the season would have a classic and unpredictable ending." —Conan O'Brien

"Jerry Bruckheimer, Steven Spielberg, and George Lucas could be locked in a room for a month and wouldn't be able to come up with a story like this." —John M. Crist, Chicago Sports Review

"It ain't over till it's over." —Yogi Berra

The ALCS: Cue the Comeback

(continued from Chapter One)

Before the beginning of Game Four, even many devout Red Sox fans had begun to question their faith in the team that had disappointed them so many times. It was the sort of lapse of faith that even religious zealots must experience from time to time. They had suffered much—more than fans of any other team in major professional sport. Their resolve had been tested in some of the most painful ways imaginable. It was not just the length of the World Championship drought (after all, Moses wandered in the desert for less than half that time—a mere 40 years). It was the way fans were enticed year after year into pursuing mirages of distant oases, and tempted to go overboard by mermaids that turned out to be manatees.

Game Four
Against the Wall

No team in baseball history had ever come back from a 3-0 post-season deficit. In total, there had been 25 times in baseball history that a team had fallen behind by three games in a best-of-seven series. All 25 times, that team lost the series. Most teams were so deflated at that juncture that they went quietly in four straight—in fact, in 20 of the 25 occasions that is just what occurred. Only two teams ever even made it to Game Six. Common sense told Red Sox fans that it was hopeless. Consider the historical record.

Times in modern baseball history, prior to the 2004 season, when one team took a 3-games-to-0 lead in a seven-game playoff series:

1907   World Series—Detroit Tigers were down 3-0 to the Chicago Cubs, then lost Game Four. SWEEP (There was also a tie game, the first scheduled game in the Series.)

1910   World Series—Chicago Cubs were down 3-0 to the Philadelphia Athletics, won Game Four, but then lost Game Five.

1914   World Series—Philadelphia Athletics were down 3-0 to the Boston Braves, then lost Game Four. SWEEP

1922   World Series—New York Yankees were down 3-0 to the New York Giants, then lost Game Four. SWEEP (There was also a tie.)

1927   World Series—Pittsburgh Pirates were down 3-0 to the New York Yankees, then lost Game Four. SWEEP

1928   World Series—St. Louis Cardinals were down 3-0 to the New York Yankees, then lost Game Four. SWEEP

1932   World Series—Chicago Cubs were down 3-0 to the New York Yankees, then lost Game Four. SWEEP

1937   World Series—New York Giants were down 3-0 to the New York Yankees, won Game Four, but then lost Game Five.

1938   World Series—Chicago Cubs were down 3-0 to the New York Yankees, then lost Game Four. SWEEP

1939   World Series—Cincinnati Reds were down 3-0 to the New York Yankees, then lost Game Four. SWEEP

1950   World Series—Philadelphia Phillies were down 3-0 to the New York Yankees, then lost Game Four. SWEEP

1954   World Series—Cleveland Indians were down 3-0 to the New York Giants, then lost Game Four. SWEEP

1963   World Series—New York Yankees were down 3-0 to the Los Angeles Dodgers, then lost Game Four. SWEEP

1966   World Series—Los Angeles Dodgers were down 3-0 to the Baltimore Orioles, then lost Game Four. SWEEP

1970   World Series—Cincinnati Reds were down 3-0 to the

Baltimore Orioles, won Game Four, but then lost Game
Five.

1976   World Series—New York Yankees were down 3-0 to the
Cincinnati Reds, then lost Game Four. SWEEP

1988   A.L.C. S.—Boston Red Sox were down 3-0 to the
Oakland Athletics, then lost Game Four. SWEEP

1989   World Series—San Francisco Giants were down 3-0 to
the Oakland Athletics, then lost Game Four. SWEEP

1990   A.L.C.S.—Boston Red Sox were down 3-0 to the Oakland
Athletics, then lost Game Four. SWEEP

1990   World Series—Oakland Athletics were down 3-0 to the
Cincinnati Reds, then lost Game Four. SWEEP

1995   N.L.C.S.—Cincinnati Reds were down 3-0 to the Atlanta
Braves, then lost Game Four. SWEEP

1998   N.L.C.S.—Atlanta Braves were down 3-0 to the San
Diego Padres, won both Games Four and Five, but then
lost Game Six.

1998   World Series—San Diego Padres were down 3-0 to the
New York Yankees, then lost Game Four. SWEEP

1999   N.L.C.S.—New York Mets were down 3-0 to the Atlanta
Braves, won both Games Four and Five, but then lost
Game Six.

1999   World Series—Atlanta Braves were down 3-0 to the New
York Yankees, then lost Game Four. SWEEP

In 20 of the 25 occasions, the team which won the first three games also
won the fourth game and thereby swept the series.

In only two instances did a series extend as far as a sixth game.

Never did a series go to a full seven games, before 2004.

This sort of a comeback is virtually without precedent in *any* sport. The
Los Angeles Times reported that there had been 73 times in NBA history
that one team had a 3-games-to-0 lead over another. Not once did the team
that was down come all the way back to win. In the NHL, it had happened
an astonishing 140 times and there had been two such comebacks, by the
1942 Toronto Maple Leafs and the 1975 New York Islanders. Over the
three sports, that makes 2 comebacks in 239 situations. If the Red Sox were
to win in 2004, they would have to do so against all odds.

Many teams would have given up and just gone through the motions in Game Four. The Sox had lost their best starter in Schilling. Their erstwhile ace had a father complex with the Yankees, and they had just beaten him like a redheaded stepchild. The team had then been humiliated, dismantled, dissected . . . oh, wait, we went through that already, back in Chapter One. Well, they were humiliated. 19-8 is a very humbling score. Having just endured that bombardment, the Red Sox were under virtual siege at Fenway Park, where their backs were literally against the Wall—the Green Monster to be exact. The Evil Empire was just innings away from playing a funeral dirge for the Red Sox right inside their "lyric little bandbox of a ballpark."

The fans couldn't have been more disheartened if Theo Epstein traded Pedro Martinez and brought back Heathcliff Slocumb. It was one thing to slug it out all the way to Game Seven as they did the year before. Our team gave the Yankees what-for. If Grady had only paid attention to Pedro's pitch count, they could have won it—probably *would* have won it. They deserved better, and by adding Schilling and Foulke while keeping the core of the team together (all the stars who would become free agents after the '04 season), they had a legitimate shot. Everything looked great on paper. They almost blew it through lackluster play in May, June, and July, but they rallied and secured the Wild Card—then swept the Angels. Maybe this was, finally, "next year."

And then Schilling went down, and Pedro lost his start, and then the sheer hopelessness of it all seemed evident. Already, fans feared those first games of 2005 when the Yankees would come to town. The taunt "19-18", the long winter ahead and then . . . that taunt again. For another year. And then what? What kind of team was going to be left after the 2004 season? If this Red Sox team couldn't win, what Red Sox team could? To be swept by the Yankees, to lose in front of the home crowd. It was with resignation more than trepidation that fans trudged into Fenway the night of October 17. They had about as much spring in their step as a condemned man heading for the gallows. Derek Lowe was to pitch for the Red Sox. Few still had faith in the man who had once thrown a no-hitter. He'd been erratic all year and won only two more games than he'd lost (14-12, with a 5.42 ERA, one of the worst records of any starter in the league). True, he *had* gotten the win in Game Three of the Division Series as the pitcher of record when David Ortiz hit a two-run walk-off homer in the bottom of the tenth to complete the sweep of the Angels. But that fact instilled little comfort throughout the cities and hamlets of Red Sox Nation. He was up against El Duque—the formidable Orlando Hernandez of the Yankees.

Not a single player for either side crossed home plate in the first two innings, something of a miracle in itself, given the unstaunchable flow of runs the night before. The Red Sox managed only one hit over the first four innings. Against all odds, however, the Sox players looked like they had some game left. Maybe we could pull one out, maybe two. Make it look respectable, anyhow. After all, back in Game One, the Sox almost came back and tied it. And Game Two wasn't such a bad score, not by any means. It was Game Three that was the crusher, but even there the Sox did score eight runs. Win one, the players told themselves. You can only play one game at a time. Win this one and worry about tomorrow when tomorrow comes.

Derek Lowe hadn't started a game in 14 days. He was arguably out of rhythm, and maybe out of sorts at the way he'd been banished to the bullpen before being called on here. The Red Sox had lost faith in him, due to his inconsistency. The lack of confidence was entirely understandable; Lowe had surrendered more runs than any pitcher in the American League. Asked before the game for his thoughts on Lowe in 2004, Jason Varitek was frank in his assessment: "Up and down, just like waves. I hope he's up and on for this one." Red Sox pitching coach Dave Wallace was asked if they had any alternative to Lowe. "I wish we did," Wallace was reported to have replied. Not exactly your standard and predictable "We believe in Derek Lowe" line.

The Yankees struck the first blow in the third inning. With two out, Captain Jeter singled to left off embattled starter Lowe. Alex Rodriguez then homered over everything in left to put the Yankees up 2-0. A few moments after A-Rod's home run went out, a baseball came flying back over the Wall from outside the park. A fan had heaved it back. Center fielder Johnny Damon picked it up and threw it back out over the Green Monster. Back it came yet again. Dominican native Nestor Garcia of Boston was out on Lansdowne Street and apparently was not the least bit interested in keeping that ball. "Nobody wants it," he told Amalie Benjamin of the *New York Times*. The umpire pocketed the boomerang ball and the game resumed.

Things were looking bleak for the Fenway faithful, but the Red Sox struck back in the home half of the fifth. Kevin Millar drew a walk. After Bill Mueller grounded into a fielder's choice, forcing Millar at second, Bellhorn walked, putting runners on first and second. Johnny Damon grounded into a fielder's choice and Bellhorn was forced at second, with Mueller advancing to third. Cabrera then singled to right, scoring Mueller with the first Red Sox run of the game. Damon moved to second on the play and Ramirez walked to load the bases. Ortiz singled, driving in both Damon and Cabrera and staking the Sox to a 3-2 lead before Varitek struck out swinging to end the inning. In Game Three—the horrible 19-8 game just the day before—the Sox actually had a one-run lead for half an inning. It was the first time in the Series they had a lead. Now they had another one-run lead. It lasted just a half-inning, too.

Once the poster boy for mound instability, Lowe had settled down and was pitching on guts, determination and pride. With one out in the top of the sixth, he gave up a triple to Hideki Matsui and was lifted. A shudder went through the crowd at the prospect of the shell-shocked Red Sox bullpen being called to the front lines. The call went out for Mike Timlin, one of the few spared from the wrath of Yankees hitters the night before. Timlin gave up a run on a Bernie Williams single, but after walking Posada, Williams was thrown out at third by Varitek. Ruben Sierra reached via an infield hit with Posada moving to third. Tony Clark drove him home to stake the Yankees to a slim, but for Sox fans grim, 4-3 lead. It was the last run that the Yankees would score in the next 5⅔ innings off the valiant quartet of Keith Foulke, Alan Embree, Mike Myers, and Curtis Leskanic. Foulke still hadn't come into a single ALCS game with a lead on the line, but he kept the Sox in the game, getting the last two outs of the seventh and throwing a scoreless eighth and ninth.

In the bottom of the ninth, with the Red Sox down 4-3 and three outs from elimination against the lead-pipe pitching cinch called Rivera, the fans of Red Sox Nation were again coaxed back to the edges of their seats. They were three outs away from the most ignominious defeat of them all. Three outs away from another long winter of criticism on talk radio and three outs away from the sacrilege of a Yankees celebration on Fenway Park turf. This was Rivera, who was a perfect 6-for-6 in playoff saves against the Red Sox, Rivera with 32 post-season saves to his credit. Rivera, who only needed those three outs to send the Yankees to the World Series for the 40th time in their history. "Just in case you had forgotten," wrote John M.

Crist in the *Chicago Sports Review*, "Rivera is the greatest closer in post-season history and had the blood removed from his veins and replaced with ice water long ago."

The cold-blooded closer began, though, by walking an equally sangfroid Kevin Millar, just as the scoreboard clock turned to midnight. Terry Francona then showed that battle strategy could overcome great odds. He inserted speedy Dave Roberts to pinch-run for Millar at first base. Turns out these guys were not idiots after all, but idiot savants because this move immediately and palpably changed the dynamic of the game. The once predictable, plodding Red Sox were now the pesky, small-ball Red Sox, and they were playing mind games with the mighty Yankees. The former Dodger proved to be an instant distraction for Rivera, drawing three pick-off throws from the ace reliever. Roberts was able to use these tosses to gauge Rivera's move and get his timing. He stole second on the very first pitch to Bill Mueller. "I hadn't played for a while," he explained later, "and it helps the jitters." Rivera later conceded that the walk-steal was the turning point of the game. "You put the walk away and it would have been totally different," he said.

When Red Sox fans generations hence discuss the comeback of '04, they will treat this moment with reverence. It will be the mirror image of the decision to leave Buckner at first in '86, the decision to leave Pedro on the mound in '03, the other side of the Bucky Dent coin. With the multitude of home runs and high averages that the Red Sox had boasted over the years since 1918, it was a singularly wise managerial decision coupled with perfect execution by a utility player that turned the tide for the 2004 Red Sox. Such was baseball in 1918. The Royal Rooters would have approved.

Credit Theo Epstein and his baseball brain trust. It was no accident that they swapped two-time batting champion and local icon Nomar Garciaparra in a complex three-way trade for Doug Mientkiewicz, Orlando Cabrera, and Dave Roberts. Everyone in the ballpark knew Roberts was going to try to steal second, and steal second he did. The steal was more akin to grand larceny than petty theft in its importance to the Sox. Bill Ballou led his column in the *Worcester Telegram*, writing "Long neglected, occasionally belittled, often shunned, and never really appreciated by the Red Sox, the humble old stolen base helped them survive last night."

Now there was a runner on second and no one out. Mueller, the defending A.L. batting champion was at the plate. He showed bunt on the first pitch, then drove a single past Rivera up the middle to score the speedy Roberts. After having successfully converted 23 consecutive save opportunities (53 season saves in all, a personal best) Rivera had blown two regular season saves to the Bosox (July 24 and September 17). In fact this blown save was the ninth in 24 opportunities against the Red Sox since 2001, raising the question: "Mo, who's *your* daddy?" But the previous eight had not been playoff games, where Rivera was consistently untouchable. Rivera had saved Game One, and then he'd saved Game Two. Not Game Four, despite a couple of days' rest since Game Two. The ice water in his veins was apparently thawing.

Did Mueller have Mo's number? It was Mueller who'd hit the three-run homer off Rivera back on July 24 to win the game for the Red Sox. Rivera was a little rocky at times facing the Red Sox. Since 2001, he'd blown seven games against Boston and only 14 against all the other teams in baseball combined.

Mientkiewicz sacrificed Mueller to second and Johnny Damon hit a grounder to Tony Clark at first. Clark failed to handle it cleanly, allowing Mueller to take third. Cabrera then struck out, but Damon moved to second uncontested. Ramirez drew a walk, loading the bases. Habitual hero Ortiz had a chance at more walk-off heroics, but he flied to right for the final out of the ninth. But now the score was tied 4-4. Extra innings beckoned. There was a beacon of hope in the home ballpark. It felt at the time as though there'd been a shift in momentum, and yet the game was still tied.

Alan Embree took over mound duties for Boston in the top of the tenth and retired the side in order. After the Sox failed to score in the bottom of the inning, Miguel Cairo kicked off the eleventh with a single to right. Jeter bunted, sacrificing to move Cairo to second. Rodriguez hit the ball hard, but right at Cabrera, who held on tight. Two outs, runner at first and Gary Sheffield up. No brainer. Intentional walk, and left-handed specialist Mike Myers was brought in to replace Embree. He walked Matsui on four pitches and was immediately pulled. With the bases now loaded with pinstripes, the call went out for Curtis Leskanic. On a 0-1 count, Bernie Williams flied out to Johnny Damon in center to end the latest panic attack by Red Sox fans.

Damon walked and stole second in the bottom of the inning, but there were two outs and Cabrera grounded out to end the inning.

Was this all just setting the stage for the man they call "Big Papi" to come back and reprise his role as hero, a role in which he was practically typecast. It was up to "The Mechanic" Curtis Leskanic to stall out the potent NY offense in the top of the 12th, and the six-foot, 185-pound 36-year old right-hander was up to the task. In fact, Leskanic proved to be a regular Mr. Badwrench for the Yankees. Mixing a decent fastball with a hard slider, he pitched the biggest inning of his career and held the Yankees bats in check. It was still 4-4 going into the bottom of the twelfth inning.

With Paul Quantrill now on the mound for the Yankees, Manny Ramirez led off with a single. Ortiz stepped to the plate once more and Red Sox fans almost expected a miracle. They had seen him come through in situations such as this time and again all season long and especially in the post-season. He had hoisted the Boston Red Sox on his shoulders and carried them countless times before. Quantrill, a wily veteran and former Red Sox pitcher, toed the rubber.

Ortiz worked the count to 2-1, stepped out of the box, slapped his gloved hands together in his trademark manner—a mannerism that had now replaced Nomar's fidgeting Barney Fife routine on vacant lots and playgrounds across New England—and stepped back in. The next pitch came in low, inside and right in Ortiz's wheelhouse. It was immediately launched into the right-field bullpen, unleashing pandemonium at Fenway.

Now it was the Red Sox turn to hoist *him* on *their* shoulders. At 1:22 A.M. on Monday, October 18, David Ortiz could have been elected mayor of Boston, Dave Roberts governor of Massachusetts, and Terry Francona conductor of the Boston Pops for the way he orchestrated the comeback. As the big man danced around third base, he flipped his batting helmet aside and was swallowed up by a jubilant horde of Red Sox teammates.

A faint, faint glimmer of hope remained. The Red Sox had secured a moral victory. They would not be swept in front of the home fans. "This is a team that never gives up," said Ortiz in the joyous glare of lights at the post-game media scrum.

The Red Sox had avoided the I.D. (Ignominious Defeat) thanks to David Ortiz. They had shown great character and resilience in coming back from a 19-8 humiliation to defeat the Yankees in extra innings. And they'd done it by working some walks, using their base-running effectively, going through Mariano Rivera, and having their clutch hitter homer in extra innings.

The Red Sox could have gone quietly, waving the white flag of surrender and avoiding another futile battle. They could have been too demoralized to fight. They could have given up. But this was the Alamo for the Boston Red Sox, and the players left to defend the honor of the venerable old franchise were a determined, if ragged-looking lot. This was the team of Jason Varitek, Johnny Damon, and Trot Nixon (for whom a coonskin hat would have been sartorially redundant): the William Travis, Davy Crockett, and Jim Bowie of baseball. Along with Manny, Mueller, and Millar, they were a cast of hirsute heroes that rivaled those who defended that god-forsaken fort against Steinbr . . . 'er Santa Anna's troops. Of course victory was out of the question. The Red Sox would certainly be defeated. But at least they would go down fighting. The Red Sox did not want to be humiliated in front of the fans that had supported them so loyally and so long.

This battle was an epic one, both in dramatics, heroics, time and proportion. It was, to be precise, a 5 hours and 2 minutes grinder, the longest game in ALCS history. Much had to happen before David Ortiz could launch his victorious volley into the bullpen and send a flare of hope soaring high above Red Sox Nation. This had been a true team effort.

Had momentum somehow already shifted, despite the Sox still being down three games to one? You'd think Joe Torre would avoid using the word, but he was apparently fearless about tempting fate. "I'm a firm believer in momentum for a short series," he admitted. "But it comes down to who pitches the best. Still, I've always felt that momentum is easily changed in a short series. We just have to make sure when we go out there for the next game we can't carry this baggage." Derek Jeter was cautious. Asked about the commanding lead the Yankees still enjoyed, he said, "We're not in command until it's over."

The Red Sox and Yankees had less than 16 hours before their next battle would commence. Francona wanted to keep it simple in his post-game press conference: "Now, our objective is to win tomorrow. That's all we have in front of us." One game at a time. All we have to do is win one game. That was the mantra.

Game Five
Our Red Sox Nation Ortiz of Thee

Scene: Later that same day. Same city, same ballpark, same hero; slightly longer script. Game Four had ended at 1:22 A.M. on October 18 and Game Five got underway at 5:10 P.M., some 15 hours and 48 minutes later.

Once again these two very different teams—the blue-collar Red Sox and the suddenly tight-collared Yankees—battled on overtime as the Boston fans looked on with something akin to mounting hope. This time, the Yankees had their game faces on and wanted to kill any momentum the never-say-die Red Sox had gained in Game Four. But among fans there was at least a smidgen of satisfaction in events of the previous evening. Red Sox fans had not yet dared to hope beyond Inning 12 of Game Four. Now they were dreaming slightly bigger dreams.

The Sox remained loose. One would think they'd be feeling tremendous pressure, since losing any one of the next three games would mean losing the pennant to the Yankees. Instead, the ballplayers had the healthiest attitude imaginable. Johnny Damon expressed it this way: "We're not supposed to win. The pressure is on them. They've got to play well. They've got to beat us. If not, history will be set. We're as loose and relaxed as we can be." Well said. The pressure on the Yankees could only intensify with each successive Red Sox win. The Sox came to Fenway with their bags packed for the trip to New York.

It was Mike Mussina against Pedro Martinez. Because Friday's game had been rained out, Pedro was able to start Game Five on his regular four days' rest. The Red Sox manufactured a pair of first-inning runs out of two walks and three singles against the shaky Yankees starter. The Yankees scored once in the second, and added three more in the sixth. Derek Jeter finally broke his RBI famine when Pedro threw his 100th pitch of the game; he hit a soft line drive over the first baseman's head with the bases loaded. The ball rattled off the grandstand for a double, scoring Posada, Clark and a hustling Miguel Cairo, who skillfully avoided Varitek's tag at the plate with a head-first slide. Jeter's batting average was languishing at .167 before the hit. Now the Yankees had a 4-2 lead. All four were earned runs, added onto Pedro's tab. Cairo should never have been in position to score. With two outs, Pedro hit the light-hitting second baseman and number nine hitter, forcing him to pitch to the always-dangerous Jeter. After Jeter's hit, Pedro plunked Rodriguez with a pitch. Gary Sheffield was up, again taunted by the Fenway crowd with chants of "Who's your deal-er?" Sheffield walked on five pitches. Godzilla was at the plate with the bases loaded. Martinez got Matsui to fly out. Boston fans exhaled as one, causing ripples on Boston Harbor. It could have been a lot worse.

The usually efficient Tom Gordon allowed the Red Sox back in the game in the eighth on a leadoff Green Monster homer by—that guy again—David Ortiz, to bring the score to 4-3. Gordon walked Kevin Millar, and Francona sent in the speed specialist Roberts to run for Millar. Trot Nixon singled to center and Roberts motored around to third. Gabe Kapler, another fast man on the basepaths, was put in to pinch-run for Nixon. With one out and runners on first and third in what was now a one-run game, Joe Torre summoned Mariano Rivera. Once again, surely lights out. Once again, not this time. Rivera got an out, but it was a sac fly by Jason Varitek that greeted Mo and the score was now knotted at 4-4. It was Rivera's second unsuccessful save attempt in as many nights, though he'd inherited a tough situation from Flash Gordon. The man with 53 regular season saves was suddenly mortal. The Red Sox were still breathing.

Arroyo took over for Keith Foulke in the tenth and set the Yankees down 1-2-3. After the unfortunate Game Three start, Foulke's confidence had to be boosted by getting Jeter to pop up and then striking out both A-Rod and Sheffield. Heredia took Rivera's place, and now both closers were out of the game. Mientkiewicz knocked a ground-rule double and moved up to third, but was left stranded. In the eleventh, Myers got his man—the mighty Matsui—and then handed the ball to Embree. After Bernie Williams singled, Embree struck out Posada and Sierra.

The Sox looked to score in the bottom of the eleventh, as Mueller and Bellhorn both singled to Sheffield. Mueller could only move up to second, though, and Damon's bunt attempt was a pop-up to Posada. Loaiza came in to pitch, the seventh pitcher of the night for the New Yorkers. He induced a double play from Cabrera, and it was on to the twelfth.

Tim Wakefield came in for the Red Sox, their seventh pitcher of the evening, which had now become morning. It was to be Loaiza vs. Wakefield for the duration. Though Manny Ramirez made a horrendous error in fielding a Miguel Cairo drive, allowing Cairo to scamper to second, with this team it wasn't as though the Weight of History had suddenly descended from the skies above. This, after all, was the team of self-confessed idiots, and what did idiots know about history? Manny was able to laugh it off, and so were the Sox. Wakefield got the job done. Loaiza did, too, with a little help. Ortiz walked, with one out—and then took off to steal second! The last time Ortiz stole a base, he was 13 years old in the Dominican Republic. Actually, that's not true. He stole a base once with the Minnesota Twins in 1998. He actually did it again once in 2000, and again one more time in 2001. In 2002, still with the Twins, he stole a fourth base but was caught stealing twice. Perhaps chastened by the experience, he didn't try once in either 2003 or 2004. To say that no one was expecting it is an understatement. The umpire ruled him out; television viewers at home ruled him safe. Fans in the park hadn't quite believed their eyes in the first place, so accepted the ruling with aplomb. Ortiz later said it was a case of mixed signals on a hit-and-run play. Whether Mientkiewicz missed the sign, or Ortiz mistook it, remains unclear. That was the second out, and Mientkiewicz whiffed on the next pitch. Maybe he thought he'd been seeing things, too.

Wakefield struck out Sheffield in the top of the thirteenth, but the knuckleball got away from Varitek and Sheffield made it safely to first. Matsui hit into a fielder's choice, forcing Sheffield at second, and Bernie Williams flied out. Posada up, and on a 2-1 count, the knuckler fooled Varitek again. A second passed ball, and Matsui took second base. The Sox decided to walk Posada and set up a force play. Ruben Sierra was up, and the count was 2-2. Wakefield's usual batterymate was Doug Mirabelli. Varitek had now been squatting behind the plate for nearly 25 innings in a little over 24 hours. Like everyone else, he was exhausted, never a good time to try to catch Wake's flutterball. The third passed ball of the inning allowed Matsui to take third, and Posada took second base. It would be a sad state of affairs if New York scored a run on four passed balls. On the 3-2 count, Sierra swung at another knuckleball, but missed. And Varitek squeezed the glove tight on the ball.

Loaiza had an easy 1-2-3 bottom of the thirteenth.

This game was becoming a long one. Don't umpires ever have to go to the men's room? Wakefield got himself a 1-2-3 inning, throwing three straight strikes past Tony Clark, before getting Cairo and Jeter. Bottom of the fourteenth. Bellhorn struck out, Damon walked. Cabrera struck out, Ramirez walked. David Ortiz came through again. He worked the count like a bulky Wade Boggs, fouling off pitch after pitch after pitch. Loaiza was now throwing nothing but strikes. Finally, on the tenth pitch of the at-bat, with the count 2-2, Ortiz put the ball in play. It was no monster homer, no gap triple, no Wall double, just a soft yet sufficient sinking line drive that dropped in front of Bernie Williams in center. Damon scored easily. The Red Sox won Game Five.

Wakefield had thrown three scoreless innings, and he got the win. "You can't imagine how happy I am that he gets to end that game," said Francona.

It had been 5 hours and 49 minutes of baseball, breaking the post-season record set just the previous evening. 26 innings of playoff baseball in just under 30 hours. Rivera had blown two saves in two straight games, and Big Papi had his second straight extra-inning walk-off RBI. Because this one came before midnight on the 18th, it was his second walk-off drive of the day. With his two-run homer in the tenth inning, which won the ALDS for the Red Sox on October 9, Ortiz now had three walk-off hits in nine days, the kind of production figures that General Motors or Ford would envy.

Between the 8:10 P.M. start on Saturday night and the Ortiz walk-off on Monday night at 10:59 P.M., the intervening 50 hours saw two teams go after each other for 15 hours and 11 minutes of baseball—over 35 innings of action. And there were less than 24 hours to recuperate before they had to go at it again, back in New York.

Doug Mientkiewicz acknowledged the many decades that Red Sox teams had tried to win a World Series, and said "If we're going to do it, we might as well do it the hard way." "New York, here we come," said Manny Ramirez after the game. Pedro Martinez, in a reference to Senor Ortiz, and his own "Daddy" quote from a few weeks before, directed a few pointed words of wisdom toward his NY foes: "The Yankees have to think about who's their Papi."

Curt Schilling had been co-MVP of the 2001 World Series, when his Arizona squad bested the New York Yankees. He'd been in The Show for years, and appeared in two World Series. He knew that coming to Boston as a gladiator in the Red Sox-Yankees rivalry would be big, but he hadn't known how big. "It's been so much more than I imagined it would be. I've never seen anything like this," he admitted.

When the Red Sox have gotten into extra innings in the post-season, they have fared fairly well. They have won 9 of the 14 October games. There was also one tie. Almost half of the extra-inning contests (6 of 14) took place in the two years 2003 and 2004.

October 16, 1912 World Series, Game Eight (there had been an extra-inning tie Game Two). Larry Gardner's sacrifice fly in the tenth inning produced the second, and tie-breaking run of the inning, for a walk-off win of a very exciting World Series.

October 9, 1916 World Series, Game Two. After giving up a solo home run in the first inning, pitcher Babe Ruth held Brooklyn scoreless for the next 13 innings. After a walk and a sacrifice, the Sox' Del Gainer pinch-hit in the bottom of the fourteenth and singled down the left-field line to break the 1-1 tie.

October 6, 1946 World Series, Game One. It was 2-2 in the top of the tenth, and the Red Sox' Rudy York hit a home run to win the game.

October 21, 1975 World Series, Game Six. After Bernie Carbo tied the game with a crucial pinch-hit three-run homer into the center field seats, catcher Carlton Fisk came up in the bottom of the twelfth inning and hit his dramatic home run that stayed fair by a matter of a very few inches.

October 11, 1986 ALCS, Game Four. Calvin Schiraldi hit a batter with the bases loaded in the bottom of the ninth, tying the game. In the eleventh inning, the California Angels' Bobby Grich singled in the winning run.

October 12, 1986 ALCS, Game Five. The second extra-inning game in a row, this one was won by Boston when Dave Henderson hit a two-run homer in the ninth inning to help overcome a three-run deficit, and then hit a sacrifice fly in the eleventh to give the Sox the lead.

October 25, 1986 World Series, Game Six. In the tenth inning, Bill Buckner reached down to take Mookie Wilson's routine grounder, step on the bag, and win the World Series for the Red Sox. The ball went through his legs. The Mets won the game.

October 3, 1995 ALDS, Game One. With two outs in the bottom of the twelfth inning, Tony Pena hit a home run to win the game. He'd played four years for the Red Sox. Unfortunately, he was playing for the Cleveland Indians in 1995.

October 1, 2003 ALDS, Game One. In the bottom of the twelfth inning, Ramon Hernandez bunted with the bases loaded, and pulled it off. Oakland beat Boston, 5-4.

October 4, 2003 ALDS, Game Three. Trot Nixon turned the tables on the A's in the bottom of the eleventh, with a two-run walk-off home run before the Fenway faithful.

October 16, 2003 ALCS, Game Seven. The memory is still fresh enough to be painful. In the bottom of the eleventh inning at Yankee Stadium, New York's third baseman Aaron Boone homered off Tim Wakefield to win the pennant for the Yankees.

October 8, 2004 ALDS, Game Three. Happier memories have David Ortiz hitting a tenth-inning two-run walk-off home run on the first pitch he saw from reliever Jarrod Washburn; the win gives Boston a sweep in the Division Series.

October 17, 2004 ALCS, Game Four. Down 3 games to none, the Red Sox faced being swept by the Yankees. After the Red Sox tied the game dramatically in the ninth inning, the two teams still found themselves facing off in the twelfth. David Ortiz homered again (see October 8) to win in a walk-off, and give the Sox new life and a little momentum.

October 18, 2004 ALCS, Game Five. Again, the two teams tangled into extra innings. This time the game went to the fourteenth inning, and again it was David Ortiz who came up big, with a single into center driving in the winning run. Momentum began to snowball.

Game Six
From the Alamo to Fort Apache, the Bronx

Momentum was clearly with the Red Sox now, as both teams were back in the Bronx. Thomas Boswell stated it clearly: "For those who love and understand baseball, it would be impossible to overstate the impact on any team of losing back-to-back extra-inning games after saves were blown in regulation time. To do it twice with the pennant in your hands is unprecedented . . . Back-to-back blown pennant saves have never happened." Damon had been right; the pressure was on the Yankees.

George Vecsey of the *New York Times* began his column that ran the morning of Game Six, "Before, it was a nuisance. Now, it has become a downright menace to the Yankees. Before, it was a swarm of gnats. Now, it is a phalanx of mosquitoes, bearing the West Nile Virus of baseball, a massive shift in momentum. The Red Sox are alive, alive and swarming." He concluded the column: "The Yankees usually know how to put away opponents but now their chief swatter has failed them twice. The Red Sox have gone from an annoyance to a threat. One more Boston victory and the Yankees will be facing an epidemic."

The Red Sox bullpen threw 14 innings in Games One, Two and Three, and served up 17 runs on 27 hits. In Games Four and Five, they threw 14⅔ innings, giving up just one run.

After the first five games, though, leadoff batter Johnny Damon was just 2-for-24, batting .083. Bellhorn was 3-for-20, with a thousand strikeouts. Well, actually it was 10. Millar was only 3-for-17. And Manny Ramirez still had not even one RBI. Half of the Red Sox offense seemed to be on life support.

With Halloween only a few days away, the Team of the Living Dead was back from the crypt for yet another harrowing assault on the good people of Gotham. They were led by that Number One Crypt-Kicker, Curt Schilling. With blood oozing though his sock (the original red sock!), the man who was acquired to rid the team of a curse helped to do just that. Schilling, whose impromptu stitching made him walk like Frankenstein, rendered cavernous Yankee Stadium as quiet as the aforementioned crypt (his stated dream to make 55,000 New Yorkers shut up was finally realized) and had Yankees fans looking as if they had seen a ghost. Finally some of the injustices of the last 86 years were resolved; thanks in large part to team umpiring that corrected two egregious calls.

Pitching courageously with the dislocated tendon temporarily sewn back into its proper place in his right ankle, Schilling may have had only a few less sutures than Frankenstein's monster (although his stiff-legged gait was reminiscent of the creature) but he petrified Yankees fans, who could only sit and exclaim: "It's alive!"

Schilling, already getting his due for leading the Red Sox to the post-season, gained Instant Legend status throughout New England with his Bunyanesque exploits. The man who could barely walk after Game One was now walking on water. His ruptured tendon sheath and dislocated tendon was a serious injury that would require post-season surgery. Dr. Bill Morgan told the media after Game Two, "If this was your problem, we would put you in a cast." Instead, Morgan looked for a way to suture the dislocated tendon in place long enough for Schilling to make his start. The concern spread beyond the ankle. Even if that could be stabilized, and the pain suppressed, any significant compensating change in his delivery could result in injury to his rotator cuff, his arm, or even his oblique muscle. The Boston newspapers had provided all the medical diagrams of his damaged *peroneus brevis* and its effect on plantar flexation and ankle eversion. Red Sox fans who previously couldn't have diagnosed the common cold were now offering their learned prognoses on talk radio. Suffice it to say, there were a lot of things that could go very seriously wrong here.

Curt Schilling pitched seven courageous innings and Mark Bellhorn chipped in with a three-run homer to lift the Red Sox to within one game of the ALCS title. We were reminded: never before had a team been down 0-3 in any post-season baseball playoff and come back even to force a seventh game, let alone win it. Only twice had a team down 0-3 pushed it to six games. The Sox had come back to the Stadium, where New York boasted the best home record (57-27, .704) in all of baseball in 2004. The Yankees also had a stellar 61 come-from-behind wins during the 2004 regular season.

It was Schilling's first start since his disastrous appearance in Game One of the ALCS. In that game, the debilitating ankle injury had led to his worst outing of the year. He gave up six runs in just three innings and left the game with the taunts of New York fans ringing in his ears. This time was different. Credit Dr. Morgan of the Red Sox staff and the orthopedic surgeons he had assembled, thank even the cadaver that Morgan practiced on if you like (who was the departed one, whose corpse helped give new life to

Schilling and the Sox?), but it was Schilling who had to take the ball and toe
the rubber. He pitched brilliantly, retiring the first eight batters to face him
and keeping zeroes on the board until there was one out in the seventh and
Bernie Williams touched him for a homer. Posada popped to second and
Sierra struck out swinging. Schill allowed just four hits and that one earned
run over seven full innings. He struck out four and, even with the blood
seeping from the sutures, didn't walk a batter. An amazing 67 of his 99
pitches were strikes. On this all-but-moribund Red Sox team, Schilling
stood out as the Lazarus of baseball, back from the dead, and with the help
of the dead.

The offense rallied behind the wounded pitcher, offering enough run
support to carry him to victory. The Sox had scored first, back in the fourth.
With two outs, Millar doubled and Jason Varitek, who bore the burden of
an 0-for-36 stretch in New York (with 19 strikeouts) before his two-run
homer in Game Two, came through with an RBI single. He finished the
Series 7-for-16 in the Stadium games. Cabrera singled and that brought up
Bellhorn, he of the disappointing offensive drought. Bellhorn had started
Game Six poorly; batting with one out and the bases loaded in the top of
the second, he grounded into an inning-ending 4-6-3 double play. But in
the fourth, Bellhorn broke out of it big-time. He popped the ball just barely over the wall in left; it bounced off a fan's chest and landed back on the
field. It was the second baseman's first post-season home run, staking
Boston to a 4-0 lead.

If there was ever a poster boy for courage on the baseball diamond, it
had to be the man who'd trundled to the mound for the Red Sox this day.
And if there was ever a time to heap praise on a team of umpires, this was
that time. Eschewing the frustrating practice of sticking to a call come hell
or high water, this team actually conferred with each other in a selfless
effort to get it right. They did so twice and the replays show clearly that
they made the correct decision in each case. The first controversy occurred
when Bellhorn's homer was initially ruled a ground-rule double. Francona
came out to argue and, after a short deliberation, the decision was reversed.
That made the score 4-0, not 2-0. Two more runs were credited to the boys
from Boston. Lieber retired the next ten Red Sox batters he faced, but the
four runs remained on the board.

The second controversial play was like something more fitting for the
Babe Ruth League than the House that Ruth Built. The Williams homer

had made it 4-1, and so it stood in the eighth, with Bronson Arroyo on in relief of Schilling. Arroyo struck out Tony Clark, but then Cairo doubled to right and Derek Jeter singled to produce the second Yankees run. Now Arroyo had to face A-Rod, the same A-Rod he had hit with a pitch back on July 24, igniting a donnybrook. The two squared off once again.

On a 2-2 count, the $22 million dollar man, Alex Rodriguez (we're talking one year's pay here), hit a soft grounder down the first base line. Arroyo fielded the ball and as he attempted to tag A-Rod, the man some call "the best player in baseball" slapped at the ball, knocking it out of the pitcher's hand. First base umpire Randy Marsh's view of the play was blocked and he called Rodriguez safe, even though he had also run right by first base without touching the bag. A jubilant Jeter clapped his hands in celebration as he crossed home plate. Yankees fans went wild with delight. The Red Sox bench exploded in outrage, as Terry Francona leaped from the dugout and confronted the umpire. Another conference ensued and this call, too, was reversed, Rodriguez ruled out due to batter interference. Call it "the slap" or a tomahawk chop, or even a sportsmanlike "low-five" in appreciation of Arroyo's heads-up hustle, it was still against the rules. Had A-Rod just let himself be tagged out, it would have been two outs but Jeter would have been on second base, in scoring position. Instead, because of the rules on an interference call, Jeter was brought all the way back and placed on first base.

Now it was the Yankees and their fans who were outraged. A-Rod, defending the indefensible, argued that Arroyo blocked his path to first base, but umpire Joe West had seen the play clearly. Viewers at home knew that A-Rod's claim was not substantiated by the video evidence, but fans at the Stadium couldn't see the replays and showered the field with debris. The scored remained 4-2 as about 40 helmeted NYPD officers were brought in for riot control and ringed the infield. Suddenly, one could imagine what baseball in Baghdad might be like. It took more than a dozen Stadium workers a few minutes to clean the mess off the field. Once order was restored, Sheffield fouled out to Varitek to end the inning. Some Yankees partisans no doubt left the Stadium feeling, "We wuz robbed!" There must have been a little sheepishness when they saw the slap on the replays after they got home. Or, wait, maybe Yankees fans don't do sheepishness.

There was a bit of a flashback here to Game One and to Game Five of the 1999 ALCS when the umpiring crew refused to review two egregious errors. When Boston's Jose Offerman was called out on the basepaths even though Yankees second baseman Chuck Knoblauch's attempt at a tag missed him by a good two feet, the Fenway faithful along the right-field side pelted the field with plastic bottles, cups, and anything else they could get their hands on. After order was restored, Yankees sympathizers wrung their hands over the boorish behavior of the Boston fans.

But that was then and this was now.

There were two baserunners for both Boston and New York in their respective parts of the ninth, but neither team scored. There was no Yankees uprising and the 4-2 score held. The Red Sox had done what no team had ever done before—come back from a 0-3 deficit and force a Game Seven. The Red Sox and Yankees were tied in the 2004 ALCS at

---

On the Slap

From the Official Baseball Rules:

Interference:

(a) Offensive interference is an act by the team at-bat which interferes with, obstructs, impedes, hinders or confuses any fielder attempting to make a play. If the umpire declares the batter, batter runner, or a runner out for interference, all other runners shall return to the last base that was in the judgment of the umpire, legally touched at the time of the interference, unless otherwise provided by these rules. In the event the batter runner has not reached first base, all runners shall return to the base last occupied at the time of the pitch.

From the MLB Umpire Manual, a casebook that guides their decisions:

Section 6.1 (Offensive Interference):

While contact may occur between a fielder and runner during a tag attempt, a runner is not allowed to use his hands or arms to commit an obviously malicious or unsportsmanlike act such as grabbing, tackling, intentionally slapping at the baseball, punching, kicking, flagrantly using his arms or forearms, etc. to commit an intentional act of interference unrelated to running the bases.

Rodriguez clearly would have preferred to talk about anything else, when asked about the incident after the game. He continued to protest his innocent intent, but noted that "the line belongs to me," as he put it to the *New York Times*. "Maybe I should have just run him over." Curt Schilling, never one to mince words, told ESPN it was "bush league." Really? "Absolutely. First of all, Bronson was not in the base line—his glove was. I've never seen anything like that. Someone in the base line is one thing, [but] he could break his arm on a play like that. That's not the way you play the game. Bottom line: would Derek Jeter ever do that? No chance. It's not unexpected, though." Kevin Millar interjected, "It was an unprofessional play and he knows that. He has to brush his teeth and look at himself in the mirror in the morning." A-Rod was supposed to be Aaron Boone's replacement at third base. Rather than drive in the winning run, he may have cost the Yankees a shot at a very crucial run. He certainly didn't win any respect.

three games apiece! It was the second year in a row the two teams had battled to the final game. A replay of the drama of 2003 would have seemed
impossible after the 19-8 loss in Game Three had the Sox down on the mat
gasping for breath. Yet here it was at 12:41 A.M. on the morning of October
20 and there was another game to be played that very evening. For all the
marbles. Sox fans had just about lost their marbles, and Yankees fans were
marbleized with shock—but still had every reason to believe their team
would, once again, prevail.

With the 4-2 win, the Red Sox had now made history, but what comfort
and satisfaction could they take from that if they lost the Game Seven they
had forced for the second year in a row? Lose now and, sure, you could talk
about how far back you came, but that's nothing like actually winning it all
and heading to the World Series. Theo Epstein had worked with one of the
two teams that had been forced into a Game Six, the 1998 San Diego
Padres. "I remember being over-confident when we were up 3-0. I think
when they won Game Four, I still felt good. But when they won Game Five,
you start looking around a little. The players were OK, but it got real quiet."
One can only imagine the tension in the Yankees clubhouse, having lost
three games in a row to their arch-rivals, the team they always seemed to
beat. This time, though, the momentum surge seemed almost palpable,
truly of juggernaut proportions.

In a little bit of gamesmanship, neither manager would name his starter
for the final showdown.

Game Seven
Lowe and Behold History Being Made

It took God seven days to create the heavens and the earth and it took the
Boston Red Sox seven games to create a miracle of their own.

Game Seven of the 2004 ALCS was a cliché. It was the most idealized,
improbable fantasy concocted in the feverish minds of every kid who ever
loved baseball and/or the Boston Red Sox. The other dreams—three night-
mares and then three daydreams—were nothing compared to this one.
Let's review, shall we? You are playing against the best team in the history
of baseball. You lose Game One, you lose Game Two, you lose Game Three
19-8, and are trailing in Game Four. Everything is stacked against you.

Somehow, you win that fourth game—though it took 12 innings to do it. Then you win Game Five, and that win takes 14 innings. A couple of bizarre plays both result in overturned rulings against your opponent—the team that won 26 World Championships, the team that always seemed to get all the breaks. You are now playing in Yankee Stadium in front of the most intimidating fans in the major leagues. History is against you. No team had ever ventured this far back from such a deep deficit. These were uncharted waters. All the odds are against you. Some cynics even suspect that God is against you.

Was there ever a more unlikely, corny, credulity-stretching scenario? This was *Field of Dreams* with attitude; *The Natural* with Jim Carrey as Roy Hobbs; *The Greatest Story Ever Told* played out on a baseball diamond. Any Hollywood scriptwriter would have been laughed out of town, coming in with a script like the 2004 ALCS. "OK," starts the jaded scriptwriter, paddling hard to peddle his idea to skeptical producers. "In Game Seven, I think we'll have that little lead-off guy—you know, the one with the Jesus complex—hit a home run . . . no, wait . . . a—whatta you guys call them— a grand slam home run. And that pitcher guy who had such a miserable year and sought therapy . . . isn't his name Lowe? We'll have him win the game in front of 56,000 rabid, hostile fans. And the Red Sox will beat the Yankees and erase the Curse of the Bambino, or whatever it's called, overturn eighty years of history, create an upset the likes of which has never, ever been seen." Cynical Hollywood producers scoff. The studio executive who gave the green light to *Lord of the Rings* terms it too much fantasy. The creators of the Harry Potter movies say "it's unbelievable." And they are right, of course.

This was not a team, though, that was going to worry too much about history. As Sean McAdam wrote, "If the last week has shown anything, it's that the Red Sox aren't consumed with history. They're intent on making it." They were knocked down, beaten, trampled on, run over, and left for dead. The obituaries were already written. Yet now the New York Yankees looked like the haunted ones. They were the ones with the "highest payroll in the history of team sports" who now found themselves "trying to fend off an embarrassment of historic proportions." [*Bergen Record*]

The Yankees pulled out all the stops. They even had Bucky Dent throw out the first pitch. Stewart O'Nan suggested they should have let Dent start the game instead of handing the ball to Kevin Brown.

Game Seven was arguably the greatest game in Red Sox history. At least in its significance, if not in its substance. The Red Sox made history this day, coming back from the brink of elimination to capture the American League pennant in the backyard of their most hated rivals. At the end, nothing could have been sweeter for Sox fans than watching their heroes cavort on Yankee Stadium grass, guarded by New York's finest, while New York fans slunk silently off into the darkness.

If Game 3 was the lowest of the low, Game 7 was surely the highest of the Lowe. A rejuvenated and rehabilitated Derek Lowe, reprieved to pitch under close scrutiny, a day pass, and tight conditions of parole, got the well-deserved win. Lowe, deeply wounded when he was sentenced to the bullpen at the beginning of the playoffs, was nothing short of brilliant in subduing the potent Yankees offense. Pitching on just two days' rest, the sinkerball specialist allowed one hit over six innings of work and retired the last 11 Yankees he faced. He induced hitters to ground out for 12 of the 18 outs he recorded. In short, he was the Lowe of old.

Yankees starter Kevin Brown was not so blessed on this day. The struggling right hander lasted only 1⅓ innings, coughing up four hits, two walks, and five runs. His post-season career record now stands at 0-5. In the very first half-inning, there was a roller coaster of ups and downs. Damon singled to lead off, and stole second. This was not looking good to the New York fans (Bill Lee later told Leigh Montville they seemed to shrink "like testicles in the cold"). But Bellhorn struck out. Manny then singled to left, and Sox third base coach Dale Sveum waved Damon around third and homeward. Out at the plate. Yankees fans were pumped. David Ortiz wasted no time re-establishing momentum, in a decisive fashion. Swinging at the very next pitch, Big Papi stroked a two-run home run. The Sox had a two-run lead.

Brown got Nixon to ground out to start the second, but then gave up a single to Kevin Millar, and walked Bill Mueller and Orlando Cabrera to load the bases. Joe Torre had seen enough. So had the Yankees fans who loudly booed the $15 million Brown. Torre called on Javier Vazquez, the off-season free agent acquisition the Yankees had slotted into the Roger Clemens role in their rotation. Johnny Damon knew the difference. This was no Rocket Roger. Sox fan Howie Singer asked the obvious question: "Vazquez, another multimillion dollar Yankees bust, comes in to relieve Brown. We thought Torre was nuts. Why not bring in a real reliever with the bases loaded? How can he expect a starter to succeed in this situation?" Vazquez wanted to get the first pitch over. It was over all right—over and out of the park—courtesy of a Damon blast that cleared the bases. "I haven't been as aggressive. With the bases loaded, I knew Vazquez would try to sneak a fastball by me," Damon explained later.

Johnny Damon had returned to his role as the hero of heroes. The man who resembled Jesus had been the team's salvation before falling into in a veritable hitting tomb, going 3-for-29 in the first six games of the ALCS. On the Seventh Day he and his bat rose from the dead and led the Red Sox to victory with a single emphatic swing. His grand slam in the top of the second staked the Bosox to a quick and shocking 6-0 lead.

Leading by an unconverted touchdown, the Red Sox could not rest on their laurels. Miguel Cairo was hit by a pitch in the third, stole second and Derek Jeter singled him home. Boston's lead was cut to 6-1. These are the Red Sox, after all. A mere five-run lead after three innings is no guarantee of much of anything. Those who could remember just a year earlier might recall a certain 4-0 lead in a certain Game Seven against a certain Yankees team. But Vazquez walked Cabrera, batting first in the Red Sox fourth. Again, Damon was first-pitch swinging. This time Damon deposited a two-run homer into the upper deck of venerable old Yankee Stadium and it was 8-1 Red Sox, and suddenly the House that Ruth Built felt as flat as the House of Pancakes.

Strange and new forces were at work here.

Red Sox principal owner John W. Henry sat with co-owners Tom Werner and Larry Lucchino and observed, "With a seven-run lead everyone in America except us thinks we're going to win this game tonight." These owners had learned their Red Sox history, though. "We weren't doing any premature celebrating," Lucchino said.

Derek Lowe cruised along almost effortlessly. When the exhilarated pitcher was finally lifted, a somewhat bizarre and annoying move by Francona sent a collective shiver down the spine of Red Sox Nation. With the capacity Yankee Stadium crowd effectively silenced by Lowe's masterful one-hit performance, Pedro Martinez, the most hated Red Sox player in New York, was brought in to relieve. The crowd was immediately energized, and taunts of "Who's your daddy?" reverberated throughout the stadium. As horrified New Englanders watched from between their fingers, the converse of last year's mind cramp by Grady Little seemed to be taking place. In 2003, the Red Sox had been five outs from the World Series when Pedro's tank emptied and the Sox engine sputtered and died. At that point Grady left Pedro in the driver's seat too long. This time Francona put him in the race when the finish line was in sight. The *Times'* Vecsey said "the death-wish insertion of Pedro Martinez into the game . . . roused Yankees fans out of their sullen stupor." Pedro promptly gave up three hits and two runs, and Yankees fans began to salivate, while Red Sox throats were suddenly dry. The score was 8-3, after he finished up the frame. The Sox still had to get six more outs.

The comeback was short-lived, though, and Mark Bellhorn responded with a home run in the eighth to boost the lead to 9-3. The Yankees were facing a very difficult task; they had to score six runs before the Red Sox got six outs. Mike Timlin came in to pitch the eighth. Three up, three down. With a couple of singles and a sacrifice fly, the Red Sox added a tenth run in the ninth. Mariano Rivera came in to get the final out. What was that all about? Maybe he needed the work?

The Yankees got a couple of runners on base in the bottom of the ninth. With two outs and two on in the bottom of the ninth, Alan Embree came in to face John Olerud. Joe Torre pinch-hit Ruben Sierra for Olerud. At one minute after midnight, Sierra grounded out to Pokey Reese, now in for defensive purposes at second, who threw to Mientkiewicz, in for defense at first. Final score, 10-3, in favor of the Red Sox. This was truly an impossible dream come true. Wild celebrations broke out on the field and across the northeast.

There were many heroes. Lowe was redeemed. His sinkerball sunk both the Yankees and their fans. Lowe allowed just the one single to Jeter in the third. The bullpen closed it out. The outcome of this one was never in doubt, and Red Sox fans began to relax, experiencing something many had never before experienced: the idea that breaks could go *their* way, that it was no longer inevitable the Sox would somehow manage to find a way to lose.

Red Sox owner John Henry, seldom given to hyperbole, called it the "greatest comeback in baseball history." That might not be hyperbole. Few would disagree. Some would also call it the "biggest choke in baseball history." The Red Sox won their trip to the World Series in the most satisfying way imaginable: by shaming the Yankees in front of their own fans. After being only three outs from a clean sweep, the Red Sox had fought back to win the American League pennant.

"All empires fall sooner or later," Red Sox president Larry Lucchino said. *The Los Angeles Times'* Tim Brown observed (noting that Boston still had to win the World Series to rid itself of the Curse), "New York owns The Choke, the most significant and shocking collapse in baseball history."

What was an epiphany for Boston was an apocalypse for New York. One team's miraculous comeback is another team's choke and the Yankees were eviscerated in the New York press after their humiliating loss. What would have been that 40th American League pennant became a crushing loss to their most despised adversary. "They played better, that's the bottom line," admitted team captain Derek Jeter after the game. "We had them on the ropes." Rodriguez chimed in, "I'm very shocked. We couldn't deliver the knockout blow. It's very frustrating, but it's something in the long run that will make me a better player and make us a better team. This is going to make us hungrier." Food for thought, indeed. The Internet was full of the usual charitable thoughts: things such as changing the World Health Organization symbol for choking from a picture of a man clutching his throat to one of the Yankees insignia.

David Ortiz was named Series MVP and the heart and soul of the Boston Red Sox summed up the feeling in the visitor's locker room. "Last year I remember we had a bad memory. So a lot of my teammates were just destroyed because we played a pretty good game and we lost, and it was a big-time opportunity to step to the World Series. We saw a lot of fans crying and feeling hurt and I think myself and all of my teammates, we were worried about it and kept that for ourselves. And that's one of the big reasons for us to come to the field and represent the way we did the last four games." There isn't an English professor in all of Harvard who could have said it better!

The Red Sox had now won the American League Championship Series in four straight games—after spotting the Yankees a three-game lead. They had now won the American League pennant. The Yankees had to pack up their champagne and put it back in storage for the fourth year in a row. Some people claimed that whatever happened next, they could now die happy. Others knew there was more work to be done.

When he saw Yankees fans in the stands at the Stadium suffering the way Sox fans have suffered for so many years, Stephen Wright thought to himself: "I almost felt bad because they weren't used to it. . . . No, screw 'em!"

ALCS Turning Points

The ALCS boasted more unexpected turning points to fans than a tourist from Oklahoma encountered in Boston during the years of the Big Dig. For many fans the turning point came in Game Four when Francona inserted Dave Roberts to run for Millar. For others it was Roberts' steal of second and subsequent scoring on Mueller's hit. Some felt that Trot Nixon's larcenous diving catch of Hideki Matsui's drive with the bases full in Game Five qualifies as a major turning point.

For others, it was a selfless act by the Red Sox elder statesman Tim Wakefield that set the stage for the Red Sox comeback. In Game Three when the Yankees were hitting every offering that Red Sox pitchers threw, manager Terry Francona asked Wakefield to come in and take one for the team. Wakefield had been scheduled to start Game Four, but instead of whining or complaining about his lot in life, he stepped into the breach and faced the barrage of hot Yankees hitters, granting the bullpen some much-needed rest and sacrificing his own ERA and chance to start. A total class act and a total team play by a total professional, and a true leader.

Still others pointed all the way back to Varitek's July 24 confrontation with A-Rod as the biggest turning point of all!

"To everything there is a season, turn, turn, turn." Whatever turned, however it turned, we know how it all turned out. Let's say it one more time: No other team had come from being down three games to none in a seven-game series and even forced a sixth game. The Red Sox not only forced a seventh game, but they won it.

The World Series: Another Familiar Feud

The Red Sox had one more river to cross before they could hope to cast off the last remnants of any curse. The mighty Mississippi. Since 1918 the Red Sox had been in the World Series five times: in 1946, 1967, 1975, 1986, and now in 2004. On two of those occasions, their opponents were the St. Louis Cardinals, and both times the Redbirds had flown off with the trophy in Series that went the entire grueling seven games. In '46, the names were Williams and Musial, Slaughter and Pesky, Doerr and Schoendienst, and Harry Brecheen, who won three games. In 1967, it was Yastrzemski and Lonborg and Gibson and Maris, and Brock. Now, in 2004, with an entirely different cast of characters, the two old foes would meet again.

If the Red Sox were truly to put any franchise curse to rest, they still had to prove themselves by going through the "Show Me" state. This was not going to be any pushover. This edition of the St. Louis Cardinals won more games than any team in the major leagues in 2004. They featured one of the most powerful offensive lineups in all of baseball, stellar defense, and possibly the most revered managerial mind in the game in Tony LaRussa.

The St. Louis lineup was loaded with talent, starting with Albert Pujols, Scott Rolen and Jim Edmonds. They also boasted the newly acquired Larry Walker, a veteran slugger hungry for a World Series ring. Only their pitching was suspect. Their best starter, Chris Carpenter, was unavailable due to an injury to his right biceps. Carpenter had been 15-5, with 152 strikeouts and a 3.46 ERA. Ted Williams had been hampered by a serious injury in '46. Tony Conigliaro was lucky to be alive, but unable to play in 1967. Jim Rice's left hand was broken in the final week of the 1975 season. Bill Buckner struggled with bad legs in '86. Injuries always play a role.

The Cardinals were 105-57 on the year, a .648 mark that out-distanced any other team. They won their division by a full 13 games over the second-place Houston Astros. They disposed of the Dodgers quickly enough, winning three of four in the NLDS. The Astros gave them a battle in the next round, taking it to the full seven games, but the Cardinals came out on top.

The Series started in Boston, thanks to the American League 9-4 win in the 2004 All-Star Game. Ironically, the winning run in the mid-season classic was scored by Derek Jeter, right after Jason Giambi notched the fourth A.L. run—both of them crossing the plate on former Yankee Soriano's three-run homer. Thank you, New York!

Game One
Fenway Park—October 23, 2004

Tim Wakefield, the noble knight of the knuckler, took the mound for Boston. Wake easily retired three of the first four batters, working around a Larry Walker double. Cardinals skipper Tony LaRussa gave the ball to Woody Williams, and that did not work out well. Johnny Damon worked a 3-2 count, then doubled. Williams hit Orlando Cabrera with a pitch. Manny flied out to right, and Damon took third but that was soon academic, thanks to David Ortiz's three-run homer inside the Pesky Pole. Kevin Millar doubled and moved up to third on the second out, which made it possible for him to score the fourth Boston run on Bill Mueller's single to left. After one inning, Boston had a 4-0 lead. The Red Sox scored first in every game of the Series.

The Cardinals manufactured a run in the second and collected another on Walker's homer in the third. But the Red Sox responded quickly with three more runs in the bottom of the third, in part thanks to a trio of bases on balls, to make it 7-2.

Wakefield walked the first three batters in the St. Louis fourth, and a sac fly, a throwing error, and a ground-out enabled St. Louis to score all three baserunners. Bronson Arroyo replaced Wakefield. Woody Williams had already departed the inning before. In the sixth, Arroyo's two-out throwing error kept the Cardinals in the game, and they took advantage, with back-to-back doubles by Renteria and Walker. The score was now tied 7-7. Ramirez and Ortiz both singled, each driving in a run, and the Red Sox took a 9-7 lead in the bottom of the seventh. Both managers made a lot of strategic, National League-style chess moves in the top of the eighth, moving their pieces defensively, while using pinch-hitting and pinch-running pawns to counter the other's bid for checkmate. Manny Ramirez misplayed a ball hit to him with one out, then made another error on the very next play. A Cardinal scored on each error, and it was tied once more, 9-9. The Cardinals had the bases loaded, but Keith Foulke induced Scott Rolen to pop up to third base and then struck out Jim Edmonds.

The Sox had now squandered three leads in one game. In the bottom of the eighth, Renteria made an error, too, allowing Varitek to reach first. Mark Bellhorn followed with a home run off the Pesky Pole in right field, and Boston took—and held—the 11-9 lead. Bellhorn had now hit a home run in three consecutive post-season games, banging one off the foul pole in back-to-back games. "Every little boy always thinks about playing in the World Series and winning the game," Bellhorn said afterwards. "I know I did, but I'm not here to try to be a hero, just to win four games." Keith Foulke got both a blown save and a win. "That was not an instructional video," said Terry Francona, stating the obvious. The Sox, with four errors, had more leaks than the Big Dig's I-93 northbound tunnel wall. And still they won.

Final score: Boston 11, St. Louis 9

Game Two
Fenway Park—October 24, 2004

A surgically-repaired Curt Schilling (will future ballplayers use the Curt Schilling surgery in the same way Tommy John surgery has made it into popular currency?) faced Matt Morris in Game Two, his tendon sutured back into place a second time. As in Game One, Boston scored first, with two runs in the bottom of the first when, with two outs, Morris walked both Ramirez and Ortiz, and Jason Varitek tripled over Jim Edmonds' head in centerfield. In the second inning, Bill Meuller caught a line drive for an unassisted double play. Pujols doubled to lead off the fourth inning; with two outs, he scored on Mueller's second error (in all, he made three errors in Game Two). With two outs in the bottom of the fourth, Mueller showed that to err is human but to double to right field is divine. The Sox had runners on second and third for Mark Bellhorn, who doubled on a 1-0 count, driving in two more Red Sox runs.

Cabrera's two-RBI Wall-ball single in the sixth put the Sox up 6-2, and that was enough of a lead to let Schilling take the rest of the night off—and the rest of the Series, as it happened. Dr. Morgan doubted that he could suture up Schill's tendons a third time. Fortunately, the procedure wouldn't prove necessary the way the Red Sox were operating at the plate. Scott Rolen hit a sacrifice fly to bring in the second St. Louis run, but since the Red Sox had six by that time, it was too little, too late. Boston had booted the ball four more times, but that didn't make a difference, either. It may not have been a baseball masterpiece, but it was beautiful to behold for Red Sox fans. "Maybe four's our lucky number," Francona joked.

Schilling's courage can scarcely be overstated. When he woke up on the morning of October 24, he was in such agony that the very thought of taking the mound was like some cruel joke. "I wasn't going to pitch," he remembers thinking. "There was no way. I couldn't walk. I couldn't move." On his way into Fenway Park from his home in Medfield, he saw the signs. Signs put up by Red Sox fans along his route. "There were signs every mile from my house to this ballpark on fire stations, on telephone poles, wishing me luck. I can't explain what it was like."

The Red Sox medical staff removed one of the four sutures and gave him relief (as well as more painkiller). "I promise you that when I walked out of that dugout today and headed to the bullpen, my wife was the most surprised person in the world." He went out and warmed up and then threw six innings of four-hit ball, allowing just one unearned run. Embree, Timlin and Foulke closed it out, and both teams flew to St. Louis for the games there. What a difference a week can make. As *Diehard*'s Jerry Beach noted, at 11:47 P.M., Foulke got Mike Matheny to ground out for the final out of Game Two. At 11:47 P.M. one week earlier, the Red Sox were three outs away from being swept by the Yankees. In the course of those seven days, the Red Sox had won six playoff games in a row. A loss in any one of the first four would have meant instant elimination.

Comrade-in-arms Alan Embree heaped praise on Schilling after the game: "You can't put into words what he's done. Gut check after gut check, especially with the way his ankle has responded. The doctor has done a great job. He's been through a lot of pain. I can't say that I've been there. What he's done has been truly amazing." He had also now become the first pitcher in history to win a World Series game for three different teams—the 1993 Phillies, the 2001 Diamondbacks, and the 2004 Red Sox.

Final score: Boston 6, St. Louis 2

Game Three
Busch Stadium—October 26, 2004

St. Louis hoped that going home to Busch Stadium would help them get on track. Jeff Suppan, a former Red Sox pitcher whose name hardly sent shivers up anyone's spine, was going for St. Louis, and Pedro Martinez for the Red Sox was making his first start in a World Series. Once again, Boston scored first, and once again it was in the very first inning, this time on a Manny Ramirez home run over the Red Sox bullpen and into the left field bleachers. Pedro had struggled with first innings a lot in 2004; this game was no exception. After getting Renteria on a grounder to Bellhorn, he walked Larry Walker. Pujols hit a shot off Mueller's glove for a single. Rolen walked. Bases loaded, one out, but Jim Edmonds flied out to left on a 2-2 count, and Walker tried to tag and score. Manny Ramirez fired a bullet to Varitek at the plate and the inning was over. In the obscure records department, this was the first time a player had ever hit a home run and thrown out a runner at the plate in the first inning of a World Series game. It was a very good thing, as far as Sox fans were concerned.

St. Louis threatened again in the third. Suppan reached first on an infield hit and Renteria doubled as Trot Nixon, battling wet field conditions, fell flat on his back. Second and third, nobody out, and Larry Walker (5-for-8 in the Series) was up. Martinez induced a grounder to second and Bellhorn went by the book, throwing to Ortiz at first for the sure out and conceding the run at the plate. Except that after Suppan broke for home, he inexplicably skittered back to third, then started for home again until hit with the realization that he really had better retreat to third base. Too late. Ortiz saw the bizarre baserunning blunder unfold, took a couple of steps toward third as Pedro ducked down, and fired a perfect strike to Bill Mueller, who put the tag on Suppan. Suddenly there were two outs, a rally-killing play if there ever was one. Suppan's explanation? "I screwed the play up. That's what happened."

Maintaining momentum, Mueller doubled in the top of the fourth, and Trot Nixon drove him in. 2-0, Red Sox. A double, a single, and another single started the scoring for the Sox in the fifth, and they got their fourth run a couple of batters later. Suppan exited to consider the cruelties of fate. Pedro doled out just three hits in seven shutout innings, retiring the last 14 batters he faced. Varitek praised Pedro after the game. It was, he said, "one of the happiest moments I've ever had for somebody. As much scrutiny as he's had sometimes, with as great a career as he's had, that was phenomenal." The only run St. Louis scored was on a Larry Walker homer in the bottom of the ninth.

As patrons filed out of Busch Stadium, the message board operator mistakenly posted an ominous message: "Thanks for a great 2004 season." The Red Sox weren't taking anything for granted, though. "Anybody here ever seen me play as a player?" asked Terry Francona. "You can understand why I would never be over-confident." One game at a time; that remained the game plan. "We're up, 3-0, and that's a good way to start a series, but we're not done," Damon declared. Everyone in the Red Sox clubhouse remembered some very recent history.

Final score: Boston 4, St. Louis 1

Game Four
Busch Stadium—October 27, 2004

The Cardinals were now down three games to none. Only one team had ever come from being down 3-0 in a seven-game series, and that was the team batting first in Game Four. No team in baseball history had ever won eight straight post-season games either. The Red Sox wanted to be the first. Manny Ramirez told his teammates before the game, "Hey, let's go. Don't let those guys breathe." The first batter up in the top of the first inning was Johnny Damon. The way this Series was going, it was only fitting that he looked at three pitches and then promptly homered off Jason Marquis to stake the visitors to a 1-0 lead. It turned out that was the only run the Red Sox needed, as they completed their total domination of St. Louis in the Series.

Derek Lowe threw seven shutout innings; like Pedro the night before, he allowed just three hits. Trot Nixon's two-run double in the third gave the Sox a 3-0 lead. It missed being a grand slam by a matter of inches. Eleven of the thirteen runs the Red Sox scored in the final three games came with two outs. Arroyo, Embree, and Foulke combined to shut down St. Louis in the final three innings, the final play being a weak grounder by Renteria to Foulke, who took a few steps toward first and underhanded the ball to Mientkiewicz. Even at that very moment, there was a great intake of air as Red Sox Nation held its collective breath, expecting something—anything—to go wrong and start the slide to another Sox defeat. It didn't happen. The toss was true. Mientkiewicz caught it, held on, and then joined the celebration. The Sox had swept St. Louis and were World Champions for the first time in 86 long and trying years.

Derek Lowe had not expected to be starting a World Series game when the playoffs began. He hadn't pitched nearly as well in 2004 as he had the previous couple of years and the Sox weren't sure they could rely on him. "We told him he was going to the bullpen. He wasn't very happy," admitted Terry Francona. "We didn't expect him to be happy. He's a competitor and nobody wants to be told that. We told him he had a day or two to do whatever he needed to do—pout, yell or whatever, because he was going to have something to say about the playoffs. We knew that. We didn't know he was going to have this much, but to his credit he did what he was supposed to do. He didn't pout, he got himself ready and look what he did." What he did was get the win in the final, clinching game of the Division Series, get the win in Game Seven of the Division Series against the Yankees, and get the win in the fourth and final game of the 2004 World Series.

In the final three games of the World Series, Boston's three starters (Schilling, Martinez, and Lowe) threw 20 innings without allowing an earned run; they had a combined ERA of 0.00. The Red Sox had scored in the first inning of every game. The Red Sox never fell behind in any game, even for just a half-inning. Game One was the only game where the Cardinals showed some pluck—after that they were the pluckees. The Red Sox had won eight consecutive games, and had never trailed in any one of the last six. They had vanquished their most storied rivals, the New York Yankees, with the greatest comeback in baseball history (alternate take: courtesy of the greatest choke in baseball history.) Now they had disposed of their other nemesis. The Cardinals had beaten the Red Sox twice in World Series play—1946 and 1967. For a player like Johnny Pesky, who'd been on that 1946 Red Sox team, that just made the moment all the sweeter.

Trot Nixon who was originally signed by the Sox and had served with the organization longer than any other current player, spoke for all of Red Sox Nation. "1918 is gone forever," he said. "We're not going to have to hear about that again." Amen.

Final score: Boston 3, St. Louis 0

Hell Had Frozen Over

Celebrations broke out in Kenmore Square and every square in Red Soxdom. Celebrations broke out in households around New England. Everyone expected all hell to break loose, should the Sox ever win the World Series. The common consensus was more that Hell had frozen over.

Days later, some dazed Red Sox fans still expected to wake up and read that some MLB ruling had reversed one of the wins and the game would have to be played over. Days after that, even after the victory parade brought out an estimated 3.5 million fans in the rain in downtown Boston, suspicious Sox fans were still checking to make sure it wasn't all a dream. No, it was true. This really happened. The Red Sox won the World Series.

And they did it in such a strange and wondrous fashion. They won the Wild Card, coming in second in the division, for the seventh year in a row, to the Yankees. They swept the Angels in the first round and swept the

Cardinals in the World Series. Those two sweeps bracketed the real contest of the 2004 post-season, the battle royal between the Red Sox and the Yankees. Down three games to none, losing even as they came to bat in the ninth inning of Game Four, they rallied, fought hard and won. They won that game and every one of the next eight games they played. It was the greatest comeback in the history of major league baseball. And, for the Yankees, so accustomed to winning, it was the biggest shock (we'll be gracious for a moment and not say "CHOKE") in franchise history, to lose the way they did and to the team they did.

Thirty-year old Boston general manager Theo Epstein, drenched with champagne after the game, tried to express the full significance of what his team had accomplished. "This is for everyone who played for the Red Sox, who's rooted for the Red Sox, whose relatives rooted for the Red Sox—it is so much bigger than the 25 guys in this clubhouse."

And so it was. Throughout Red Sox Nation, folks flocked to—of all places—graveyards. No, not because of the full moon or the arrival of Halloween and some supposed Curse, but to visit the final resting place of Red Sox fans of days gone by. People remembered those who had passed away, and never known the Sox as World Champions. A father, a mother, a favorite uncle or aunt. We're not talking about one or two people here. We're talking literally of thousands of people who were moved to visit the graves of friends or relations who'd followed the Red Sox, and to try and share the moment of victory with them. The depths within us were touched profoundly in ways that many who are not devoted Sox fans might find hard to comprehend. It sounds a little hokey, but it was real and sincere and heartfelt.

There was also another notable phenomenon across New England, as many elderly people died a week or two following the World Series win. They'd wanted to see the Red Sox win the World Series, and now they could let go, literally die in peace. Apparently, this is a medically recognized and accepted phenomenon in relation to other highly anticipated events one might encounter in life.

For the living, life would go on, but everyone knew that it would never be quite the same ever again. One reason that people keep pinching themselves, even weeks and months later, is that we question our own senses. The blind still can't see. The lame still can't walk. It wasn't as though credit card debt was wiped out, or that personal shortcomings were overcome.

But the burdens of life seem a little lighter, the anticipation of the year to come much easier to bear. Those winter days around the hot stove won't have the anguish of wondering *why* Denny Galehouse was given the ball, *or where* Dave Stapleton was, or *how* Pedro could be left in, or for *what* possible reason Willoughby was taken out. Or *who* could assemble a team that would beat the Yankees. Or *when* the Red Sox would finally win the World Series.

In the bigger picture, the victory of the Boston Red Sox in the 2004 World Series scarcely matters. Indeed, most people on the globe don't even know it happened. In a world racked by wars, starvation, disease, and instability it would be obscene to assign it a higher significance than it deserves. But it *was* significant enough to make lonely servicemen in Iraq pause in their hard and dangerous task long enough to smile and celebrate and remember what America is all about. It was significant enough to bring tears of joy to stoic men and women from Nova Scotia to the southernmost part of New England. It was significant enough for grandsons and grand-daughters to remember grandfathers and grandmothers long departed. It was significant enough for us.

The Red Sox won the World Series.

"The players' exuberant faith in themselves was contagious. It changed the character of the fans. We were no longer afraid of what the next batter or the next inning might bring. Whatever happened, they would see us through. And they surely did, bringing us the greatest victory in sports history, one that, with luck, may have forever altered our temperaments as Red Sox fans." —Doris Kearns Goodwin

"The Red Sox and their fans now emerge, blinking, from a deep fog of superstition into a brighter, more rational day. Welcome to Year Zero in Red Sox Nation . . . .The great curse of the baseball gods is gone. With all respect to my great pal Dan Shaughnessy, I never thought it was a curse. Not even a milder hex. A shadow maybe, but not that of the Babe. The shadow of Willie Mays, when the Sox did not sign him back in 1949 when they had first shot . . . ."
—David Halberstam

Chapter 10
What Now? The Morning After

"They that sow in tears shall reap in joy." —Psalm 126:5

"You have turned my mourning into dancing . . . " —Psalm 30:11-12

"I'm embarrassed right now. Obviously that hurts—watching them on our field celebrating." —Alex Rodriguez, New York Yankees

"A batter may not be intimidated by Pedro or Schilling, but a grinning Stephen King will haunt your dreams forever." —Conan O'Brien

"There's no way the Sox can be the first team to lose the World Series after winning the first four games, right?" —still-nervous Sox fan Frank Solensky, a day or two after the World Series

We all know there's got to be a morning after, but over the years Red Sox fans grew accustomed to the *mourning* after. Not this time. This time the post-Series dawn broke across a physically unaltered Red Sox Nation landscape, but this time the rising sun shone on citizens in a state of disbelief, if not outright and utter shock.

Prozac sales plummeted, psychologists sat twiddling their thumbs in lonely offices, and area bridges no longer had long jumping queues. The talk shows were momentarily rendered speechless and even Bill Lee was struck dumb for 24 hours or so. Somewhere in Idaho, Bill Buckner emerged from his burrow, bent down to pick up the morning paper, saw his shadow, and stayed out anyway.

The DVD produced by Major League Baseball sold out of the box almost double that of any other World Series highlight video. It was the horror movie of the year for Yankees fans, but a romance and a suspense thriller for Sox fans, and would even evoke some fond laughter now and again.

Somewhere on a cloud—probably Cloud 9 in honor of Ted Williams—the Splendid Splinter was meeting an old baseball rival for a cup of cold ambrosia. The conversation went something like this:

Ted Williams:	Hey Joe, what's new?
Joe DiMaggio:	I'm thinking of doing some Mr. Ambrosia ads.
Ted Williams:	Anything else?
Joe DiMaggio:	Word on the street is that Hell's frozen over.
Ted Williams:	That can only mean one thing
Babe Ruth (entering):	"The Red Sox just won the World Series!"
Ted Williams:	Thank God!
God's voice:	"You're welcome, Teddy."

Yes, Red Sox Nation would never be the same again. On CNN's NewsNight, Aaron Brown asked writer Stephen King the question that was on many people's minds: "If Charlie Brown kicks the football, somehow the magic of Charlie Brown is lost. The beauty of Charlie Brown is that she, Lucy, always pulls the football away. He never kicks the football. The Red Sox, if you will, have now kicked the football. How can they be as lovable, as romantic? They're just another team."

If King's response accurately represents the sentiments of Red Sox fans, it is indeed a brave new world for us all. "The answer is, they will never be the same Red Sox as they were," said the writer. "We've entered a different age. And I'm not man enough to predict what that age will bring. All I can say is that, from this man's heart, I am delighted to leave that ancient mariners' albatross, if you will, to the Cubs."

But if Red Sox Nation would never be the same, neither would New

York. In a *Washington Post* column titled "Those Post-Election, Pitiful Yankees, Big Apple Blues," Tina Brown had this bleak assessment of her city, post-ALCS: "New Yorkers are feeling a severe case of heat withdrawal. They were used to being the red-hot center of American news and opinion. Suddenly they're flyover country, relics from a dying tribe, seedy and unloved. They are as forlorn as those fiery partisan books that once pulsed with an angry beat on the bestseller list and now linger on the remainder tables in Barnes & Noble."

Brown continued, "The psychiatrist Hadassah Brooks Morgan says that John Kerry's defeat, coming on the heels of the Yankees' collapse in the playoffs against the Red Sox, plunged many of her patients into near-catatonic distress. 'In my whole 40 years of practice here I have never heard patients as bereft by a result as this,' she told me on the phone. 'There was a feeling in session after session of the insult to one's tribe, a loss of purpose and direction. For men, their sports team being beaten at the same time made them feel New York is no longer the command center, no longer the winning city they identify with or that so many people move here to find.' "

Away from the cities of Boston and New York, Red Sox fans in every condition and circumstance exhibited an entire array of human emotion.

Sports Illustrated related a touching story about the impact of the Red Sox ALCS win in Corrigan-Radgowski, a Level IV security prison in Connecticut. Jared Dolphin, a prison guard and Sox fan was watching Game 7 on the cellblock TV. In the cells all around him, prisoners wearing crude improvised Red Sox caps also watched. They were scarcely the demographic that Fox TV would have bragged about. These were hardened criminals, one of whom had murdered his girlfriend's entire family including the family dog.

When the final out of Game 7 of the amazing comeback was recorded, Dolphin wept silently. He was startled from his reverie by a spontaneous outpouring of raw emotion from virtually every cell.

"I bristled immediately," Dolphin told SI. "Instinctively my hand reached for my flashlight. It was pandemonium—whistling, shouting, pounding on sinks, doors, bunks, anything cons could find. This was against every housing rule in the book, so I jumped up, ready to lay down the law.

"But as I stood there looking around the block I felt something else. I felt hope. Here I was, less than 10 feet away from guys that will never see the outside of prison ever again in their lives. The guy in the cell to my immediate left had 180 years. He wasn't going anywhere anytime soon. But as I watched him scream, holler and pound on the door I realized he and I had something in common. That night hope beamed into his life as well. As Red Sox fans we had watched the impossible happen, and if that dream could come true, why couldn't others?

"Instead of marching around the block trying to restore order I put my flashlight down and clapped. My applause joined the ruckus they were making and for five minutes it didn't stop. I applauded until my hands hurt. I was applauding the possibilities for the future." Amen to that.

Dan Good, writing in *The Digital Collegian*, placed the magnificence of the Red Sox win over the Evil Empire in historical perspective:

"The Roman Empire deteriorated in 476 after emperor Romulus Augustus was disposed. The Mongol Empire ended with Kublai Khan's death in 1294 when the kingdom split into khanates, thus weakening central power to the point of oblivion.

"And just moments into Thursday, October 21st, 2004, after nearly a century of rule over the Western world, the New York Yankees' dynasty, now in the Torre Era, was officially destroyed in one of sport's greatest collapses, conquered at Yankee Stadium by the historically inferior and traditionally tragic Boston Red Sox."

He goes on to put an interesting financial twist in the Yankees loss.

"The 2004 Yankees will go down as the greatest loser money could buy. In the 10-3 Game Seven loss, New York used six pitchers and eleven hitters, players whose combined season salaries, totaled $138,952,992—more than the individual GNPs of Kiribati, Tonga, and the Falkland Islands."

Finally, he opines about the citizenship rights to Red Sox Nation, now that is has become such a desirable location.

". . . the Sox have become the 'in' thing, a means for casual and nonexistent baseball fans to connect to America's Pastime. As a result, the Red Sox Nation has seen more illegal immigration in the past week than Laredo, TX. Speaking of which, what are the requirements for full citizenship in the Red Sox Nation? Is there a period of continuous rooting presence and loyalty? Is there some sort of comprehension test, such as differentiating between Gabe Kapler, Rico Petrocelli, and Johnny Pesky? Is there a requisite of withstanding the brutal hardship and vicious suffering that has formerly come with Red Sox fandom? Now that'd be something."

After the ALCS, ESPN columnist Bill Simmons, a passionate Red Sox fan, was at loose ends. "Honestly, I don't know what to do," wrote Simmons. "I just watched my beloved Red Sox win the American League pennant. That's only happened twice in my lifetime. I watched them rally back from three games down in a playoff series. That's never happened before, not in the history of baseball. I also just watched the Sox beat the Yankees in a deciding playoff game. Not only has that never happened before, it's a possible sign of the apocalypse.

"So what happens now? Where do I go from here? Should I throw myself into politics? Backpack across Europe? Take up gourmet cooking? Learn how to fly airplanes? Should I take the bus to Fort Hancock, cross the border and wander the beaches of Zihuatenejo looking for Andy and Red? You tell me. What should I do? . . . the Red Sox were celebrating at Yankee Stadium . . . Exchanging high-fives and heterosexual man-hugs, I couldn't stop glancing at the TV. *It's official, right? We definitely beat them, right?*

" 'What's wrong with you?' [my friend] Sully asked. 'Honestly? I keep waiting for them to announce that there's a Game 8.' "

Roger Angell, arguably the most evocative of all baseball writers of our age, saw the Red Sox win for what it was: a joyous gift to America from a just God. In the November 11, 2004 issue of *The New Yorker*, he observed:

"The Boston Red Sox, after eighty-six years of dreary or spectacular failure, stand as Champions of the World; the Evil Empire and the St. Louis Cardinals and the Curse of the Bambino have been carried away, one after the other, dead as doornails; and the engrossing anxieties and preposterous turns of fortune that had run up cell-phone charges and damaged sleep up and down the land ever since September . . . Non-fans can expect relief from the daily clutter of reference and nicknames and "how 'bout that"s, but even the loftiest of them must sense that this time around a professional sport produced something like a unifying jolt of happiness at the end, a national smile."

Richard Crepeau also saw the religious overtones that enveloped the Red Sox miraculous win. "To end the season with eight straight wins is one thing, but to do it against the two teams with the best records in their respective leagues is another. The end came during an eclipse of the moon, an event that will be regarded forevermore in New England as an omen of abundant blessings from the Lord. The Puritan Divines would have loved this. Those congregational churches that dot the New England landscape should be jammed tight with Red Sox fans this Thanksgiving Day for never before have God's blessings come in such abundance to the land of John Winthrop and John Cotton."

In another article called "Long Voyage Home," Angell decided to ponder the spiritual nature of the win. "The Redbird collapse can probably be laid to weak pitching, unless you decide that the baseball gods, a little surfeited by the cruel jokes and disappointments they have inflicted on the Boston team and its followers down the years, and perhaps as sick of the Curse of the Bambino as the rest of us, decided to try a little tenderness."

Not surprisingly, the faith of Red Sox fans had been sorely tested so many times that Angell, like so many others, could see disaster around every corner. It seemed to arrive in Game Six of the ALCS with one man on for the Yankees. Gary Sheffield hit a dribbler that bounced off the third-base bag for a fluke base hit. Angell saw this as the first raindrop in another disastrous flood for the Sox. Another Buckner miscue. Another Boone homer. Was God toying with us like a cat with a wounded mouse?

"You could almost envision the grin upstairs," wrote Angell. "Instead, looking back at the action up till now: the Yankees' daunting three-game lead after the first three meetings of this championship elimination; their nineteen runs in the Game Three blowout; and then the Sox' two comeback wins achieved across the next two games or twenty-six innings or ten hours and fifty-one minutes of consuming, astounding baseball—the old god feels an unfamiliar coal of pity within. 'Ah, well,' he murmurs, turning away. 'Let it go.' "

The ever-stylish Thomas Boswell, in a piece entitled "From Woebegone to Champions," also looked sky-ward and found that any such celestial explanation for this particular event fell short. "This evening, there was a lunar eclipse that began about an hour before the game, a rarity that would have produced a blood-red moon during the game if only the sky had been clear instead of cloudy. Perhaps the overcast was better. Lunar eclipses are so mundane, if you think about it. Why, another one is due in 2007—barely a blink in baseball time.

"The victory that arrived on this evening for the Red Sox and their true believers was far too rare and precious, too long overdue and spectacular in its consummation, to be upstaged by something so commonplace as the earth, moon and stars."

Postscript

You won't see this on television, but for many years now after NFL football games, several players from both teams gather at midfield on the 50-yard line and go down on one knee for a joint prayer ceremony. This is something we doubt we'll ever see after a Red Sox-Yankees game.

Scarcely more than a month after the Red Sox finally broke his curse, Babe Ruth, in the guise of pitcher David Wells, returned to Boston to play for the Red Sox. As fans in both NY and Boston know, Wells is the reincarnation of the Babe. Not only is he of similar girth, his sometimes outrageous behavior has caused Yankees ownership to cringe more than once. Wells spent four years in pinstripes and, in June of 1997, donned a vintage Babe Ruth cap from 1934 during a game with Cleveland. The comparison breaks down a bit when Wells steps to the plate to hit, but fortunately he won't have to do that much until the next World Series.

Will the Sox repeat? Even without Pedro, without Derek Lowe? Will we see Good continue to prevail, or will the Forces of Darkness regroup? We can assume a counter-attack will be mounted. No one ever said it would be easy. Faith is strengthened by tests, and surely no Higher Power would ever want to simply be taken for granted. True believers among the ranks of the Red Sox faithful can take comfort in the Miracle of 2004, while agnostics can still marvel at the improbable wonder of it all. The Flat Earth Society may suggest it never happened; Yankees fans still don't believe that it could have.

The world will always know Evil. It may often triumph over Good, but like the platonic ideal, Good will endure as the symbol of what is right and what is just, and Good will always inspire hope in the souls of humankind. The year 2001 marked the beginning of a New Millennium. In this new era, the New York Yankees have never yet won a World Series, but the Boston Red Sox have a golden trophy to their credit. May the light from that trophy shine forth and inspire men and women around the world to strive for betterment and beatitude. A New Day has dawned: the Boston Red Sox won the World Series!

Evolution of the Rivalry

"I spent more years in Boston than any city in the major leagues. I spent seven years there and I loved every minute of it except a minute and a half." —Don Zimmer

February 6, 1895: George Herman "Babe" Ruth is born, in Baltimore.

April 26, 1901: The new American League is launched and the Boston franchise plays its first game ever, in Baltimore. The Baltimore franchise will move to New York two years later and eventually become the New York Yankees. The Boston Americans lose their first game, 10-6, despite a starting pitcher named Win. Boston loses its first three games, before Cy Young turns his second start into a victory on April 30.

January 9, 1903: Frank Farrell and Bill Devery purchase Baltimore AL. franchise for $18,000 and announce plans to move it to New York City.

March 12, 1903: New York Highlanders officially join the American League

April 22, 1903: The New York franchise plays its first game, in Washington, a 3-1 loss handed to Jack Chesbro.

May 7, 1903: First game ever between Boston and New York A.L. clubs results in a Boston win (in Boston, at the Huntington Avenue Grounds) by the score of 6-2. Big Bill Dineen beats Hal Wiltse.

May 8, 1903: New York comes back and beats Boston 6-1, Chesbro beating Winter. Boston's Hobe Ferris hits a home run for second day in a row, this time in a losing cause.

June 1, 2 & 3, 1903: Boston comes to New York and sweeps a three-game series.

September 7, 1903: Eleven Boston batters earned walks off New York Highlander pitcher John Deering.

September 15, 1903: The two teams finish head-to-head competition for the season, with Boston winning 13 games and New York winning 7. Boston would go on to win the pennant, and also to win the very first World Series.

December 20, 1903: Boston trades "Long Tom" Hughes to New York for Jesse Tannehill, despite Hughes having won 21 games that season (21-7). With New York in 1904, he would only win 7 while losing 11. Tannehill turns out to be the much better pitcher in 1904 and the years to come.

April 14, 1904: New York's Happy Jack Chesbro gets his first win of season, 8-2, in New York, beating Boston and Cy Young. Chesbro finishes the season with a record 41 wins. New York team challenges Boston for A.L. pennant.

June 19, 1904: Boston trades popular outfielder Patsy Dougherty to NY for infielder Bob Unglaub, a trade thought to be engineered by A.L. president Ban Johnson, who sought more parity between the clubs by deliberately strengthening New York in that major market.

September 14 and 15, 1904: Boston and New York play back-to-back doubleheaders, with the second game each day ending in identical 1-1 tie scores.

October 7, 1904: Parity seemingly achieved, New York takes the lead in the pennant race as Chesbro beats Gibson 3-2, with but four games to play—every one of them head-to-head matchups with Boston.

October 8, 1904: Young and Dineen pitch Boston to a doubleheader sweep, in Boston, restoring their lead to the "Bostons."

October 10, 1904: Back in New York, the Highlanders and the Boston Americans play a season-ending doubleheader at Hilltop Park. Should Boston win either game, they win the pennant. New York's ace pitcher Chesbro threw a wild pitch in the top of the ninth, and Boston's Lou Criger scored from third, to give Boston a 3-2 lead. Dineen kept New York from scoring in the bottom of the ninth, and Boston won its second straight pennant. Boston would win four more pennants for a total of six, before the team that became the Yankees finally won their first pennant 17 years later. New York second baseman Jimmy Williams (no relation to Jimy Williams) committed an error earlier in the game which let in the first two Boston runs.

October 7, 1905: Boston closes an otherwise undistinguished season with four straight wins over the Highlanders, capped by a doubleheader sweep on this day.

May 1, 1906: New York pitcher Billy Hogg threw a one-hitter against Boston and beat Cy Young 8-0. In the seventh inning, Freddy Parent got the only Boston hit. It was the first of 20 consecutive losses, the worst losing streak in Boston A.L. history.

July 5, 1906: Boston makes nine errors in front of the home crowd and loses to New York, 8—3

September 4, 1906: New York Highlanders sweep fifth doubleheader in six days with 7-0 (Walter Clarkson) and 1-0 (Al Orth) shutouts of Boston.

October 5 and 6, 1906: New York wins last two games of the season, in Boston, and finishes ahead of Boston in the standings. New York had also won the first three games of the year. In all, New York won 17 games and only lost four (there was one tie) in its battles against Boston. New York finished the season just three games out, but Boston was in last place, 45½ games behind the pennant-winning White Sox.

May 31, 1907: Kid Elberfeld stole home plate twice in one game against Boston, in the sixth inning and again as part of a double steal with Hal Chase in the very next inning.

October 13, 1907: New York, Boston, and the White Sox pull off a three-way trade. Jake Stahl, who had been on the 1903 World Championship team for Boston, was sent to New York by the White Sox, who forwarded Frank LaPorte to Boston. Chicago received shortstop Freddy Parent from Boston.

June 30, 1908: Cy Young wins one of his 511 career victories with an 8-0 no-hitter over New York. He faced the minimum number of batters (the only man to reach base was Harry Niles, who walked to lead off the game and was then cut down stealing). Young got himself three hits in the process. It was the best day any pitcher ever had against the New York team, but not yet declared a state holiday in Massachusetts.

October 6, 1908: Boston fans with exceptionally long memories, though, can recall the 11-3 defeat of New York, which saddled them with a final 1908 record of 51-103. This year it was the Highlanders who finished in the cellar. Boston finished 24 games ahead of New York, but had nothing to be proud of; the Sox were only in fifth place, 15½ games out of first.

September 11, 1909: New York sells Happy Jack Chesbro to the Red Sox. He'd been 0-4 for New York, and was 0-1 for the Red Sox. A sad ending to an often-stellar career.

April 14, 1910: Red Sox and New York play to a 4-4 tie, in a 14-inning Opening Day game in New York, Eddie Cicotte against Hippo Vaughn.

May 26, 1910: Red Sox purchase catcher Red Kleinow from New York.

May 6, 1911: New York pulls off its first triple play, against the Red Sox. Top of the ninth, down 6-3, Boston's Bill Carrigan is up as a pinch-hitter with two men on and no one out. A liner to the shortstop starts a 6-4-3 triple play that ends the game.

October 3, 1911—Red Sox sweep a doubleheader in New York, then win the next day's game. Opening Day 1912 is in New York, and the Red Sox sweep a three-game series to kick off the season. In June, they sweep five games in New York and take both halves of a twin bill on September 2. In fact, from October 3, 1911 until September 29, 1913, the Sox under manager Jake Stahl don't lose a single game in the Big Apple. There was one tie on May 24, 1913; that must have felt like a moral victory for the hapless Yankees.

April 11, 1912: New York team dons the pinstripes for the first time, in home opener. Smoky Joe Wood wins for Boston, 5-3.

April 20, 1912: New York plays Boston at the Opening Day of Boston's new Fenway Park. 7-6, Boston (11 innings)

September 2, 1912: Smoky Joe Wood beats the Yankees 1- 0 in New York for his 30th win of the season. It's also his eighth shutout of the 1912 campaign.

September 25, 1912: Smoky Joe Wood beats New York 6-0 for his 34th win of the season (and his tenth shutout).

September 26, 1912: In the final home game of the championship season, it looked like the Sox were going through the motions, losing 12-7 after 7½ innings, but in the bottom of the eighth they scored eight times off New York pitching. First, two triples knocked out rookie starter Ray Keating. One run was in, but there were two outs. Then followed a single and a double—and six consecutive bases on balls, four by Ray Caldwell and two more by his replacement, Tommy Thompson. Tris Speaker deliberately swung and missed at three bad pitches to end the farce. By the time the inning finally ended, it was too dark to play any more and the game was called.

October 1, 1912: How many Red Sox fans still survive to savor this day, when New York lost its 100th game of the season? 1912 saw the biggest gap ever between the two teams. New York finished the season a full 55 games behind Boston, with a 50-102 record.

October 16, 1912: The Red Sox win their second World Championship on a tenth-inning sacrifice fly by Larry Gardner.

September 29, 1913: For the first time in two years of play in New York, the Yankees actually beat the Red Sox. Twice. The next day, the Red Sox took both halves of a doubleheader.

May 13, 1914: The Yankees purchase Les Nunamaker from the Red Sox.

May 27, 1914: The Yankees sell pitcher Guy Cooper to the Red Sox.

July 8, 1914: Boston makes a wise investment, purchasing both pitchers Babe Ruth and Ernie Shore from Baltimore (and obtain catcher Ben Egan to boot) for $8000.

January 11, 1915: Col. Jacob Ruppert and Col. Tillinghast L'Hommedieu Huston purchase Yankees for $460,000.

May 6, 1915: Babe Ruth's major league pitching debut, for the Red Sox against the Yankees, in New York. He also hits his first career home run, but loses 4-3 in 13 innings.

June 2, 1915: Ruth beats the Yankees 7-1 in New York. He hits his second homer, following which he is walked intentionally twice. The Babe lashes out and kicks the bench in frustration, fracturing his toe.

October 13, 1915: Red Sox win the World Series, beating the Phillies 4 games to 1.

May 5, 1916: Fenway fans went home unhappily as the Sox fritter away a 4-2 two-out lead in the ninth, on a Larry Gardner error. Yankees win in 13 innings, 8-4.

June 20, 1916: Red Sox shortstop Everett Scott begins his 1,307 consecutive game streak; by the time he ends it, he's playing for the Yankees.

June 21, 1916: Red Sox pitcher George Foster pitches no-hitter against New York at Fenway Park, 2-0. It's the first no-hitter at Fenway.

June 22, 1916: Babe Ruth throws a three-hitter and holds New York scoreless, 1-0. It's one of his nine shutouts in 1916, the final one being his 3-0 win over the Yankees on September 29.

September 30, 1916: The Red Sox clinched at least a tie for the pennant in the bottom of the tenth inning of a scoreless game against New York. A single and then two bunts, both of which went for hits, had the bases loaded for the Sox with nobody out. Pinch-runner Mike McNally scored on a very short Hooper fly to right field, a strong wind perhaps causing the throw to the plate to be just a hair off.

October 6, 1916: Red Sox pitchers Ernie Shore, Dutch Leonard, and Carl Mays combined to throw a 2-0 shutout of the Yankees.

October 9, 1916: Babe Ruth was Boston's starting pitcher in Game Two of the World Series. After surrendering a solo homer in the first inning, Ruth threw 13 scoreless innings. Del Gainer's pinch-hit single won the game for the Sox in the fourteenth inning.

October 12, 1916: The Red Sox win their second consecutive World Series, dominating Brooklyn 4 games to 1.

December 3, 1916: The secret purchase of the Red Sox by Harry Frazee (from Joe Lannin) is exposed by the Boston press. The deal is officially announced the next day.

April 11, 1917: On Opening Day, Babe Ruth pitches a 3-hitter for Boston and beats the Yankees 10-3. Ruth won 24 games in 1917.

April 24, 1917: George Mogridge wins 2-1 no-hitter against Red Sox at

Fenway Park. The left-hander was the first Yankees southpaw ever to throw a no-hitter.

September 11, 1918: Sox win third World Championship in the last four years. The season is shortened due to World War II, so the Series is over (Boston 4 wins, Cubs 2) in mid-September. Sox staff ERA is 1.70. The Cubs pitchers are even better, with a 1.04 ERA, but Boston prevailed.

December 21, 1918: The Red Sox trade outfielder Duffy Lewis and pitchers Dutch Leonard and Ernie Shore to the Yankees for pitchers Ray Caldwell and the wonderfully-named Slim Love, catcher Roxy Walters, outfielder Frank Gilhooley and $15,000. The 195-pound Love (who was born in Love, Mississippi) had just been acquired from the Tigers and never played for the Red Sox. The prospect of being a Yankee in this era was perhaps too distressing for Leonard and he refused to report to New York; he wound up in Detroit.

June 13, 1919: New York sells Good Time Bill Lamar to the Sox.

June 28, 1919: Boston's Carl Mays—later to become a Yankees great—throws two complete games against New York (both halves of a double-header), winning one 2-0 but losing the second 4-1. Mays was clearly not on a tight pitch count.

July 13, 1919: Sox starter Carl Mays walks off the team between innings, due to shoddy Sox fielding, reminiscent of Dutch Leonard's desertion just the summer before.

July 29, 1919: Red Sox send ace pitcher Carl Mays to the Yankees for either $25,000 or $40,000 (accounts differ), a minor league PTBNL, and pitchers Bob McGraw and Allan "Rubberarm" Russell. A flurry of lawsuits saw the American League instructing its umpires not to let Mays pitch, but the Yankees prevailed. See October 29, however.

September 20, 1919: It was Babe Ruth Day at Fenway Park and, as it turned out, his last day in town as a Boston Red Sox. Ruth hit his 27th homer of the season, tying the 1884 record held by Ned Williamson, and won the game for Boston.

September 24, 1919: In New York, Boston's Babe Ruth sets a new home run record with his ninth-inning, game-tying 28th home run of the season, off the Yankees' Bob Shawkey. Three days later, Ruth plays what will be his final game for the Red Sox—on the very day Johnny Pesky was born.

October 29, 1919: The Yankees are officially deprived of their third-place finish because of their reinstatement of banned pitcher Carl Mays. Players did not receive their third place money, but if you look in the record books, the team is listed in third place. [See July 29 entry.]

December 26, 1919: As a Christmas present, the Red Sox formally sell Babe Ruth to the Yankees, though the deal is not announced until January 3, 1920.

January 3, 1920: The Yankees officially announce the purchase of Babe Ruth for $100,000, and loan Red Sox owner Harry Frazee $300,000, secured by a mortgage on Fenway Park. Ruth was 89-46 as a Red Sox pitcher. For New York, he never lost a game, going 5-0 in appearances scattered over the next 14 years. He'd hit 49 homers for Boston, but poled out 665 for the Yankees. The next time the Red Sox team wins more than half its games is 1935.

May 1, 1920: Babe Ruth got his first home run as a New York Yankee—the 50th of his young career—and helped beat the Red Sox 6-0. His last home run for Boston against New York cleared the roof of the Polo Grounds. So did his first for the Yankees.

October 29, 1920: Boston general manager Ed Barrow quits the Red Sox to become the Yankees' business manager. Barrow had managed the Red Sox to a World Series win in 1918. While serving as Yankees GM until 1945, he oversaw 14 Yankees pennants and 10 World Championships.

December 15, 1920: The Yankees acquire another nice batch of players from Boston: pitchers Waite Hoyt and Harry Harper, catcher Wally Schang, and infielder Mike McNally in exchange for ten Boston subway tokens.

Actually, Boston obtained third baseman Del Pratt, catcher Muddy Ruel, outfielder Sam Vick and pitcher Herb Thormahlen.

February 5, 1921: The Yankees purchase 20 acres in the Bronx, on which they will build Yankee Stadium

June 10, 1921: Babe Ruth sets new career home run mark, with his 120th roundtripper. The previous recordholder was former Red Sox, White Sox, and Phillies slugger Gavvy Cravath (119 HR).

September 5, 1921: The Yankees' Bob Meusel has four outfield assists in one game, and the Yankees set a record with five. Despite having all those runners cut down, the Red Sox won 8-2.

October 2, 1921: The Yankees close out their first pennant-winning season with a 7-6 win over Boston. The New York Giants beat the Yankees in the World Series, with every one of the games played at the Polo Grounds—home to both teams.

December 20, 1921: Yankees get more players from Boston. Shortstop Everett Scott and pitchers Sam Jones and Joe Bush depart Boston for the Big Apple, and New York sends shortstop Roger Peckinpaugh plus three pitchers to Beantown: Harry Collins, Bill Piercy and Jack Quinn.

June 13, 1922: Mel Parnell born. Parnell threw four shutouts against New York in 1953.

July 24, 1922: The Red Sox trade premier third baseman Joe Dugan and outfielder Elmer Smith to New York for pitcher Frank O'Doul, shortstop John Mitchell, and outfielders Elmer Miller and Chick Fewster. Other teams are upset by the Red Sox supplying the Yankees a big boost during a competitive pennant race, and this trade prompts Commissioner Landis to institute a trading deadline for earlier in the season (June 15).

September 5, 1922: In the last game the Yankees play at the Polo Grounds before moving to Yankee Stadium, Babe Ruth homers off Red Sox pitcher Herb Pennock. Boston wins nonetheless, 4-3. It was Pennock who had also surrendered the first home run Ruth hit after joining the Yankees. Not that long afterward, Pennock became a Yankee himself.

September 30, 1922: The Yankees clinched the pennant with 3-1 win over Boston.

October 8, 1922: The Yankees lose Game Four of the World Series, swept by the Giants.

October 12, 1922: The Red Sox give Lefty O'Doul to the Yankees, completing the trade of July 24.

January 3, 1923: The Yankees announce acquisition of pitcher George Pipgras from Red Sox in exchange for catcher Al DeVormer. In a separate deal announced the same day, the Yankees purchased infielder Harvey Hendrick for cash, also from the Red Sox.

January 30, 1923—The Yankees obtain Herb Pennock from the Red Sox, for three players and more cash. Players obtained by Boston were pitcher George Murray, infielder Norm McMillan and outfielder Camp Skinner.

April 18, 1923: Yankee Stadium opens. NY beats Boston 4-1. Babe Ruth hits 3-run homer.

August 1, 1923: Harry Frazee sells the Red Sox to a group headed by Bob Quinn.

September 11, 1923: Howard Ehmke retires 27 consecutive Yankees batters—after giving up a single to the first batter in the game, Whitey Witt, a single which could equally well have been scored an error.

September 27, 1923: Lou Gehrig hits his first home run, off Boston pitcher Bill Piercy at Fenway Park. Yankees win 8-3.

September 28, 1923: The Yankees beat the Red Sox 24-4 in one of their most lopsided victories against the longtime rivals. Boston pitcher Howard Ehmke was left in to face 16 batters in the sixth inning, giving up 17 runs and 21 hits in the six innings he pitched. All told, Yankees batters racked up an A.L. record 30 hits.

October 15, 1923: Yankees finally prevail over the Giants and win their first World Series four games to two. Ruth had three homers in the Series.

September 27, 1924: At the close of the 1924 pennant race, Washington clinched the A.L. pennant by defeating the Red Sox at Fenway Park, 4-2. Boston fans cheered the Senators, as their victory meant the New York Yankees were denied the pennant.

December 10, 1924: The Yankees acquire infielder-outfielder Howie Shanks from Boston, for infielder Mike McNally. Boston had sent McNally to New York in the earlier December 15, 1920 trade.

December 11, 1924: Newly acquired infielder Mike McNally is traded the very next day for Senators' third baseman Doc Prothro.

December 12, 1924: The Yankees obtain catcher Steve O'Neill from the Red Sox on waivers. O'Neill will later serve as Red Sox manager.

May 5, 1925: The Yankees trade pitcher Ray Francis to the Red Sox for pitcher Alex Ferguson, outfielder Bobby Veach, and $8,000 cash.

May 6, 1925: Yankees shortstop Everett Scott, once a Red Sox, completes 1,307 consecutive game streak—the longest in majors before Gehrig's.

June 1, 1925: Wally Pipp has a headache and Lou Gehrig fills in. Gehrig doesn't vacate first base position until 2,130 games later.

April 13, 1926: The Yankees defeat the Red Sox 12-11 in Opening Day matchup.

June 15, 1926: The Yankees get outfielder Roy Carlyle from the Red Sox on waivers.

May 29, 1927: Seven runs in the bottom of the eighth help the Yankees secure a 15-7 win over the Red Sox.

June 23, 1927: Gehrig hits three homers in Fenway to help defeat Boston 11-4

September 5, 1927: In an 18-inning game, Boston beat New York 12-11—reversing the Opening Day defeat by the identical score. Red Ruffing had pitched the first fifteen for Boston and Yankees must have liked what they saw, as they later moved to pick up Ruffing from the Red Sox. The Yankees won the second game of the day's doubleheader.

September 6 and 7, 1927: Ruth hits five home runs in three games over two days. Of the 60 homers he hit in 1927, 11 were hit off Red Sox pitching.

April 23, 1929: At Fenway Park for their first road game of the young season, the Yankees wear numbers on their uniforms—the first team to do so. Big Ed Morris beats George Pipgras, 4-2.

May 19, 1929: Two killed and 62 hurt at a Yankees-Red Sox game. The Yankees were leading 3-0 after 4½ innings (hence an official game) when torrential downpours caused the over-capacity crowd to run for cover. A 17-year-old Hunter College sophomore and a 60-year-old truck driver were killed in the right-field bleachers crush.

July 3, 1929: New York batter Babe Ruth hits seventh-inning grand slam off Red Sox' Red Ruffing.

May 6, 1930: Yankees obtain Red Ruffing from Red Sox for outfielder Ced Durst and $50,000 cash.

June 1, 1930: Sox execute triple play against the Yankees, started by first baseman Phil Todt.

September 28, 1930: In the final game of the season, Babe Ruth wins a 9-3 complete game pitching against Boston, in Boston, years after he'd been converted to a full-time position player. He hadn't pitched since 1921. Gehrig asked if he could play left field, when he heard Ruth was pitching. Seeing the

Babe on the mound may have shaken the Sox. He struck out three, and ini-
tiated two double plays. Until the sixth inning, not a single Sox player
reached second base. It wasn't until tiring in the eighth that Boston scored
its first earned run. Ruth contributed two singles and drove in one run.

April 22, 1931: It was a battered Babe Ruth who featured frequently in a 7-
5 Yankees win which spoiled the Fenway Park home opener. He had three
hits, including an RBI single in the fourth and an RBI double in the sixth.
In the sixth inning, he suffered not one, but three separate injuries.
Running from second to third in the top of the sixth, he turned his instep.
A few moments later, he crashed into catcher (and former football star)
Charlie Berry, who was unsuccessfully blocking the plate for Boston. Ruth
scored on a sacrifice fly. Taking the field in the bottom of the sixth, he tore
a left-thigh ligament chasing down a line drive down the foul line in left.
Both runners on base scored, and Ruth had to be carried from the field.

May 4, 1931: Babe Ruth and Lou Gehrig switched positions, due to linger-
ing effects of Ruth's injury. Ruth played first and Gehrig right field. They
punched out five hits between them, but a Gehrig error figured in the Red
Sox 7-3 victory.

August 2, 1931: Playing a Sunday doubleheader against the Yankees at
Braves Field (before mid-1932 any Sunday Sox home games had to be
played at Braves Field, since Fenway was situated too close to a house of
worship), former Sox pitcher Red Ruffing won the first game for New York
(4-1), and former Yankees pitcher Wilcy Moore won the second game for
Boston (beating future Red Sox pitcher George Pipgras, 1-0).

September 1, 1931: Red Sox pitcher Ed Morris gives up a grand slam to
Lou Gehrig. The following spring, Morris is stabbed to death at his farewell
party as he prepares to leave for spring training.

June 5, 1932: The Yanks give the Red Sox $50,000 and pitchers Ivy
Andrews and Henry Johnson to obtain pitcher Danny MacFayden.

June 29, 1932: The Yankees reach into the Sox backyard and sign Harvard
pitcher Charlie Devens.

July 3, 1932: In the first Sunday game ever played at Fenway Park, the Yankees prevailed 13-2. Earle Combs hit two doubles in the same inning—and so did teammate Lyn Lary.

August 1, 1932: The Yankees reacquire Wilcy Moore, their relief hero of the 1927 season, from Boston for the waiver price. In a separate waiver deal, the Sox obtain Yankees pitcher Gordon "Dusty" Rhodes.

November 7, 1932: Dick Stuart's birthday. As a Pirate, Stuart really hit the Yankees hard in the 1960 World Series. In 1963, Red Sox first baseman Stuart led the league in RBIs.

February 25, 1933: Tom Yawkey purchases the Red Sox from Bob Quinn for a reported $1,500,000.

May 12, 1933: New Boston owner Tom Yawkey purchases infielder Billy Werber and pitcher George Pipgras from Yankees for an even $100,000.

June 6, 1933: Even though he gave up 11 hits, Herb Pennock throws a 4-0 shutout in New York.

June 14, 1933: Both Lou Gehrig and Joe McCarthy are thrown out of the game for arguing a seventh-inning play involving Rick Ferrell at Fenway during a 13-5 Boston victory.

August 14, 1933: Red Ruffing was the first Yankees pitcher to hit a grand slam. The unlucky victim was Boston's Bob Weiland.

September 23, 1933: In a messy game, New York commits seven errors but beats Boston 16-12. Frank Crosetti made three of the errors.

October 1, 1933: Another Ruth pitching performance against his old team, the Red Sox—his last game as a pitcher. Yankees won 6-5, and Ruth hit the game-winning home run. In this Stadium game, the Yankees outfield did most of the work, making 18 putouts.

May 9, 1934: New York trades infielder Lyn Lary to Boston for infielder Fred Muller and $20,000.

June 6, 1934: New York outfielder Myril Hoag sets record with six singles

(6-for-6) in a 9-inning game, as New York beats Boston 15-3. Hoag goes 1-for-5 as Yankees lose second game of twin bill.

August 12, 1934: For Babe Ruth's last American League game in Boston, over 46,000 fans pack Fenway and between 15,000 and 20,000 more had to be turned away. All cheered Ruth as he hit safely twice in the first game. During the second game, he left mid-game to a tremendous ovation, stopping to shake hands with the umpires while leaving the field.

September 24, 1934: Ruth plays final game in New York as a Yankee in 5-0 loss to Boston. Ruth walked, then was replaced by a pinch-runner.

February 26, 1935: The Yankees give Babe Ruth his release, so that he can accept an offer to return to Boston (this time, the Boston Braves).

April 16, 1935: In his last professional appearance at Fenway Park, and his first appearance as a member of the Boston Braves, Babe Ruth hit a home run off New York Giants pitcher Carl Hubbell.

June 1, 1935: The Yankees hit six one-run homers in a 7-2 win over Boston at the Stadium. The Sox' two runs came on a two-run shot by Mel Almada.

September 22, 1935: Even more fans jammed Fenway than for the Babe's last game in 1934. This time, a reported 47,627 fans packed in. The Yankees swept, 6-4 in the first game. They won the second game 9-0, hitting seven ground-rule doubles (balls hit into the roped-off crowd were considered doubles under the ground rules of the day).

April 26, 1936: The Yankees spot the Sox six runs in bottom of the first at Fenway, but rebound with seven of their own in top of second, and win game 12-9.

September 5, 1936: The Sox win 3-2 in first game; in game two, Yankees not only hit into a triple play but commit four errors and are lucky to hold onto a 7-7 tie in a game called because of darkness.

February 17, 1937: The Yankees purchase Babe Dahlgren from the Red

Sox. Dahlgren later takes Gehrig's place in New York lineup.

April 2, 1937: Yankee-killer Dick "the Monster" Radatz born. Legends sometimes become larger than life and the oft-repeated story that the Monster struck out Mantle 47 out of the 63 times he faced him is more than a little exaggerated. Nevertheless, there's never been a bullpen ace the Sox would have rather put on the mound to stare down the Yankees.

July 5, 1937: Joe DiMaggio hits his first career grand slam off of Boston pitcher Rube Walberg

September 8, 1937: The Yankees win game one of the day's doubleheader in New York. It looked like a split with the Yankees losing 6-1 in the ninth inning with two outs. New York comes alive, scores eight times and wins the second game.

May 30, 1938: Record attendance at Yankee Stadium, where a reported 81,841 fans watch New York take two from Boston. Joe Cronin and Jake Powell have a famous fistfight on the field, which continues under the stands after both players had been ejected.

September 18, 1938: The Yankees win a pennant because the Red Sox do NOT play. Sox are rained out of a doubleheader. In this era, games which were rained out were not made up. Even though the Yankees lost both games of their own doubleheader, the failure of the Red Sox to win theirs gave the Yankees the clinch. Imagine the clubhouse celebration after dropping two games to the St. Louis Browns.

April 20, 1939: At Yankee Stadium, rookie Ted Williams gets his first major league hit off the Yankees' Red Ruffing, doubling after striking out twice. This game features play by amazing number of future Hall of Famers: Cronin, Dickey, DiMaggio, Doerr, Foxx, Gehrig, Gordon, Grove, Ruffing, and Williams. Lefty Gomez was suited up and watched from the bench.

May 2, 1939: Lou Gehrig takes a game off, after 2,130 consecutive games. The Yankees win 22-2, with Gehrig's replacement, former Bosox Babe Dahlgren, hitting a homer and a double.

July 9, 1939: Boston completes a five-game series sweep of the Yankees at Yankee Stadium with a twin-bill triumph, 4-3 and 5-3.

July 11, 1939: The Yankees host the All-Star Game at the Stadium. Yankees fans see six NY starters, and Joe DiMaggio hits homer in 3-1 AL win.

September 3, 1939: Red Sox win first game of a Fenway twin bill by a score of 12-11, but in the second game the score was tied 5-5 in the top of the eighth when the Yankees scored two runs with nobody out. In those days, the Red Sox played under a 6:30 P.M. Sunday curfew and the Yankees runs scored at 6:19. If the inning was not played to completion, the runs would not count so the Red Sox took their time walking Dahlgren. Meanwhile, the Yankees for their part sent George Selkirk running from third on a sup-posed steal of home (really, to be tagged out so they could close out their half of the inning and get the Red Sox up to bat). Dahlgren refused to be walked by swinging to miss on what would have been ball three and ball four. At this point, Joe Gordon "stole home" and was easily thrown out.

Boston manager complained that the Yankees were deliberately making outs, but umpire Cal Hubbard found no rule against it. Boston fans threw so much garbage on the field that the umpires declared a forfeit and award-ed the game to New York.

May 15, 1941: Joe DiMaggio hits a single off Chicago's Eddie Smith. It would be the first game of his 56-consecutive-game hitting streak. Two months later, on July 15, he hit a single and a double off Smith in the 55th game of the streak.

May 25, 1941: When Joe DiMaggio hits a single off Lefty Grove, as part of his streak, Grove finds himself the only pitcher to have surrendered one of Babe Ruth's 60 homers in 1927 and one of DiMaggio's hits in the streak of 1941. Needless to say, Grove's teammate Ted Williams was in the midst of his .400 season.

May 30, 1941: New York won the first game at Fenway, scoring three unearned runs after Jim Tabor's ninth-inning error. Joe DiMaggio made three errors all by himself in the second game and the Red Sox won, 13-0, as three other Yankees pitched in with their own miscues. In the fifth inning of game two, the Sox stole four bases in one inning. Skeeter

Newsome stole second, and a couple of batters later found himself on third with the bases loaded and Dom DiMaggio at the plate. The Red Sox pulled off a triple steal, with Newsome stealing home, Frankie Pytlak taking third and pitcher Mickey Harris taking second. Ted Williams had six hits in the doubleheader, helping him build up hit totals toward a .406 season.

June 28, 1941: Joe DiMaggio's ankle pain suddenly disappears, and he joins Yankees lineup at Fenway, contributing a homer in 5-4 New York triumph.

July 1, 1941: Joe DiMaggio ties 19th century Wee Willie Keeler's record of 44 consecutive games with a hit, singling off Boston's Jackie Wilson. New York won that game, as they had the first game of the day's doubleheader.

July 2, 1941: Boston pitcher Heber Newsome is touched up for a home run by DiMaggio, who now has hit in 45 straight games, a new major league record. New York won the game.

July 8, 1941: Ted Williams hits two homers, including the two-out, three-run game winner, in the 1941 All-Star Game.

July 16, 1941: In the last day of the streak, Joe D manages three hits off two pitchers. After failing to hit successfully on the 17th, DiMaggio went on and hit for another streak of 16 games in a row. Because he walked on the 17th, and walked in the game before the hitting streak began, all told DiMaggio had crafted a stretch of 74 straight games in which he reached base. Society for American Baseball Research member Herm Krabbenhoft terms this statistic CGOBS (Consecutive Games On Base Safely). Ted Williams had a stretch of 69 CGOBS in 1941, and then in 1949, Ted exceeded Joe D's CGOBS mark.

September 3, 1941: Yankees clinch the earliest in a season, beating Boston 6-3.

September 27, 1941: Ted Williams is batting .401 but declines Joe Cronin's offer to sit out the game and preserve his .400 average. Ted goes 1-for-4 and drops under the magic mark to .3995.

September 28, 1941: In a doubleheader season finale in Philadelphia, Ted Williams goes 6-for-8 and boosts his average well over the .400 mark to a spectacular .406. Had the sacrifice fly rule not been eliminated the previous December, he would have hit .411 on the season (and not faced the need for the final day's drama). Williams ended the season with an on-base percentage of .553, the best ever until Barry Bonds obliterated the mark in 2003 and upped the ante again in 2004. Ted still holds the highest career on-base percentage of any player, ever.

April 14, 1942: Johnny Pesky makes his major league debut with a single and a triple in the Fenway home opener.

September 27, 1942: Tony Lupien Day at Fenway is also the last day before Ted Williams, Johnny Pesky and Dom DiMaggio enter military service. Tex Hughson helps Boston win 7-6. Johnny Pesky ended the season leading the league with 205 hits, and would clearly have been "rookie of the year" if the award had been instituted yet. Ted Williams won the Triple Crown.

November 3, 1942: The Yankees' Joe Gordon wins the A.L. MVP award despite leading the league in strikeouts, and leading all second basemen in errors. Gordon also led the league into hitting into double plays. Ted had 137 RBIs and Joe had 103. Ted had 36 HR and Joe had 18, only half as many. Ted had 34 doubles and Joe had 29; Ted had 5 triples and Joe had 4. Ted scored 141 runs and Joe scored 88 runs. Ted batted .356 and Joe averaged .322. Ted's on-base percentage was .499 and Joe's was .409. Ted's slugging percentage was .648 and Joe's was .491. For what it's worth, Ted's fielding average was .988 and Joe's was .966.

January 25, 1943: The Yankees sell Lefty Grove to Boston Braves

June 26, 1943: His 4-1 win on this day gave Tex Hughson eight straight wins over the Yankees.

July 12, 1943: To raise money for war bonds, both Ted Williams and Joe DiMaggio play on the same team, managed by Babe Ruth, in an exhibition game against the Boston Braves at Braves Field. Ted's home run wins it for the Ruth All-Stars, 9-8.

September 12, 1943: The Yankees begin a five-game sweep from the Sox at Fenway Park.

January 4, 1944: "Jumpin' Joe" Dugan, briefly with the Red Sox but then a seven-year veteran infielder for the Yankees, had apparently lost a bit of the spring in his step and was injured some 13 years after retirement, hit by a car in Boston while crossing the street.

April 16, 1945: The Red Sox offer tryouts to three black players (Jackie Robinson, Sam Jethroe and Marvin Williams) and claim to not see adequate talent in any one of the three. Fifteen more years—and a tremendous opportunity—pass before the Red Sox have an African-American player on their major league roster.

April 17, 1945: The Yankees salvage their home opener by scoring seven runs in the seventh inning, beating Boston 8-4.

June 16, 1945: Dave "Boo" Ferriss lost to New York, 3-2. It was the first loss of his career. He'd won the previous eight, four of which were shutouts.

June 21, 1945: The Yankees score 13 runs in the fifth inning against Boston.

May 10, 1946: Joe DiMaggio's Stadium grand slam provides all the Yankees runs in a 5-4 Red Sox win, their 15th in a row. The Sox' streak was snapped next day by a 2-0 New York win.

June 18, 1946: The Red Sox get pitcher Bill Zuber from the Yankees on waivers.

July 2, 1946: Yankees hurler Spud Chandler has a no-hitter going against Boston for 8⅓ innings until Bobby Doerr breaks it up with a single. Chandler had incredibly walked nine Sox batters in the first four innings, but got the win 2-1.

September 13, 1946: With a 1-0 win, the Red Sox clinch the pennant on an inside-the-park home run by Ted Williams, the only one of his career. It was their first pennant since 1918.

October 6, 1946: The Red Sox open the World Series in St. Louis with a 3-2 win in the tenth inning on a Rudy York homer.

October 15, 1946: With the Series tied at three wins each, it's sudden death in St. Louis. Boston scored first, in the first, but was down 3-1 after six innings. The Red Sox then scored two runs to tie the game, but lost on Harry Walker's hit to left-center as Enos Slaughter was off and running before contact. Slaughter unexpectedly churned all the way around third base and streaked to the plate as Leon Culberson lofted a routine return throw to cutoff man Johnny Pesky. Pesky's throw to the plate was inevitably late, given Slaughter's "mad dash." The Cardinals hold on in the ninth and win the World Series. Pesky allowed himself to be portrayed as the goat for "holding the ball" although none of the players fault him, and existing film shows no clear hesitation.

April 14, 1947: The Yankees release pitcher Johnny Murphy, and the Red Sox sign him up.

May 26, 1947: A staggering 74,747 jam the Stadium and watch the Yankees win over Boston, 9-3.

September 3, 1947: The Yankees win the first game of a Fenway double-header 11-2 by making 18 hits, every one of which was a single. Yanks won second game, too, with 16 hits, some of which were extra base hits.

September 28, 1947: Ted Williams wins his second Triple Crown. No player has ever won three. Again, he falls short in the MVP voting.

September 29, 1947: Former Yankees manager Joe McCarthy is brought out of the retirement and hired to manage the 1948 Red Sox. McCarthy had led the Yankees to nine pennants, and came as close as one can (without succeeding) to winning two more for Boston. The Sox would fall short on the final day in both 1948 and 1949.

November 27, 1947: Joe DiMaggio gets one more vote for A. L. MVP than Ted Williams, despite the fact that Williams won the Triple Crown. One voter listed Williams in ninth place and another in tenth place. Ted hit .343 to Joe's .315, hit 32 HR to Joe's 20, and knocked in 114 runs to Joe's 97. Ted also led the league in runs scored, walks, on-base percentage, and slugging. Joe did not lead the league in a single offensive category.

March 29, 1948: Battling it out even in spring training, the Yanks and the Red Sox play a 17-inning-long game and end with a 2-2 tie. The Yankees came from behind in the ninth inning to tie the score, and then Tommy Byrne walked four batters in the tenth to give the Sox the lead, but the Yankees tied it up yet again. In eight innings of relief, Byrne gave up just one hit. The Sox threw 14 players into the fray, and the Yankees used 19.

October 2 and 3, 1948: Boston beat the Yankees 10-5 on the final two days of the season, placing them in a tie with the Cleveland Indians and forcing a single-game playoff which a coin toss determined would be at Fenway Park.

October 4, 1948: Boston manager Joe McCarthy unexpectedly hands Denny Galehouse (8-7 on the season) the ball as starting pitcher in the first playoff game in A.L. history. Cleveland player-manager Lou Boudreau gave the ball to 19-game winner Gene Bearden and himself made four hits, including a couple of homers. The Red Sox lose the sudden-death game, just as they had in Game Seven of the '46 Series.

June 29, 1949: Dom DiMaggio begins his team-record 34-game hitting streak.

July 1, 1949: Beginning on July 1 and ending on September 27, Ted Williams reached base safely in every game he played, for a Consecutive Games on Base Safely (CGOBS) streak of 84 straight games. That's the record. In fact, in all of 1949, Ted only failed to reach base five times: June 3, 7, 26, 30, and September 28. For more than 10 years, Williams never had back-to-back games of not getting on base safely, from July 14, 1940, through September 26, 1950.

September 25, 1949: Mel Parnell wins his 25th game of the year, as the Red Sox beat the Yankees, 4-1. The win brings the Red Sox into a tie with New York, with six games to play. According to Ed Walton, Bobby Doerr, lying on the ground after being taken out in a double play, is told by either Joe McCarthy or Birdie Tebbetts, "C'mon Bobby, get up. You don't want all these people in the stands to think you are a Yankee, do you?"

September 30, 1949: With an 11-9 win against the Washington Senators, Boston travels to New York for the two final games of the '49 season. Winning either game will give the Red Sox the pennant.

October 1, 1949: New York caught league-leading Boston (and Mel Parnell) with a win this day, bringing the two teams to a first-place tie. Yankees were down 4-0, but won the game 5-4. Joe Page gets the win, after five innings of strong relief. Whichever team wins the following day's game wins the pennant.

October 2, 1949: For the second year in a row, the Red Sox face sudden-death elimination on the final day of the season. They lose, 5-3, Ellis Kinder losing to Vic Raschi. After a four-run eighth, the Yankees carried a 5-0 lead into the ninth, but then Boston scored three runs and had the tying run at the plate. Dramatic, but the Yankees prevailed. It is the third time in four years that the Sox were facing sudden death, and died. Joe McCarthy managed the Red Sox for just two full seasons. In both years (1948 and 1949) the team lost the pennant on the final day.

April 18, 1950: Shut out and down by nine runs in the sixth inning, New York catches up and spoils Opening Day for Red Sox fans with a 15-10 victory after a nine-run eighth inning. The Sox use five pitchers in one inning.

June 8, 1950: Boston beats St. Louis, 29-4 in a game at Fenway. Red Sox rookie Walt Dropo has two homers and seven RBIs, topped only by Bobby Doerr's three homers and eight RBIs.

August 15, 1950: The season seemed a lost cause for the Sox, but twin-bill triumphs over the Philadelphia Athletics kick off a stretch where Boston wins 27 of 30 games and makes a real run for the flag.

September 26, 1950: From July 14, 1940 through this date, Williams never had back-to-back games without reaching safely, if a couple of pinch-hit appearances in 1941 and '48 are discounted.

October 2, 1950: Again, two Sox tie for the RBI crown, this year both Vern Stephens and Walt Dropo have 144 RBIs. Stephens and Williams had both driven in 159 the previous year. Dropo falls one short of Williams' rookie record 145 RBIs in 1939. Williams had broken his elbow in the All-Star Game, but wound up the season with 97 RBIs in just 89 games.

April 17, 1951: Mickey Mantle's major league debut comes at home in 5-0 win against the visiting Red Sox. Mantle singles and drives in one run, going 1-for-4.

May 30, 1951: Mantle strikes out five times in a row against Sox, on the same day Williams scores from second base on a sacrifice bunt.

September 28, 1951: Allie Reynolds no-hits Boston, and wins 8-0—his second no-hitter of the year. Ted Williams was the last batter up in the ninth, and Berra dropped Ted's pop foul. Given new life, Williams popped up foul all over again—this time Berra held on tight.

January 9, 1952: It is announced that both Jerry Coleman of the Yankees and Ted Williams of the Red Sox will be recalled to military service with the Marine Corps.

April 2, 1952: Ted and Jerry Coleman both pass physicals before a Marine Corps medical board at Yukon, Florida (near Naval Air Station Jacksonville). Both were found physically fit for return to active duty. Neither had flown a plane for six years.

April 30, 1952: Ted Williams Day at Fenway Park, just before his departure for the Marines. In what might have proved to be his last at-bat in major league baseball, Williams hits a two-run HR his last time up to break a 3-3 tie with the Tigers and win the game for the Red Sox, 5-3.

August 16, 1952: Boston loses to New York, 5-4. The Red Sox lose 12 games in a row to the Yankees, before next winning on May 8, 1953.

August 22, 1952: New York obtains pitcher Ray Scarborough from Boston on waivers

September 2, 1952: The Yankees sweep a doubleheader with two shutouts of the Sox, 5-0 (Tom Gorman) and 4-0 (Ewell Blackwell).

February 16, 1953: Ted Williams shot down over Korea, crash-lands his Phantom F9F jet and escapes as the plane becomes engulfed in flame.

May 8, 1953: An 11th inning homer by Billy Goodman gives the Sox their first win against the Yankees since the previous August. Sox then lose the next four matchups.

May 25, 1953: One of the longest nine-inning games in history was between the Red Sox and Yankees, at 3 hours and 52 minutes. Boston 14, New York 10. A Baltimore-New York game in 1996 topped out at 4 hours and 21 minutes.

July 1, 1953: Mel Parnell's 4-0 shutout of New York is his 100th career victory.

September 19, 1953: Mel Parnell shuts out the Yankees for the fourth time in the 1953 campaign. Walter Johnson was the last pitcher to shut out an opponent four times in one season, and he did that in 1908.

April 11, 1954: The Yankees obtain Enos Slaughter from Cardinals. Slaughter's "mad dash" did in the Red Sox during the seventh game of the 1946 World Series.

May 28, 1954: In a game featuring 20 bases on balls (12 walks by Sox pitchers and 8 by Yanks), New York was losing 5-0 after three, and 9-3 after five. They scored six runs in the sixth inning to tie the score, then won the game 10-9 in the ninth inning with a walk to Collins, who was sacrificed to second by McDougald and driven home by an Andy Carey single.

June 30, 1954: Yankees pitcher Tom Morgan hits three Red Sox batters in one inning. With two outs and nobody on in the third, Morgan hit Billy Goodman, saw an error committed on the next play, then hit Ted Lepcio and Milt Bolling after that. The plunking of Bolling brought in a run, and the Red Sox scored two more, eventually winning 5-1.

September 6, 1954: Yankees use 10 pinch-hitters in doubleheader and split with Boston. New York wins first game 6-5, using 20 players and scoring two runs in the bottom of the ninth. New York manager Stengel used 18 players in the second game, but came up short, 8-7, as Boston battled back from being down 7-0.

April 14, 1955: Elston Howard became the first African-American to play for the Yankees. He entered the game in the top of the sixth inning after leftfielder Irv Noren had been ejected for arguing a close play at the plate. Howard played left and came up to bat in the eighth, with the Yankees down 6-2. Mantle and Skowron both walked, and Howard singled in his first at-bat, scoring a run. The *New York Times* reported that he "received a fine ovation."

May 5, 1955: The musical *Damn Yankees* opened on Broadway.

July 4, 1955: In the first game of the Independence Day doubleheader in New York, the Yankees sent up four pinch-hitters to the plate and Boston pitchers struck out all four. Cerv, Robinson, Byrne, and Howard all whiffed in the fifth, seventh, ninth, and ninth, respectively. Jensen's grand slam in the second game helped the Sox sweep, 4-2 and 10-5.

September 11, 1955: Ted Williams gets his 2000th hit in 5-3 loss to New York.

September 23, 1955: Needing one win to clinch the pennant, the Yankees lost the day game, 8-4, but won the night game, 3-2. The pennant was the 21st for the Yankees, and the sixth of the last seven seasons under Casey Stengel.

April 22, 1956: Don Larsen hit a grand slam off Sox pitcher Frank Sullivan. Later in the year, Larsen would become more famous.

August 7, 1956: Yankees pitcher Don Larsen started and threw ten innings, scattering just four hits. Willard Nixon was pitching a gem for the Red Sox, and after ten-and-a-half innings, neither team had scored. Larsen had some bad luck and, thanks to two Yankees errors and a walk, found the bases loaded in the bottom of the eleventh with nobody out and Ted Williams in the on-deck circle. Stengel called on Tommy Byrne to relieve Larsen, but Byrne promptly walked Williams, forcing in the winning run, and the Sox won 1-0. It was reported to be the largest crowd in Fenway history. Williams flipped his bat in the air—in a foul mood on the day and a little disgusted, since he always loved to hit—and started walking to the dugout until coach Del Baker reminded him he had to touch first base. Earlier in the game, Terrible Ted had spit at the fans after dropping a Mantle fly ball.

September 21, 1956: The Yankees lose in Boston 13-7, ending the game with 20 runners left on base, despite five Boston errors. Three different times, New York left the bases loaded.

September 30, 1956: The Yankees win another pennant—no surprise there—and Mickey Mantle wins the Triple Crown, leading both leagues in homers, RBIs, and batting average. His .353 beat out Ted Williams' .345; Williams had only batted .196 against New York pitching.

October 8, 1956: Don Larsen throws a perfect game in the World Series, against the Brooklyn Dodgers. Midway through the game, some Red Sox fans began to actually root for a Yankees pitcher to throw strikes and for Yankees fielders to play error-free ball.

April 20, 1957: Moose Skowron homers over the old center-field wall at Fenway Park. He was only the third player to do so.

August 7, 1957: Before one of the largest crowds in the history of Fenway Park (36,350), Ted Williams spits at the crowd. Sox lose 2-1, and Williams loses $5,000 when he is fined by owner Tom Yawkey. It is widely understood that the fine was never collected.

September 17—23 1957: Soon after he turned 39 on August 30, Williams reached base in 16 consecutive plate appearances, the final 13 against the Yankees.

    Sept. 17 vs. KC—pinch-hit home run

    Sept. 18 vs. KC—pinch-hit walk

    Sept. 20 at NY—pinch-hit home run

    Sept. 21 at NY—home run, three walks

    Sept. 22 at NY—home run, single, two walks

    Sept. 23 at NY—single, three walks, hit by pitch

November 22, 1957: Mickey Mantle gets one more vote for A. L. MVP than does Ted Williams. The 39-year-old Williams hit .388 in '57, and had a .528 on-base percentage with a .731 slugging average (all of which led the league). Mantle led the league in walks and runs scored, and had four fewer home runs than Ted but seven more RBIs.

July 5, 1958: Boston and New York play to 3-3 tie in 10 innings.

September 2, 1958: Mickey Mantle and Yogi Berra hit back-to-back home runs, two solo shots off Dave Sisler in the sixth to break a scoreless tie. Final score, 6-1 New York.

September 3, 1958: Yankees losing, 5-3, after seven innings. Mantle hit a homer in the eighth to cut Boston's lead to 5-4. Berra singled, then Skowron singled, Berra holding up at second—only to be picked off moments later. McDougald and Kubek each managed infield hits to tie the score, but Yogi had to wait until the bottom of the ninth to redeem himself. His 3-run home run off Leo Kiely won the game for New York, 8-5.

April 12, 1959: Opening Day at the Stadium, and Norm Siebern blasted a solo homer off Boston's Tom Brewer in the bottom of the eighth to break the 2-2 tie. Bob Turley won his first start as a Yankee. It was Siebern's first major league game wearing eyeglasses; he'd missed two fly balls in the 1958 World Series.

April 17, 1959: Turley and Brewer match up again, this time in Boston, and Brewer tosses a two-hitter, winning it for Boston 4-0.

July 11, 1959: With the Yanks ahead 3-1 after 7½ innings, the Sox scored three runs and went ahead in the bottom of the eighth on Tony Kubek's throwing error which let in two of the three runs. Kubek, batting in the ninth, tied it on a home run. In the bottom of the tenth, the Yankees battery of Ryne Duren and Yogi Berra were both ejected in an argument over a pitch called a ball. Jim Bronstad (who would finish the season 0-3) couldn't get either of the next batters out, and so Turley was trotted in. His first pitch was blasted over the Green Monster just down the line for a grand slam. The batter? An unlikely hero—Don Buddin.

July 13, 1959: The Sox complete a five-game sweep of New York. Gene Stephens came in to run for Ted Williams in the sixth, and the Red Sox bat around, bringing Stephens up to bat later in the inning with the bases loaded. Stephens hit a grand slam to punctuate the nine-run inning.

January 21, 1960: Birthdate of Yankees pitcher Andy Hawkins, who had a 162.00 ERA in starting three games at Fenway Park in 1990. Total innings pitched in the three starts: one. Hawkins managed to surrender 18 runs on 13 hits and 6 walks.

April 19, 1960: Ted Williams hits homer #494, providing a bit of excitement for the Fenway faithful, but the day belonged to Roger Maris, who kicked off the 1960 season with two home runs and a double, driving in four runs as the Yankees beat Boston, 8-4.

September 6, 1960: Mantle's homer gave the Yankees one run in a 7-1 loss to the Red Sox at the Stadium. It was the last game Ted Williams would ever play there, and he homered (#518).

September 25, 1960: The Yankees clinch the 1960 pennant with cliffhanger 4-3 win over Boston. The Red Sox had pulled within a run of the Yankees and had runners at first and third. Stengel called on Luis Arroyo in relief of Ralph Terry. Arroyo was facing Pete Runnels, the 1960 batting champion. Arroyo threw one pitch, and Runnels popped up foul to the third baseman. Game over. Season over. The Yankees had clinched their tenth pennant in twelve years.

October 2, 1960: New York wins its 15th game in a row, and the last game of the season, when first baseman Dale Long homers in the bottom of the ninth to lift the Yankees to an 8-7 Yankee Stadium win over the Red Sox. Japan's Crown Prince Akihito and Princess Michiko attend the game and the prince threw out the first ball.

April 26, 1961: Roger Maris hits first HR of 1961 season. 60 more follow.

May 29, 1961: Three mistakes in a pitcher's duel between the Yankees' Whitey Ford and Boston's Ike Delock give the Red Sox a home win, 2-1. Ford made two mistakes and Delock only one.

May 30, 1961: Many mistakes result in seven New York homers (1 by Berra, and 2 each by Mantle, Maris, and Skowron) as Yankees cruise to a 12-3 victory.

May 31, 1961: Mantle and Maris homer again—a theme for 1961—and New York's bullpen holds off a late Red Sox surge to win, 7-6.

July 21, 1961: In the first inning, both Mantle and Maris homered off Bill Monbouquette, but it was Johnny Blanchard's ninth-inning pinch-hit grand slam which sunk the Sox, 11-8.

July 22, 1961: Johnny Blanchard came up the second day in a row in a pinch-hitting role, and hit a game-tying homer in the ninth. The Yankees went on to win.

October 1, 1961: In the last game of the year, Roger Maris hit his 61st home run, off a fourth-inning waist-high fastball from Bosox pitcher Tracy Stallard. Stallard struck Maris out his next time up. Yankees win a well-pitched game,1-0.

January 22, 1962: Red Sox outfielder Jackie Jensen announces his retirement from baseball for good.

May 17, 1962: Mickey Mantle almost single-handedly won the game for the Yankees in the top of the ninth inning, by working a walk, stealing second, taking third on a bad peg to third by Boston catcher Pagliaroni, and then scoring on an Elston Howard sacrifice fly. His was the winning run in a 2-1 game. The other Yankees run was set up by a wild pitch by Gene Conley.

June 12, 1962: The Yankees trade infielder Billy Gardner to Red Sox for Sox Triple A outfielder Tommy Umphlett and cash

July 27, 1962: After a game in New York, Bosox pitcher Gene Conley and infielder Pumpsie Green hop off team bus for a drink (well, quite a few, apparently) and don't come back until July 29th (Green) and 30th (Conley). Conley is spotted at the New York airport after buying a ticket to fly to Israel, but lacks a passport and is denied boarding.

September 9, 1962: The Yankees were swept for the ninth time in a doubleheader loss to the Red Sox, 9-3 and 5-4. The second game lasted a full 16 innings, with Dick Radatz pitching nine innings of relief for the Red Sox. With a man on third and one out in the top of the 16th, Radatz was up to bat and Sox manager Pinky Higgins put in Billy Gardner (see June 12 above), who bunted hard to the charging pitcher Marshall Bridges. Bridges "went sprawling head first" and Bob Tillman scored easily. Chet Nichols, on in relief of Radatz, held off the Yanks in the bottom of the sixteenth.

June 23, 1963: Dick Stuart, of all people, makes three assists in the first inning, gloving the ball and throwing it accurately to Boston's Bob Heffner three times in a row for the putouts. He's also 2-for-4 at the plate with a double, but Boston bows to New York, 8-0.

August 27, 1963: New York swept two from the Red Sox, 5-0 (Jim Bouton) and 3-0 (Ralph Terry).

April 16, 1964: After being postponed twice, the Yankees and Red Sox finally get in Opening Day at Yankee Stadium, Yogi Berra's first game as a manager. Twice, Yankees hit what looked like a walk-off homer in the tenth inning and a game-tying one in the eleventh—but both hooked just foul. One 440-foot drive by Mantle was hauled in by Yastrzemski. In the eleventh, Boston's Bob Tillman tripled even deeper to center—460 feet—and was on third with one out. Whitey Ford's sinker to Roman Mejias sunk too much and bounced off the plate, getting by Howard and allowing Tillman to score.

August 29, 1964: Mickey Mantle tied Babe Ruth's career strikeout record of 1,330 Ks in game two of a doubleheader against Boston.

November 2, 1964: CBS became the first corporation to own a baseball team, buying the Yankees for $11.2 million. They later sold the team at a loss to a group headed by George Steinbrenner.

May 10, 1965: Red Sox rookie Jim Lonborg wins a tight 3-2 game in Boston. Mantle drove in both New York runs, but Yaz hits two homers and drove in all three Red Sox runs.

July 20, 1965: Mel Stottlemyre won the game with an inside-the-park grand slam for New York at the Stadium. It was the first by a pitcher since the Pirates' Deacon Phillippe in 1910. The grand slam was hit off Boston's Bill Monbouquette and made all the difference in the final 6-3 score.

January 20, 1966 Ted Williams is elected to the Hall of Fame on the first ballot.

June 29, 1966: On the 28th, Mickey Mantle hit two homers his last two times up in a game against the Sox in Boston. On the 29th, he did it again, kicking off the day with a three-run homer in the first and driving in four runs total to help New York build up a 6-0 lead. Final score, 6-5, as a hard shot by Yaz glanced off Yankees reliever Hal Reniff to shortstop Dick Schofield, who started a game-ending double play.

September 27, 1966: The Red Sox beat the White Sox, 2-1, in the last game of the year. The Yankees won two of their last three games against the White Sox (the Yankees' season extended five days after the Red Sox had wrapped up theirs). Nevertheless, the season ended with the Red Sox 26 games out of first place, in ninth place—but the Yankees were in tenth place, 26½ games out.

April 14, 1967: Billy Rohr threw a no-hitter for 8⅔ innings and the Red Sox won, 3-0. Elston Howard's single spoiled the rookie's no-hit bid. Reggie Smith's leadoff homer in the first inning was all Rohr needed.

April 15, 1967: The drama of the first series between the rivals continued, as Mel Stottlemyre pitched a 1-0 gem against Boston's Dennis Bennett.

April 16, 1967: Yanks beat Red Sox 7-6 in 18 innings in a 5 hour, 50 minute Stadium game. Yaz got five hits, Tony Conigliaro got five hits, but it was Joe Pepitone's single off Lee Stange (the 571st pitch of the game) with two outs in the bottom of the 18th that won it for New York.

April 21, 1967: It looks like the Red Sox have a new Yankee-killer in Billy Rohr. In his second major league start, he again handcuffs New York allowing just one eighth-inning run, as Boston beats the Yankees, 6-1. Lionized in Boston, Rohr ran out of roar and never won another game for the Red Sox. He lost three, and finished out the season 2-3. In 1968, he was 1-0 for Cleveland. He never won another game in the major leagues.

June 21, 1967: A battle of beanballs erupts between the Red Sox and the Yankees at Yankee Stadium, as the New Yorkers lose their fifth straight game (and ten of their last thirteen). The Red Sox scored four times in the first inning, and Yankees pitcher Thad Tillotson may have felt that Joe Foy had to pay the price for a fifth-inning grand slam the day before. In the second inning, Tillotson's pitch hit Foy on the helmet. This was back before the DH and Tillotson had to bat against Lonborg in the bottom of the second. He was hit in the back, between the shoulder blades and both benches emptied for five minutes. A few punches were thrown and Pepitone had to leave the game with a strained left wrist. No one was ejected, perhaps a mistake. The very next inning, Reggie Smith was floored, buzzed by a close one, and in the fifth inning, pinch-hitter Dick Howser was hit in the helmet by another one of Lonborg's throws. The Red Sox won, 8-1.

August 3, 1967: Elston Howard is traded to the Red Sox for some cash and players to be named later, who prove to be pitchers Peter Magrini and Ron Klimkowski.

August 8, 1967: The Yankees purchase catcher Bob Tillman from the Red Sox on waivers. Consequently, it's Howard and not Tillman behind the plate when the "Impossible Dream" team wins the pennant.

August 29, 1967: A Yankee Stadium doubleheader sees Boston win the first game 2-1, but lose a 20-inning nightcap 4-3 as sixth Sox pitcher Darrell Brandon yielded a single to John Kennedy, then hit Jim Bouton, moving Kennedy into scoring position. Jose Santiago was brought in, but Horace Clarke slapped a single through the infield into right, driving in Kennedy to end the game at 1:57 A.M.

August 30, 1967: The day after the 20-inning marathon, Boston beat New York, 2-1, in 11 innings. Yaz won it with a solo shot off Al Downing.

October 1, 1967: The Red Sox won the pennant on the final day of the season. Spared last place only because Kansas City was much, much worse, the Yankees still ended the season a full 20 games behind the league-leading Red Sox.

May 10 and 11, 1968: The first two games in 1968 between the rivals result in 2-1 and 1-0 New York wins, in New York, but Boston sweeps a twin bill the next day, 8-1 and 4-2.

May 18, 1968: The Yankees purchase pitcher John Wyatt from the Red Sox.

September 20, 1968: In the third inning, Mickey Mantle hits the last home run of his career, #536. Jim Lonborg is the winning pitcher in a 4-3 Sox win.

September 21, 1968: Ray Culp shuts out Yankees on a one-hitter in New York. It's Culp's third straight shutout, the no-hit bid spoiled only by Roy White's seventh-inning single.

September 27, 1968: Mantle is given a first-inning standing ovation by Fenway fans, who believe it's his last ballgame in Boston. Mantle goes 0-for-3, and Sox win 12-2.

September 28, 1968: Mantle's actual last game. He flied out in the first, and was removed with a sore ankle. Overcoming a 3-0 deficit, the Yankees tied the score in the eighth inning on Andy Kosko's homer. Kosko had been the one to take Mantle's place. A Joe Pepitone homer won it for New York in the top of the ninth, 4-3.

February 21, 1969: Ted Williams is named as manager of the 1969 Washington Senators. In his first year as manager, Williams' Senators finished five games above the Yankees in the standings, and Ted was voted Manager of the Year.

April 28, 1969: After hitting 27 home runs in 11 consecutive games, Boston bats were nearly silenced as New York pitcher Fritz Peterson let them have just three hits and shut them down, 1-0. The Red Sox squeaked out a win the next day, 2-1.

June 21, 1969: Joe Pepitone had a grand slam rained out on the 20th, but things were looking up for the Yankees when they scored three runs in the top of the eleventh to take a 5-2 lead over the Sox at Fenway. It might have been worse had not first baseman George Thomas pulled the hidden ball trick and caught Jerry Kenney off first. Yankees reliever Ken Johnson, though, loaded the bases and then saw two runs score on a double by Joe Lahoud. After walking Dick Schofield, the afore-mentioned Thomas hit a little single to center off his fists and the Red Sox won, 4-3. In an evening game (it was a separate-admission doubleheader), the Yankees were down 3-0 after two innings, but scored four runs in the top of the ninth to win, 6-3.

June 22, 1969: A Bronx Bomber he was not, and Len Boehmer was sitting on the bench having gone 0-for-26 for the Yankees (he was 0-for-3 with the Reds in 1967). Both Joe Pepitone and manager Ralph Houk were ejected during the game, perpetuating a three-day running feud with the umpiring crew. Boehmer filled in for Pepitone at first, and saw his teammates tie the game 3-3 in the top of the ninth. Come the tenth, Horace Clarke was at second base on a walk and a sacrifice. Bobby Murcer struck out, and here came Boehmer, 0-29 in his major league career. Boston's hardly-legendary Garry Roggenburk was on the mound. He singled between third base and shortstop and drove in what would prove the winning run.

September 24, 1969: Ken Brett vs. Ron Klimkowski, in Boston. Both went the full nine, with neither team scoring a run in support. After 13 innings, the score was still knotted 0-0, Sonny Siebert in relief of Brett, with four New York pitchers having spelled Klimkowski. George Scott reached first on an infield hit (how often did that happen?) and was sacrificed to second by Satriano. Siebert was taken out and Dalton Jones walked. Mike Andrews swung on the first pitch and doubled about 10 feet up on the left-field Wall to score Scott. 1-0 Boston.

January 17, 1970: The Yankees drafted Fred Lynn, but the future Red Sox outfielder chose not to sign with New York. He went on to play major league ball for 17 years, the first seven of which were with Boston and he was on the All-Star team every full year he was with Boston, even leading the league in hitting in 1979.

June 19, 1970: The Sox' Sonny Siebert took a no-hitter into the ninth against Yankees, at Fenway. Suddenly, it all fell apart. On five pitches, the Yankees got four hits. Horace Clarke singled to right-center. Jerry Kenney doubled off the Wall on the next pitch. Two pitches later, Bobby Murcer singled in two runs with a hit down the right-field line, and Roy White banged the first pitch he saw over the bullpen in right. The Sox had had a 7-0 lead, but Siebert had now given up four runs and it seemed time to call it a day. Sparky Lyle came in and set down the first three Yankees he faced.

June 21, 1970: Looking to break up an 8-8 tie, the Yankees pounced on Jose Santiago and Lee Stange for six runs in the top of the eleventh, then survived a two-run Red Sox rally to win, 14-10.

March 22, 1972: The Yankees trade relief pitcher Sparky Lyle to the Red Sox for first baseman Danny Cater and shortstop Mario Guerrero.

May 21, 1972: Fritz Peterson and Mike Kekich combined to beat Boston in a doubleheader, 6-3 and 3-2. Had either loss been swapped for a win, Boston would have won the pennant. In the strike-shortened '72 season, Boston won 85 games and lost 70, but the Detroit Tigers won 86 and lost 70. It had been decided that all teams would play out the season, even should it end (as it did) with teams not having played an equivalent number of games.

August 2, 1972: The Red Sox lost the first game of a home doubleheader. They won the second game and then, with the exception of one loss on July 31, 1973, they won every home game they hosted the Yankees until September 9, 1974.

January 4, 1973: George Steinbrenner and partners purchase the Yankees from CBS for $12 million. Steinbrenner says he will not be active in day-to-day operations of club. The only time this held true was between 1990 and 1993, when "he was serving a 'lifetime' ban from baseball." Even with this attention, his shipping company filed for bankruptcy in 1993.

April 6, 1973: The first use of DH in baseball is Yankee Ron Blomberg, who is walked by Luis Tiant in his first at-bat in game at Fenway Park. Yanks lose 15-5, though Blomberg is 1-for-3 with 1 RBI. Fisk hits two home runs on this Opening Day. Sox DH is Orlando Cepeda, who goes 0-for-6.

April 7, 1973: In George Steinbrenner's first two games as Yankees owner, the Red Sox scored 25 runs and win both games. In fact, the Sox won the third game as well, and then the fourth, after both teams had moved from Boston to Opening Day in New York. Maybe the Boss decided he had better get involved in day-to-day operations. Boston finished the season winning 14 of 18 games from the Yankees.

July 30, 1973: The Yanks and the Sox were battling for first place. To kick off a series at Fenway, pinch-hitter Jim Ray Hart homered in the ninth inning to drive in two runs for New York and tie the score. The Yankees lost it when Boston batted in the bottom of the ninth. Sparky Lyle came in to pitch for the Yankees. Rico Petrocelli singled. A wild pitch and a couple of grounders got him to third, and Rick Miller singled him in.

July 31, 1973: The Yankees scored three runs in the ninth and won their first game at Fenway Park since August 2, 1972. A home run off Bill Lee, then a single, and he was replaced by Bob Veale who whiffed Horace Clarke. Matty Alou singled. So did Roy White, and Bobby Murcer then hit a two-run single to give the Yankees the 5-4 advantage.

August 1, 1973: The Red Sox and Yankees were tied at two apiece after four innings. Then the ninth inning rolled around and Yankees catcher Thurman Munson led off the top of the ninth with a double. He moved up to third on a grounder by Nettles. After an intentional walk to Felipe Alou, Gene Michael tried to squeeze Munson home—but missed the ball. Munson barreled home and crashed into Carlton Fisk, who was flattened but held the ball for the out. Fisk then "flipped Munson over to get rid of him. Munson threw a punch, they clinched and then Michael (ball one, strike one) jumped over Munson to throw a few for the visitors." [*New York Times*] Both dugouts cleared, both bullpens cleared. Both catchers were ejected, but Michael was not. Lyle lost his fifth straight game to Boston since being traded in 1972, as, after two outs in the bottom of the ninth, replacement catcher Bob Montgomery singled, Rick Miller walked and Mario Guerrero (the player to be named later in the Lyle-for-Cater trade) singled off Sparky to win the game. Munson admitted throwing the first punch, but argued, "Fisk was lucky he didn't get into a fight last night after the way he blocked the plate on Roy White."

September 13, 1973: Munson extracted some revenge for the August 1 melee, singling in a run in the bottom of the eighth to give the Yankees a 1-0 lead. The Sox tied it in the ninth on a Rick Miller homer. Munson walked in the tenth, but didn't score. In the bottom of the twelfth, Clarke and White singled, and Munson singled to center to break the tie and win the game. Bob Veale took the loss.

July 29, 1974: On the 27th, Bob Montgomery singled off Sparky Lyle in the bottom of the ninth to win the game for the Red Sox, 5-4. Boston won again on the 28th, 8-3. On the 29th, a Dwight Evans homer tied the game 1-1 in the bottom of the eighth, and it went into extra innings. Lyle walked Yaz, then threw wide to first when Montgomery laid down a bunt. With two on and no one out, he walked Burleson intentionally. With a force at every base, and the Yankees infield in, Doug Griffin was up. He bunted and Lyle couldn't handle that one, but the plate umpire ruled that the ball had struck Griffin while he was still in the batter's box. Griffin then grounded to short and Yaz was thrown out at the plate. Terry Hughes got one of his six RBIs of the season with a sacrifice fly to center. It won the game for the Red Sox, 2-1.

September 9, 1974: The Yankees beat the Red Sox at Fenway Park, 6 -3. They hadn't won in Boston for over a year, since July 21, 1973—and that was their only Boston victory in all of 1973.

September 10, 1974: The Yankees purchase designated hitter Alex Johnson from the Texas Rangers, and Johnson flew to Boston. He arrived in the middle of a tied game, put on the pinstripes, and hit a homer to give New York a 2-1 victory.

July 27, 1975: Bill Lee shut out the Yankees 1-0; the sole Sox run coming in the top of the ninth when Fred Lynn reached on an error. With two outs, he stole second and then scored on a single by Rick Miller and an error by Alomar. Roger Moret and the Sox more handily won the second game of the day, 6-0. The Red Sox won the pennant, too.

September 27, 1975: The Yankees secure the pennant for the Red Sox, by winning two games against Baltimore.

October 21, 1975: In Game Six of the World Series, Carlton Fisk's home run in the bottom of the twelfth inning is one of the most dramatic walk-off home runs in history.

May 20, 1976: It was the first meeting of the year between the two rivals, and the Yanks were ahead, 1-0. It was the bottom of the sixth at the

Stadium, and there were two outs. Lou Piniella was on second when Otto Velez hit to right field. Even though Dwight Evans had already cut down Fred Stanley at the plate in the third inning, Piniella decided to go for it. Evans cut him down, too, when Fisk held onto the ball (just as he had on August 1, 1973 when Munson tried to bowl him over). Piniella upended Fisk, who bounced up and onto Piniella. Both players got into it, and things seemed to be settling down again when Graig Nettles started punching Sox starter Bill Lee. The fight resumed with redoubled intensity. Nettles later said he'd thrown Lee on the ground, and apparently hurt his shoulder. Then, he said, Lee was yelling at him "until I couldn't take it any longer. I socked him in the eye, and he hit me." [*New York Times*] Lee had to leave the game—rushed to Lenox Hill Hospital—suffering a torn shoulder and some torn ligaments and looked to be through for the season. Though Ed Figueroa had kept the Sox scoreless until this time, Boston immediately exploded in the top of the seventh and went on an eight-run rampage over the final three innings. The Sox had never hit a home run off him, but he gave up a two-run shot by the Rooster (Rick Burleson) in the seventh. Yaz hit homers in both the eighth and the ninth, and Boston won, 8-2.

May 21-23, 1976: The Yankees won the next day's game, 6-5, in twelve innings. The day after that, they won again in extra innings, 1-0 (11 innings, Catfish Hunter going all the way). Boston took the fourth game of the set, 7-6, when Yaz walked in the top of the ninth and forced in what proved to be the winning run.

April 5, 1977: The Yankees acquire Bucky Dent from White Sox for outfielder Oscar Gamble and pitchers Bob Polinsky and Dewey Hoyt.

June 17, 1977: At Fenway, the Sox bang out four home runs in the first inning against Catfish Hunter, and win 11-1.

June 18, 1977: The Yankees fight amongst themselves as manager Billy Martin feels Reggie Jackson is loafing on a Jim Rice bloop to right. Martin stops at the mound and relieves pitcher Mike Torrez, then embarrasses Reggie by walking out to right field and removing Jackson from the game. Martin has to be restrained from attacking Jackson after both argue in the Fenway visitors dugout. Boston wins 10-4, powered by five Sox home runs.

June 19, 1977: Red Sox hit five more homers and again beat Yankees 11-1. In three-game series, Boston hit 16 homers while the Yankees failed to hit one.

June 24, 1977: Roy White hits a game-tying two-run homer in bottom of the ninth, and Yankees go on to win game the (6-5) the next inning. This game is seen to be a major Yankees turning-point victory as New York wins its next two games as well, nearly erasing the Sox lead in standings.

July 19, 1977: The All-Star Game is held once again at Yankee Stadium. The National League wins 7-5. Boston's George Scott hits two-run HR in ninth.

August 14, 1977: Carl Yastrzemski's 506th career double moves him past Babe Ruth in the two-bagger department.

August 15, 1977: Jim Rice doubles and becomes first Sox player since Ted Williams (1939) to have 20 homers, 20 doubles, and 10 triples in a single season. The only other post-WWII players to have done this were all Yankees—Charlie Keller, Joe D, & Mickey Mantle.

October 1, 1977: Baltimore beats Boston at Fenway, thus handing the '77 pennant to New York, who won it while watching TV in the clubhouse, in the midst of a nearly three-hour long rain delay.

July 19, 1978: As of the close of play on the 14th, the Red Sox hold a seemingly insurmountable 14-game lead over the Yankees in the standings.

August 2, 1978: Red Sox and Yankees battle to a 4-4 tie in a game which is suspended after 14 innings, because of the 1:00 A.M. curfew. The game was picked up the next evening, and won by Boston 7-5 in 17 innings. The Red Sox then went on to win the regularly scheduled August 3 game, 8-1, this game being cut short by rain. Despite the two wins, the Red Sox lead over New York had shrunk to 8½ games.

September 7, 1978: The so-called "Boston Massacre" begins. The Bosox lead had eroded and the Yankees arrived in Boston four games behind. New York battered Boston, 15-3, on 21 hits.

September 8, 1978: Part two of the Boston Massacre saw the Yankees win, 13-2, as the Yanks accumulated 17 more hits and are helped by seven Red

Sox errors. The Yankees are now just two games behind.

September 9, 1978: With 11 more hits and a seven-run fourth inning, the Yankees won again (7-0) as the massacre continues; the Yankees are now just one game behind Boston.

September 10, 1978: The Yankees win game four of the Boston Massacre, 7-4. Eighteen more hits. They outscored Boston 42 runs to 9 over the four-game series, courtesy of 67 hits and 12 Sox errors. The 19 bases on balls doled out by Red Sox pitchers didn't hurt the Yankees cause. The Yankees took the lead on the 13th.

September 16, 1978: New York builds up a 3½ game lead over the Red Sox. Boston then comes back to life and wins twelve of its next fourteen games.

October 1, 1978: The Yankees lose their final game of the year, to Cleveland, while Boston wins theirs over the Blue Jays—it's the eighth straight win for Boston. The result is a dead tie for first place at the end of the regular season, setting the stage for a single-game playoff to be held in Boston the following day.

October 2, 1978: Yankees are losing 2-0 after six innings, but score four times in the top of the seventh with the famous Bucky Dent three-run home run being the big blow. The less said about it, the better, in the view of most Boston fans. The Yankees brought back Bucky Dent to throw out the first pitch in a 2004 ALCS game, hoping to fend off a Boston comeback. That time, it didn't work.

November 7, 1978: Red Sox leftfielder Jim Rice won the M.V.P. and Yankees pitcher Ron Guidry won the Cy Young Award, coming in second in the M.V.P. voting.

November 13, 1978: Yankees sign Luis Tiant, a free agent who had starred for the Sox for several seasons. Tiant won 13 for New York in 1979.

May 18, 1979: In the first contest between the Yankees and the Red Sox that followed the October 2 playoff game, the Yankees come to Fenway and win, 10-0.

June 29, 1979: In the top of the 13th inning, Jerry Remy singles home Rick Burleson to provide a 3-2 Red Sox win in New York.

September 12, 1979: Carl Yastrzemski gets hit 3000th hit off Yankees pitcher Jim Beatttie. Yaz becomes first A.L. player with 3000 hits and 400 home runs. As a bonus, Boston beats New York 9-2.

October 27, 1980: Falling deeply behind New York in the standings, the Sox turn to another former Yankees manager (they'd hired Joe McCarthy in the 1940s), seeking salvation. They hire "the Major", Ralph Houk. It doesn't really work, though the Sox get back to within four games of the lead in 1981.

September 12, 1981: Boston's Bobby Ojeda has a no-hitter going into the ninth inning. The first two batters up are both pinch-hitters (Rick Cerone and Dave Winfield) and they both double. Ojeda is only holding a 2-1 lead at this point, with Winfield on second and no one out. Houk calls in Mark Clear, who struck out two, walked a man, then got the final out on a Reggie Jackson fly ball to left field.

September 19, 1981: Losing 5-1 as they entered the bottom of the eighth inning at Fenway Park, the Yankees brought in Ron Davis in relief of Ron Guidry. After two routine outs, the Red Sox routed Ron Davis and dominated Dave LaRoche, scoring seven runs in the bottom of the eighth to take an 8-5 lead. Mark Clear held the lead in the ninth.

June 8, 1982: In the first meeting of the year, the Red Sox scored once in the bottom of the tenth to top New York, 4-3. Mark Clear got the win.

October 3, 1982: Not that it really mattered, given that the Sox were in third place and the Yankees were in fifth place, but on the final game of the season, Boston beat New York, 5-3, in eleven innings. The first Sox hit during the final frame was by Roger LaFrancois, who was 2-for-5 on the day. Three batters later, he scored the winning run. LaFrancois had been with the team for the entire year, and finished the season batting an even .400. Trouble is, he was only 4-for-10, some 492.2 plate appearances short of qualifying for the batting title.

February 6, 1983: Commissioner Bowie Kuhn says that Mickey Mantle is no longer welcome in baseball due to his affiliation with an Atlantic City casino.

March 25, 1983: George Steinbrenner is fined $50,000 for accusing N.L. umpires of favoring N.L. teams during spring training games. Other notable Steinbrenner fines:

> $300,000 for comments after the famous Pine Tar game

> $25,000 plus $200,000 in damages for tampering in Dave Winfield trade

> $25,000 for criticizing umpires' competence during the 1998 American League Championship Series

> numerous $5,000 fines for tampering with unsigned players, questioning the integrity of an umpire and calling the co-owners of the White Sox "Abbott and Costello"

> [Source: Art McDonald's book *This Date in Yankee Hating*, p. 103]

July 4, 1983: Dave Righetti pitched a 4-0 no-hitter against the Red Sox in Yankee Stadium. Rice walked in the first, Nichols walked in the fifth. Two men left on base. An excellent performance.

June 14, 1984: After seven innings, Boston was losing 7-5. They scored six times in the eighth to take the lead, but Bob Stanley coughed up four in the top of the ninth. Score tied, heading into the tenth. Willie Randolph's solo home run in the top of the tenth beat Stanley and the Sox.

May 8, 10, and 11, 1985: The Sox season gets off to a promising start as Boston sweeps its first three games, all against the visiting Yankees at Fenway Park. The Red Sox win the first two in New York as well, including a 5-4 11-inning win on April 23. Losing all six games to New York in August wasn't helpful, though, and the Sox were never really in serious contention.

January 14, 1986: Pitching prospect Curt Schilling is selected by the Red Sox in the second round of the free-agent draft.

March 28, 1986: The Yankees trade Don Baylor to the Red Sox for designated hitter Mike Easler.

April 29, 1986: Roger Clemens set a major league record, striking out 20 Mariners. "Rocket Roger" Clemens won both the Cy Young Award and MVP in 1986. Later, he became perhaps the most hated former Red Sox player. After leaving the Yankees, though, Clemens won his seventh Cy Young Award for the Houston Astros and won a new measure of respect from Red Sox fans—at the same time that a lot of Yankees fans in turn felt spurned.

October 4, 1986: Dave Righetti got the save in both halves of a doubleheader, 5-3 and 3-1. His 46 saves on the season set a new record.

October 5, 1986: The Red Sox lost the last four games of the season to the Yankees—but it didn't matter. They'd already clinched the pennant days beforehand.

October 18 and 19, 1986: Boston got off to a great start in the World Series against another New York team, winning the first two games on the road, in Shea Stadium. When the Series came back to Shea, though, on the 25th, the Red Sox found themselves one strike away from the Championship—and things went awry.

June 26, 1987: The Red Sox built up a 9-0 lead early, with the Rocket on the mound—but the Yankees didn't wait long to respond. They scored 11 runs of their own in the third, and ultimately won the game 12-11 in 10 innings. Despite all the scoring, and Boston's 15 hits, not one of them was a Wade Boggs hit. His 25-game hitting streak had ended.

September 29, 1987: Don Mattingly hit his sixth grand slam of the season—a record—this one off Red Sox pitcher Bruce Hurst. Yankees won 6-0.

October 2, 1988: Despite dropping six of their last seven games, the Red

Sox won the A.L. East, 3½ games ahead of the fifth-place Yankees. The Oakland A's swept the Sox in the ALCS, 4 games to 0.

September 25, 1989: Boston's Wade Boggs—later to become a Yankee—went 4-for-5 against New York. Boggs became the first player in modern baseball history to obtain 200 hits and 100 walks for four years in a row.

January 9, 1990: George Steinbrenner makes a payment of $40,000 to Howard Spira, for which he is later banned from baseball for life. Sort of. For a while.

June 6, 1990: Bucky Dent is fired as manager of Yankees. His .404 winning percentage was the worst of any Yankees manager since Babe Ruth was purchased from the Red Sox.

June 7, 1990: The day after Dent was fired, a two-out single in the fifth inning by Jesse Barfield was the only hit the New Yorkers could muster. Greg Harris (eight innings) and Jeff Reardon (one inning) combined to throw a one-hitter and the Red Sox won, 3-0. The Yankees only had two hits the day before, both in the second inning. Boddicker then held them hitless the last seven innings.

September 1, 1990: Mike Greenwell hits an inside-the-park grand slam in the fifth inning, and helps the Sox crush New York 15-1. It's not as though the Yankees didn't try; two outfielders were injured, both having to leave the game, in the same seven-run Red Sox fifth inning.

October 3, 1990: The Red Sox finished first in the A.L. East, and the Yankees finished last. Come the ALCS, though, and just as in 1988, the Oakland A's won four games and swept. Boston scored a total of four runs in the four games, one run per game.

November 12, 1992: Yankees pitcher Steve Howe, suspended eight times already for drug offenses, was reinstated by an arbitrator.

December 15, 1992: Wade Boggs, five-time American League batting champion for the Red Sox, signed with the Yankees as a free agent. He'd only hit .259 for the Sox in 1992, but recovered to post four more over-.300 seasons with New York.

September 18, 1993: The Yankees were losing 3-1 in the ninth when a fan ran on the field, interrupting the game just as Yankee Mike Stanley popped up to the Red Sox left-fielder. The out did not count and, when play resumed, the Yankees rallied for three runs to win 4-3.

May 2, 1995: V for Victory. In the third inning, John Valentin hit a grand slam off New York's Sterling Hitchcock. The very next inning, Mo Vaughn hit a grand slam off Hitchcock's replacement, Brian Boehringer. That was all the scoring in the 8-0 Red Sox win before a subdued Yankee Stadium crowd.

September 8, 1995: Sox players Scott Hatteberg, Lee Tinsley, Carlos Rodriguez, and Chris Donnels all hit consecutive pinch-hits against the Yankees, setting a major league record. Boston only mustered seven hits in the game, though, and lost 8-4.

October 6, 1995: As in 1988 and 1990, the Red Sox had again won the A.L. East. As in 1988 and 1990, the Red Sox couldn't win a single game in the post-season, this time being swept by the Indians. The wild card Yankees at least won a couple of games in the new Division Series, but didn't advance to the ALCS.

May 7, 1996: Yankees pitcher David Cone is diagnosed with an aneurysm in his right arm, requiring surgery. Cone, a two-time Cy Young Award winner, pitched well for New York until a disastrous 4-14 season in 2000. He signed with Boston as a free agent for 2001; he won 9 and lost 7.

July 17, 1996: Boston was at home, ahead 9-2 after six. The Yankees scored three in the seventh, two in the eighth, and four in the ninth to take an 11-9 lead. John Wetteland had saved 27 straight games, but after getting one out in the bottom of the ninth, he walked Tim Naehring on four pitches and then gave up a double off the Wall to former Yankee Mike Stanley. He struck out Kevin Mitchell, and walked Reggie Jefferson to load the bases. Pinch-hitter Troy O'Leary doubled off the Wall to tie the score, and Jeff Frye (0-for-5 on the day) finally connected, singling to right field to win the game for the Red Sox.

December 11, 1996: The Yankees sign free agent relief pitcher Mike Stanton, who had played with the Red Sox in 1996.

May 22, 1997: The Sox got 19 hits, and left 16 men on base, but scored eight times and beat the Yankees, 8-2. Cordero was 5-for-6 and Naehring was 4-for-6. Tom Gordon started and won for the Red Sox.

May 30, 1997: Mo Vaughn hit three homers for the Red Sox, as Boston beat New York 10-4 at Fenway. New York pitchers gave up six HRs in all; reliever Danny Rios made his major league debut, only to surrender homers to the first two batters he faced.

August 13, 1997: Boston traded Mike Stanley—a catcher and DH—back to New York after a year and a half with the Red Sox.

April 11, 1998: Pedro Martinez' first Fenway start with the Red Sox. The Red Sox win 5-0 and Pedro strikes out Dan Wilson for his 1000th career K.

May 31, 1998: Over 55,000 fans at Yankee Stadium see the Red Sox score 11 runs in the third inning, and beat the Yankees, 13-7.

September 27, 1998: Does a team finishing 22 games out of first place deserve to make the playoffs? The Yankees won their 114th game on September 27, and the Red Sox won their 92nd. Those 92 wins were enough to win the Wild Card slot for the Red Sox, despite finishing 22 games behind the Yankees. The 92 wins placed them ahead of even the winners in the other two divisions.

September 29, 1998: After losing 13 consecutive post-season games, the Sox finally won one, beating the Indians by a convincing 11-3 margin. They promptly lost the next three, and the Division Series as well.

January 5, 1999: George Steinbrenner apologized and on this day Yogi Berra announced the end of his self-imposed exile and boycott of the Yankees, some 14 years after Berra was dismissed as Yankees manager after only a 16-game stint.

February 18, 1999: Toronto traded five-time Cy Young Award winner Roger Clemens to the Yankees for pitchers David Wells and Graeme Lloyd, and infielder Homer Bush, thus assuring that both Boston and Toronto fans would unite in dislike for their (former) ace pitcher.

May 22, 1999: Roger Clemens won his 19th consecutive game for the Yankees, setting a new A. L. record.

July 13, 1999: In the All-Star Game (held at Fenway Park) Pedro Martinez strikes out the first four batters he faces: Barry Larkin, Larry Walker, Sammy Sosa, and Mark McGwire.

September 10, 1999: At Yankee Stadium, Pedro Martinez threw a complete game one-hitter, 3-0. Martinez faced only one batter over the minimum, and racked up 17 strikeouts—the most Yankees ever to strike out in a single game. Getting stronger as the game progressed, he struck out the side in the fifth, seventh, and ninth innings. New York only hit one ball in fair territory after the fourth.

October 13, 1999: For the very first time, the Sox and Yankees face each other in post-season competition. Boston got off to a quick 3-0 lead, but New York tied it up and Bernie Williams won it with a walk-off home run off Rod Beck in the bottom of the tenth inning, 4-3. The Yankees won again on October 14th, 3-2.

October 16, 1999: A classic matchup featuring New York's (ex-Red Sox) Roger Clemens against Boston's new ace Pedro Martinez in Game Three of the American League Championship Series. Clemens was chased early, and the final score was Red Sox 13 (21 hits) to the Yankees 1 (on just three hits). New York won the war, though, with an easy 9-2 the next day.

October 18, 1999: "El Duque" (Orlando Hernandez) pitched eight shutout innings and Derek Jeter hit a two-run homer in this 6-1 Yankees win of Game 5 of the ALCS. Yankees win their 36th pennant.

May 28, 2000: Pedro beat former Boston ace Roger Clemens in a 2-0 game at Yankee Stadium, decided by a two-run Trot Nixon HR in the top of the ninth off Rocket Roger.

June 19, 2000: Longtime Red Sox season ticket holder Lib Dooley died on the morning of the 19th. The very day before, the White Sox had beaten the Yankees 17-4, so the New Yorkers were spoiling for a fight. The evening of Lib Dooley's death, the Yankees dealt the Red Sox the most lopsided loss ever suffered at Fenway, whipping the Sox 22-1. Nine runs were scored in the eighth and seven more in the ninth, as New York piled on late. Winning pitcher for New York was Ramiro Mendoza, who allowed just six hits in seven innings. The two mop-up pitchers didn't allow a single hit in the last two frames.

November 30, 2000: Mike Mussina, courted heavily by the Red Sox, signed with the Yankees instead. He could have become a true hero in pennant-starved Boston, instead of just another fine pitcher for the Yankees. Ask Curt Schilling what that feels like. The last World Series the Yankees won was the one they won the month before Mussina signed.

April 13, 2001: In the first meeting of the year, the Yankees scored once in the top of the tenth, but Boston banged out two runs in the bottom of the tenth to take a 3-2 win. When the Yankees grabbed the lead, they brought in their closer, Mariano Rivera, to face the Sox. An out, a single, an out, a single. Nixon and Everett moved up on a wild pitch. With first base open, Rivera had the choice: face Manny Ramirez, or walk him to set up a force at every base and face Troy O'Leary? He decided to face Ramirez, because Manny was 0-for-12 lifetime against Rivera, and six of those at-bats had been strikeouts. Not this time. Manny singled up the middle, drove in two, and won the game.

May 23, 2001: The first time ex-Yankee David Cone faced his old team, he also faced Andy Pettitte. Cone allowed 3 earned runs in five innings, pitching pretty well, but Pettitte pitched better. The Yankees won, 7-3. Cone hit both Bernie Williams and old battery mate Jorge Posada. Jeter went 5-for-5.

May 24, 2001: Pedro Martinez faced Mike Mussina. Both pitchers struck out 12, and both pitchers allowed only six hits, but the Yankees scored one more run and won the game, 2-1. Were the Yankees Pedro's daddy? Was Pedro cursed? The Sox had lost Pedro's last five starts against the Yankees, dating back to June 14, 2000.

May 30, 2001: Pedro's next start against New York (and Mussina) was also a strong one, and he won this time, allowing just four hits (to Mussina's five). Final score: 3-0 in Boston's favor. After the game, Pedro said, "I'm starting to hate talking about the Yankees. The questions are so stupid. They're wasting my time. It's getting kind of old. Maybe they should just wake up the Bambino, and have him face me and maybe I'll drill him in the ass." Maybe, also, Pedro shouldn't have said that. The Red Sox and Yankees matched up seven more times in 2001, and the Red Sox lost every one of them. Three of those seven games were Pedro starts, including the September 7 game at the Stadium where Pedro was bounced after three innings. It would be more than a year later (July 19, 2002) before he beat the Yanks once again.

September 2, 2001: You can't get any closer to a perfect game than to retire the first 26 batters in order and have two strikes on batter #27. David Cone already had a perfect game on his resume, and he pitched a whale of a game on September 2, shutting out the Yankees for eight innings, allowing just one run to come across in the top of the ninth. Cone was up against Mike Mussina, though, and it was Mussina who was working on a perfecto. Carl Everett was the batter, a pinch-hitter. Mussina got two quick strikes on him, then threw a ball bringing the count to 1-2. In the May 24 game noted above, Mussina struck out Everett four times, every time on high fastballs. He fired in a high fastball, but Everett was ready and lined a clean single into left-center field.

August 27 and 28, 2002: Hosting the Yankees for two games, the Sox failed to score even once. Casey Fossum lost to starter David Wells, 6-0, and Mike Mussina beat Pedro Martinez, 7-0. The Yankees had not blanked the Boston back-to-back at Fenway since World War II (September 11 and September 12, 1943).

December 26, 2002: The day after Christmas, Red Sox president Larry

Lucchino ignites a bit of a firestorm by tweaking George Steinbrenner, declaring "The Evil Empire extends its tentacles even into Latin America." Lucchino tweaked because he was piqued: the Red Sox had put on a full-court press to sign Cuban exile Jose Contreras and thought they had the inside track, only to be scooped by New York.

Steinbrenner fired back, saying that the Sox offered more than the Yankees had, and that clearly Contreras simply preferred to play for the Yankees. Other Yankees officials said that Contreras had been offended by Boston's attempt to cut him off from other teams by, for instance, booking all the rooms in the hotel where the pitcher was staying. It was implied that the Sox had Contreras tailed, too. Steinbrenner called Lucchino "baseball's foremost chameleon of all time." The invective reached such a peak that the Commissioner urged both parties to cool it. Contreras went just 7-2 for the Yankees, and was traded away after the 2003 season.

October 8, 2003: New York and Boston meet again in post-season play. At Yankee Stadium, Boston wins Game One behind the pitching of Tim Wakefield, while Mike Mussina yields home runs to David Ortiz, Todd Walker, and Manny Ramirez. Boston 5, New York 3.

October 9, 2003: Andy Pettitte out-pitched Derek Lowe, who was pitching on short rest. New York 6, Boston 2.

October 11, 2003: At Fenway Park, the Yankees overcome an early Red Sox lead, in a classic Clemens/Martinez matchup. Manny Ramirez takes exception to a Clemens pitch, and both benches clear. Yankees coach (and former Sox skipper Don Zimmer) charges Pedro Martinez and is flipped to the ground; after the game, Zimmer apologizes. In the ninth inning, blood is drawn as Yankees reliever Jeff Nelson suddenly assaults groundskeeper Paul Williams, objecting to Williams' rooting for the Red Sox. Yankees outfielder Karim Garcia leaps over bullpen wall and attacks the groundskeeper, too. Both Yankees players are charged by police, and ultimately sentenced to perform community service. New York 4, Boston 3.

October 13, 2003: Wakefield again outduels Mussina, and the Red Sox even the Series at two each. Boston 3, New York 2.

October 14, 2003: It's another one run game as the "other Boomer" David

Wells holds the Sox to just one run in seven innings, and New York takes a 3-games-to-2 lead. New York 4, Boston 2.

October 15, 2003: Back at the Stadium, the Sox took an early 4-1 lead but then gave up five runs to go down 6-4. Garciaparra, Ramirez, and Ortiz all hit reliever Jose Contreras safely in the seventh and the Sox tied it up. The call went out to the bullpen and Felix Heredia threw a wild pitch, moving runners to second and third, then walked Trot Nixon intentionally—but also walked Johnny Damon quite unintentionally, forcing in what was the go-ahead run. Boston 9, New York 6.

October 16, 2003: Game Seven of the ALCS. With the Red Sox taking a 4-0 lead early in the game, Boston's hopes soar. Boston manager Grady Little chooses to stick with his tiring ace Pedro Martinez a little too long and the Red Sox lead evaporates. After midnight, it becomes October 17 and New York ultimately wins 6-5 in the 11th inning on Aaron Boone's home run.

October 27, 2003: Choosing not to pick up the option on Grady Little's contract for 2004, the manager was not technically fired—but he certainly wasn't coming back to work for the Red Sox.

October 29, 2003: The Red Sox offer Manny Ramirez on irrevocable waivers, available to any team in baseball for $25,000 (and assuming his contract). No one bites.

November 28, 2003: Curt Schilling is acquired from the Arizona Diamondbacks in exchange for Casey Fossum, Brandon Lyon, Jorge de la Rosa, and Michael Goss.

December 14, 2003: The Red Sox sign free agent reliever, 2003 Fireman of the Year Keith Foulke.

February 16, 2004: The New York Yankees trade with the Texas Rangers and acquire Alex Rodriguez. Boston was trying to reach a deal for A-Rod two months earlier. The potential for dissatisfaction in the Red Sox clubhouse is great, given the preference that Sox ownership seemed to show for Rodriguez over Nomar Garciaparra, and given the placing of Manny Ramirez on waivers (no takers).

April 24, 2004: Mark Bellhorn hits a sacrifice fly in the top of the twelfth inning at Yankee Stadium for a 3-2 Red Sox win. It is one of three Sox sac flies in the game.

July 1, 2004: Manny Ramirez homers in the top of the 13th inning, but the Yankees come back with two runs to win. The highlight film shows Derek Sanderson Jeter (he was named after the famous Boston hockey player) diving headfirst into the stands to snare a foul ball, emerging bloodied and bruised moments later—with the ball.

July 24, 2004: Bill Mueller hits a three-run homer off Mariano Rivera in the bottom of the ninth inning and wins the game for the Red Sox, 11-10. Earlier in the games, both benches emptied and punches were thrown, with Jason Varitek sticking his glove in Alex Rodriguez's face.

September 17, 2004: Rivera blows another save, yielding ninth-inning homers to both Orlando Cabrera and Johnny Damon in 3-2 Red Sox victory.

October 5, 2004: The visiting Red Sox beat the Anaheim Angels handily, 9-3, in the first game of the American League Division Series.

October 6, 2004: The Red Sox roll again, winning 8-3.

October 8, 2004: A Sox lead of 6-1 is wiped out by a five-run Angels seventh inning. Tied after regulation, David Ortiz hits a walk-off two-run homer in the bottom of the tenth inning. The Sox complete a sweep of the Angels and move on to face the Yankees in the League Championship Series.

October 12, 2004: An obviously sub-par Curt Schilling is banged around for six runs in the first three frames, and the Yankees post an 8-0 lead after six innings. The Red Sox put a scare into them with five runs in the seventh and two more in the eighth, but New York wins, 10-7.

October 13, 2004: A close 3-1 win for the Yankees as 55,000-plus patrons jeer Pedro Martinez. John Olerud's two-run homer seals Pedro's fate in the sixth inning. Boston fans learn that 21-game winner Schilling is most likely lost for the rest of the year due to a crippling tendon problem in his ankle.

October 16, 2004: Though the score is 6-6 after three innings, the Yankees begin to tee off on Boston pitching, and post a final score of 19-8, a crushing and seemingly fatal blow to Boston's pennant hopes for 2004. The Yankees had now won the first three games in the League Championship

Series. Never in baseball history has a team faced a 3-0 deficit in a seven-game series and won.

October 17, 2004: The Red Sox take a deep breath and stay alive another day, as they tie a 4-3 game in the bottom of the ninth, battle for three more innings, and win in the bottom of the twelfth inning on a walk-off home run by David Ortiz. The blown save by Mariano Rivera is his third against the Red Sox in 2004. The game lasted 5 hours and 2 minutes, a playoff record.

October 18, 2004: Deja-vu all over again? This game lasts 5 hours and 49 minutes, and is decided in the bottom of the fourteenth inning with another walk-off hit, this time a single, by the same David Ortiz (see October 8 and see October 17). Boston 5, New York 4.

October 19, 2004: Curt Schilling, after temporary surgery to hold his tendon in place, pitches a courageous game as blood seeps through his socks. Mark Bellhorn's three-run homer in the top of the fourth inning makes the difference in a 4-2 Boston win that—incredibly—ties the Series at three games each and sets up a Game Seven showdown between the two rivals for the second year in a row.

October 20, 2004: History is made as the Red Sox score early and often, largely thanks to Johnny Damon's two home runs (one a grand slam). Derek Lowe's strong pitching limits the Yankees, and the Red Sox cruise to a win, 10-3.

October 23, 2004: Game One of the 2004 World Series. Despite Boston taking an early 7-2 lead, the St. Louis Cardinals fight back to tie it in the top of the eighth, 9-9. The Sox make four errors but still win as Mark Bellhorn hits the tie-breaker, a two-run shot off the Pesky Pole. Boston 11, St. Louis 9.

October 24, 2004: Schilling, sutured once more, takes the mound and holds the Cardinals back (despite four more Red Sox errors). Boston 6, St. Louis 2.

October 26, 2004: The Series shifts to St. Louis and the Cardinals hope to win at home, but their offense remains anemic and Pedro Martinez is in fine form. Manny Ramirez drives in two, and the Red Sox win, 4-1. No one has ever come back from a deficit of 3-0 in a seven-game series—until one week beforehand. It doesn't look good for the winningest team in 2004, the 105-win St. Louis Cardinals.

October 27, 2004: For the first time in 86 years, the Boston Red Sox win the World Series. The Sox scored first, as they had in every game of the Series, and Derek Lowe never let the Cardinals score, nor did the Boston bullpen. Boston wins, 3-0. The Sox swept the Angels. The Yankees pushed them right to the brink, but Boston won four in a row to win the pennant— and then won four more in a row, sweeping the World Series.

Players Who Played for Both Teams

	Boston Red Sox, 1901-2004						New York Yankees, 1903-2004					
	Years	G	AB	BA	HR	RBI	Years	G	AB	BA	HR	RBI
Doc Adkins	1902-1902	4	9	.222	0	0	1903	2	3	.000	0	0
Ivy Andrews	1932-1933	63	93	.172	0	3	1931-1938	41	47	.149	0	6
Pete Appleton	1932	11	17	.176	0	1	1933	1	0	.000	0	0
Neal Ball	1912-1913	41	103	.184	0	10	1907-1909	155	519	.241	0	45
Scott Bankhead	1993-1994	67	0	.000	0	0	1995	20	0	.000	0	0
Willie Banks	2001-2002	34	0	.000	0	0	1997-1998	14	0	.000	0	0
Don Baylor	1986-1987	268	924	.238	47	151	1983-1985	420	1504	.267	71	265
Juan Beniquez	1971-1975	233	799	.274	8	62	1979	62	142	.254	4	17
Lou Berberet	1958-1958	57	167	.210	2	18	1954-1955	7	10	.400	0	5
Doug Bird	1983-1983	22	0	.000	0	0	1980-1981	39	0	.000	0	0
Wade Boggs	1982-1992	1625	6213	.338	85	687	1993-1997	601	2240	.313	24	324
Darren Bragg	1996-1998	340	1144	.264	20	136	2001	5	4	.250	0	0
Ken Brett	1967-1971	79	61	.295	3	6	1976	2	0	.000	0	0
Hal Brown	1953-1955	72	83	.253	1	14	1962	2	1	.000	0	0
George Burns	1922-1923	293	1109	.317	19	155	1928-1929	13	13	.154	0	0
Joe Bush	1918-1921	136	325	.286	0	40	1922-1924	137	332	.313	3	45
Ray Caldwell	1919	33	48	.271	0	4	1910-1918	472	951	.250	7	98
Jose Canseco	1995-1996	198	756	.298	52	163	2000	37	111	.243	6	19
Roy Carlyle	1925-1926	138	441	.311	9	65	1926	35	52	.385	0	11
Danny Cater	1972-1974	211	638	.262	14	83	1970-1971	276	1010	.290	10	126
Rick Cerone	1988-1989	186	560	.255	7	75	1980-1990	587	1842	.249	31	203
Ben Chapman	1937-1938	240	903	.324	13	137	1930-1936	910	3539	.305	60	589
Jack Chesbro	1909	1	2	.500	0	1	1903-1909	270	730	.201	4	53
Jack Clark	1991-1992	221	738	.236	33	120	1988	150	496	.242	27	93
Tony Clark	2002	90	275	.207	3	29	2004	106	253	.221	16	49
Roger Clemens	1984-1996	383	1	1.000	0	0	1999-2003	8	13	.154	0	1
Tex Clevenger	1954	25	14	.214	0	0	1961-1962	43	8	.125	0	1
Lou Clinton	1960-1964	412	1427	.252	49	198	1966-1967	86	163	.227	5	23
Michael Coleman	1997-1999	10	29	.172	0	2	2001	12	38	.211	1	7
Rip Collins	1922	33	76	.158	0	4	1920-1921	64	118	.161	0	8
David Cone	2001	1	1	.000	0	0	1995-2000	28	12	.167	0	2
Dusty Cooke	1933-1936	404	1257	.284	15	161	1930-1932	122	255	.267	7	35
Guy Cooper	1914-1915	11	7	.000	0	0	1914	1	1	.000	0	1
Lou Criger	1901-1908	628	1943	.208	6	193	1910	27	69	.188	0	4
Babe Dahlgren	1935-1936	165	582	.265	10	70	1937-1940	327	1143	.248	27	163
Al DeVormer	1923-1923	74	209	.258	0	18	1921-1922	46	108	.269	0	18
Patsy Dougherty	1902-1904	296	1223	.325	4	97	1904-1906	234	922	.269	9	55
Joe Dugan	1922	84	341	.287	3	38	1922-1928	785	3043	.286	22	320
Cedric Durst	1930	102	302	.245	1	24	1927-1930	239	485	.249	6	71
Mike Easler	1984-1985	311	1169	.288	43	165	1986-1987	211	657	.297	18	78
Clyde Engle	1910-1914	512	1680	.265	6	163	1909-1910	140	505	.277	3	71
Todd Erdos	2001	10	0	.000	0	0	1998-2000	7	1	.000	0	0
Steve Farr	1994	11	0	.000	0	0	1991-1993	159	0	.000	0	0
Doc Farrell	1935	4	7	.286	0	1	1932-1933	70	156	.231	0	10
Alex Ferguson	1922-1925	119	217	.111	0	13	1918-1925	39	35	.171	0	3

	Boston Red Sox, 1901-2004						New York Yankees, 1903-2004					
	Years	G	AB	BA	HR	RBI	Years	G	AB	BA	HR	RBI
Wes Ferrell	1934-1937	188	396	.308	17	17	1938-1939	8	20	.150	0	2
Chick Fewster	1922-1923	113	367	.248	0	24	1917-1922	228	642	.271	3	45
John Flaherty	1992-1993	48	91	.176	0	4	2003-2004	87	232	.259	10	30
Tony Fossas	1991-1994	239	0	.000	0	0	1999	5	0	.000	0	0
Eddie Foster	1920-1922	285	907	.265	0	79	1910	30	83	.133	0	1
Ray Francis	1925	6	8	.125	0	0	1925	4	0	.000	0	0
Billy Gardner	1962-1963	89	283	.247	0	13	1961-1962	45	100	.210	1	0
Milt Gaston	1929-1931	100	214	.192	1	15	1924	29	27	.222	0	1
Frank Gilhooley	1919	48	112	.241	0	1	1913-1918	250	907	.277	2	55
Joe Glenn	1940	22	47	.128	0	4	1932-1938	138	385	.252	1	54
Tom Gordon	1996-1999	170	0	.000	0	0	2004	4	1	.000	0	0
Randy Gumpert	1952	10	5	.000	0	0	1946-1948	73	61	.115	0	1
Chris Hammond	1997	29	0	.000	0	0	2003	5	0	.000	0	0
Harry Harper	1920	27	50	.120	0	1	1921	8	16	.125	0	1
Greg Harris	1989-1994	287	0	.000	0	0	1994	3	0	.000	0	0
Joe Harris	1922-1925	402	1401	.315	23	209	1914	2	1	.000	0	0
Fred Heimach	1926-1926	26	44	.295	0	3	1928-1929	54	79	.177	1	4
Charlie Hemphill	1901	136	545	.261	3	62	1908-1911	386	1238	.271	1	90
Rickey Henderson	2002	72	179	.223	5	16	1985-1989	596	2302	.288	78	258
Tim Hendryx	1920-1921	148	500	.304	0	95	1915-1917	153	495	.251	5	50
Butch Hobson	1975-1980	623	2230	.252	94	358	1982	30	58	.172	0	3
Fred Hofmann	1927-1928	165	416	.250	0	40	1919-1925	213	584	.245	7	53
Ken Holcombe	1953	3	2	.000	0	0	1945	23	15	.133	0	0
Elston Howard	1967-1968	113	319	.207	6	29	1955-1967	1492	5044	.279	161	733
Waite Hoyt	1919-1920	35	81	.123	0	3	1921-1930	365	805	.219	0	59
Tom Hughes	1902-1903	45	123	.301	1	16	1904	22	54	.241	0	2
Jackie Jensen	1954-1961	1039	3857	.282	170	733	1950-1952	108	257	.249	9	32
Deron Johnson	1974-1976	29	73	.192	1	5	1960-1961	19	23	.174	0	2
Hank Johnson	1933-1935	70	103	.214	0	4	1925-1932	166	264	.212	2	28
Roy Johnson	1932-1935	515	1954	.313	31	327	1936-1937	75	198	.273	1	25
Sam Jones	1916-1921	168	340	.197	2	25	1922-1926	210	352	.210	2	26
John Kennedy	1970-1974	265	783	.243	13	101	1967	78	179	.196	1	17
Red Kleinow	1910-1911	58	161	.155	1	8	1904-1910	522	1496	.219	2	127
John Knight	1907	98	360	.217	2	29	1909-1913	435	1494	.267	6	171
Andy Kosco	1972	17	47	.213	3	6	1968-1968	131	466	.240	15	59
Jack Kramer	1948-1949	50	108	.185	1	11	1951	19	10	.100	0	0
Frank LaPorte	1908	62	156	.237	0	15	1905-1910	516	1850	.274	6	227
Bill Lamar	1919	48	148	.291	0	14	1917-1919	50	167	.228	0	5
Lyn Lary	1934	129	419	.241	2	237	1929-1934	496	1717	.274	21	54
Louis Leroy	1910	1	1	.000	0	0	1905-1906	14	22	.136	0	1
Duffy Lewis	1910-1917	1184	4325	.289	27	779	1919-1920	248	924	.272	11	150
Jim Leyritz	1998	52	129	.287	8	24	1990-2000	577	1682	.263	58	191
Tim Lollar	1985-1986	50	2	.500	0	0	1980	14	0	.000	0	0
Joe Lucey	1925	10	15	.133	0	0	1920	3	3	.000	0	0
Sparky Lyle	1967-1971	260	49	.163	0	2	1972-1978	420	22	.182	0	1
Danny MacFayden	1926-1932	190	384	.161	1	24	1932-1934	64	122	.082	0	6
Jeff Manto	1996	22	48	.208	2	6	1999	6	8	.125	0	0
Josias Manzanillo	1991	1	0	.000	0	0	1995	11	0	.000	0	0
Carl Mays	1915-1919	181	379	.243	0	29	1919-1923	167	416	.279	3	49
Mickey McDermott	1948-1953	182	306	.281	3	44	1956-1956	46	52	.212	1	4
Jim McDonald	1950	9	3	.333	0	0	1952-1954	71	79	.177	0	7
Lynn McGlothen	1972-1973	28	53	.189	0	4	1982-1982	4	0	.000	0	0
Bob McGraw	1919	10	10	.100	0	1	1917-1920	24	13	.000	0	0
Deacon McGuire	1907-1908	7	5	.600	1	0	1904-1907	225	695	.230	0	8

	Boston Red Sox, 1901-2004						New York Yankees, 1903-2004					
	Years	G	AB	BA	HR	RBI	Years	G	AB	BA	HR	RBI
Marty McHale	1910-1916	8	9	.000	0	1	1913-1915	52	96	.156	0	2
Norm McMillan	1923	131	459	.253	0	42	1922	33	78	.256	0	11
Mike McNally	1915-1920	278	592	.231	0	17	1921-1924	202	465	.252	1	45
Bob Melvin	1993-1993	77	176	.222	3	23	1994	9	14	.286	1	3
Ramiro Mendoza	2003-2004	30	0	.000	0	0	1996-2002	133	3	.000	0	0
Elmer Miller	1922	44	147	.190	4	16	1915-1922	357	1230	.250	12	132
Buster Mills	1937	123	505	.295	7	58	1940	34	63	.397	1	15
Fred Mitchell	1901-1902	21	45	.156	0	4	1910	68	196	.230	0	18
Johnny Mitchell	1922-1923	151	550	.235	1	27	1921-1922	17	46	.239	0	2
Bill Monbouquette	1958-1965	263	498	.096	0	15	1967-1968	50	58	.138	0	2
Wilcy Moore	1931-1932	90	78	.128	0	1	1927-1933	171	127	.087	1	3
Jerry Moses	1965-1970	155	472	.278	13	57	1973	21	59	.254	0	3
Johnny Murphy	1947	32	11	.273	0	1	1932-1946	383	287	.150	0	19
Rob Murphy	1989-1990	142	0	.000	0	0	1994	3	0	.000	0	0
George Murray	1923-1924	67	77	.169	0	1	1922	22	18	.278	1	4
Bobo Newsom	1937	31	75	.253	0	4	1947	17	42	.095	0	1
Gus Niarhos	1952-1953	45	93	.140	0	6	1946-1950	153	311	.264	0	27
Harry Niles	1908-1910	180	635	.243	3	44	1908	96	362	.249	4	24
Otis Nixon	1994	103	398	.274	0	25	1983	13	14	.143	0	0
Les Nunamaker	1911-1914	131	356	.247	0	34	1914-1917	369	1076	.262	2	107
Mike O'Berry	1979	43	59	.169	1	4	1984	13	32	.250	0	5
Lefty O'Doul	1923	36	35	.143	0	4	1919-1922	40	37	.243	0	6
Steve O'Neill	1924	106	307	.238	0	38	1925	35	91	.286	1	13
Bob Ojeda	1980-1985	140	0	.000	0	0	1994	2	0	.000	0	0
Joe Oliver	2001	5	12	.250	0	1	2001	12	36	.250	1	2
Spike Owen	1986-1988	263	820	.244	8	76	1993-1993	103	334	.234	2	20
Ben Paschal	1920	9	28	.357	0	5	1924-1929	346	750	.309	24	133
Herb Pennock	1915-1934	204	354	.195	1	29	1923-1933	346	762	.188	3	62
Bill Piercy	1922-1924	82	126	.143	0	7	1917-1921	15	30	.200	0	2
George Pipgras	1933-1935	29	47	.191	0	4	1923-1933	247	492	.161	2	38
Bob Porterfield	1956-1958	55	72	.264	1	7	1948-1951	41	46	.174	0	1
Del Pratt	1921-1922	289	1128	.312	11	188	1918-1920	420	1578	.295	10	208
Curtis Pride	1997-2000	11	22	.273	1	1	2003	4	12	.083	1	1
Paul Quantrill	1992-1994	93	0	.000	0	0	2004	6	1	.000	0	0
Jack Quinn	1922-1925	145	281	.157	1	18	1909-1921	228	447	.179	4	34
Jeff Reardon	1990-1992	150	0	.000	0	0	1994	11	0	.000	0	0
Bill Renna	1958-1959	53	78	.218	4	20	1953	61	121	.314	2	13
Gordon Rhodes	1932-1935	127	236	.178	2	22	1929-1932	41	45	.244	0	4
Aaron Robinson	1951	26	74	.203	2	7	1943-1947	233	743	.284	29	128
Carlos Rodriguez	1994-1995	70	204	.294	1	18	1991	15	37	.189	0	2
Buddy Rosar	1950-1951	85	254	.252	2	25	1939-1942	252	751	.273	7	119
Braggo Roth	1919	63	227	.256	0	23	1921	43	152	.283	2	10
Muddy Ruel	1921-1931	262	802	.269	1	79	1917-1920	170	517	.251	1	47
Red Ruffing	1924-1930	237	438	.269	5	57	1930-1946	631	1475	.270	31	218
Allan Russell	1919-1922	112	177	.113	0	5	1915-1919	122	156	.179	0	6
Babe Ruth	1914-1919	391	1110	.308	49	230	1920-1934	2084	7217	.349	659	1971
Rey Sanchez	2002	107	357	.286	1	38	1997	38	138	.312	1	15
Ray Scarborough	1951-1952	65	86	.198	0	8	1952-1953	34	26	.231	1	3
Wally Schang	1918-1920	323	942	.291	4	126	1921-1925	529	1627	.297	16	214
Johnny Schmitz	1956	2	1	.000	0	0	1952-1953	8	5	.600	0	2
Dick Schofield	1969-1970	170	365	.230	3	34	1966	25	58	.155	0	2
Everett Scott	1914-1921	1096	3887	.246	7	346	1922-1925	481	1698	.254	13	173
George Scott	1966-1979	1192	4234	.257	154	562	1979	16	44	.318	1	6
Bob Seeds	1933-1934	90	236	.242	0	24	1936	13	42	.262	4	10

| | Boston Red Sox, 1901-2004 | | | | | | New York Yankees, 1903-2004 | | | | | |
	Years	G	AB	BA	HR	RBI	Years	G	AB	BA	HR	RBI
Howie Shanks	1923-1924	203	657	.256	3	82	1925	66	155	.258	1	18
Rollie Sheldon	1966	23	18	.111	0	0	1961-1965	92	117	.103	0	6
Ben Shields	1930	3	3	.000	0	0	1924-1925	6	8	.125	0	0
Ernie Shore	1914-1917	125	283	.117	0	17	1919-1920	34	39	.154	0	0
Bill Short	1966	8	1	.000	0	0	1960	10	15	.200	0	3
Norm Siebern	1967-1968	60	74	.149	0	7	1956-1959	308	1002	.273	29	129
Camp Skinner	1923	7	13	.231	0	1	1922	27	33	.182	0	2
Elmer Smith	1922	73	231	.286	6	32	1922-1923	91	210	.290	8	40
Lee Smith	1988-1990	139	0	.000	0	0	1993	8	0	.000	0	0
Jake Stahl	1903-1913	486	1648	.277	21	293	1908	75	274	.255	2	42
Mike Stanley	1996-2000	459	1425	.274	73	254	1992-1997	426	1372	.285	72	263
Mike Stanton	1995-1996	81	0	.000	0	0	1997-2002	87	5	.200	0	0
Tom Sturdivant	1960	40	22	.182	0	1	1955-1959	115	174	.218	0	5
Frank Tanana	1981	24	0	.000	0	0	1993	3	0	.000	0	0
Jesse Tannehill	1904-1908	135	347	.225	1	28	1903	40	111	.234	1	13
Lee Thomas	1964-1965	258	922	.265	35	117	1961	2	2	.500	0	0
Jack Thoney	1908-1911	148	476	.244	2	35	1904	36	128	.187	0	12
Hank Thormahlen	1921	23	23	.174	0	0	1917-1920	76	145	.166	0	17
Luis Tiant	1971-1978	274	77	.117	0	5	1979-1980	55	0	.000	0	0
Bob Tillman	1962-1967	527	1617	.236	49	224	1967	22	63	.254	2	9
Mike Torrez	1978-1982	161	0	.000	0	0	1977	31	0	.000	0	0
Frank Truesdale	1918	15	36	.278	0	2	1914-1914	77	217	.212	0	13
Bob Turley	1963-1963	11	14	.214	0	2	1955-1962	234	407	.113	2	21
Bob Unglaub	1904-1908	263	944	.251	2	100	1904	6	19	.211	0	2
Bobby Veach	1924-1925	143	524	.294	5	101	1925-1925	56	116	.353	0	15
Sammy Vick	1921	44	77	.260	0	9	1917-1920	169	564	.246	2	41
Jake Wade	1939-1939	20	12	.000	0	0	1946	13	9	.111	0	1
Jimmy Walsh	1916-1917	71	202	.257	0	14	1914	43	136	.191	1	11
Roxy Walters	1919-1923	268	764	.204	0	62	1915-1918	193	568	.243	0	49
Pee-Wee Wanninger	1927	18	60	.200	0	1	1925	117	403	.236	1	22
Gary Waslewski	1967-1968	51	37	.054	0	0	1970-1971	50	11	.091	0	1
Bob Watson	1979-1979	84	312	.337	13	53	1980-1982	196	642	.282	19	83
Billy Werber	1933-1936	529	2045	.281	38	234	1930-1933	7	16	.250	0	2
George Whiteman	1907-1918	75	226	.261	1	29	1913	11	32	.344	0	2
Mark Whiten	1995	32	108	.185	1	10	1997	69	215	.265	5	24
Bill Wight	1951-1952	44	48	.083	0	2	1946-1947	15	11	.000	0	0
Stan Williams	1972-1972	3	0	.000	0	0	1963-1964	51	70	.114	0	5
Archie Wilson	1952	18	38	.263	0	0	1951-1952	7	6	.167	0	1
Harry Wolter	1909	54	121	.240	2	10	1910-1913	396	1370	.277	10	123
John Wyatt	1966-1968	110	23	.043	0	0	1968	7	1	.000	0	0
Bill Zuber	1946-1947	35	31	.129	0	2	1943-1946	66	113	.159	0	6

194 players played for each of these teams

Pitchers Who Played for Both Teams

	Boston Red Sox, 1901-2004						New York Yankees, 1903-2004					
	Years	**G**	**IP**	**ERA**	**W-L**	**K**	**Years**	**G**	**IP**	**ERA**	**W-L**	**K**
Doc Adkins	1902	4	20	4.05	1-1	3	1903	2	7	7.71	0-0	0
Ivy Andrews	1932-1933	59	281⅔	4.38	15-19	67	1931-1938	41	156	3.12	8-6	47
Pete Appleton	1932	11	46	4.11	0-3	15	1933	1	2	0.00	0-0	0
Scott Bankhead	1993-1994	67	102	3.88	5-3	72	1995	20	39	6.00	1-1	20
Willie Banks	2001-2002	34	49⅔	2.72	2-1	36	1997-1998	14	28⅓	6.04	4-1	16
Doug Bird	1983	22	67⅔	6.65	1-4	33	1980-1981	39	104	2.68	8-1	45
Wade Boggs	1982-1992	0	0	0.00	0	0	1993-1997	1	1	0.00	0-0	0
Ken Brett	1967-1971	79	239⅔	4.58	10-15	237	1976	2	2⅓	0.00	0-0	1
Hal Brown	1953-1955	72	288⅓	4.40	13-14	130	1962	2	6⅔	6.72	0-1	2
Joe Bush	1918-1921	111	779⅔	3.27	46-39	312	1922-1924	115	783	3.44	62-38	297
Ray Caldwell	1919	18	86⅓	3.96	7-4	23	1910-1918	248	1718⅓	3.00	95-99	803
Rick Cerone	1988-1989	0	0	0.00	0	0	1987	2	2	0.00	0-0	1
Jack Chesbro	1909	1	6	4.50	0 1	3	1903-1909	269	1952	2.58	128-93	913
Roger Clemens	1984-1996	383	2776	3.06	192-111	2590	1999-2003	157	1004	3.99	77-36	946
Tex Clevenger	1954	23	67⅔	4.79	2-4	43	1961-1962	42	69⅔	3.74	3-1	25
Rip Collins	1922	32	210⅔	3.76	14-11	69	1920-1921	64	324⅔	4.16	25-13	130
David Cone	2001	25	135⅔	4.31	9-7	115	1995-2000	145	922	3.91	64-40	888
Guy Cooper	1914-1915	10	24	4.87	1-0	5	1914	1	3	9.00	0-0	3
Todd Erdos	2001	10	16⅓	4.97	0-0	7	1998-2000	20	34	5.03	0-0	22
Steve Farr	1994	11	13	6.23	1-0	8	1991-1993	159	169	2.56	9-9	136
Alex Ferguson	1922-1925	119	650	4.20	32-48	199	1918-1925	39	112⅓	6.73	7-3	30
Wes Ferrell	1934-1937	118	877⅔	4.11	62-40	314	1938-1939	8	49⅓	6.75	3-4	13
Tony Fossas	1991-1994	239	160⅔	3.98	7-5	118	1999	5	1	36.00	0-0	0
Ray Francis	1925	6	28	7.71	0-2	4	1925	4	4⅔	7.66	0-0	1
Milt Gaston	1929-1931	100	635⅔	3.95	27-52	215	1924	29	86	4.50	5-3	24
Tom Gordon	1996-1999	170	495⅓	4.45	25-25	432	2004	80	89⅔	2.21	9-4	96
Randy Gumpert	1952	10	19⅔	4.11	1-0	6	1946-1948	72	214	3.20	16-4	100
Chris Hammond	1997	29	65⅓	5.93	3-4	48	2003	62	63	2.86	3-2	45
Harry Harper	1920	27	162⅔	3.04	5-14	71	1921	8	52⅔	3.76	4-3	22
Greg Harris	1989-1994	287	651	3.91	39-43	489	1994	3	5	5.40	0-1	4
Fred Heimach	1926	20	102	5.65	2-9	17	1928-1929	48	202⅔	3.77	13-9	51
Ken Holcombe	1953	3	6	6.00	1-0	1	1945-1945	23	55⅓	1.79	3-3	20
Waite Hoyt	1919-1920	35	226⅔	3.85	10-12	73	1921-1930	365	2272⅓	3.48	157-98	713
Tom Hughes	1902-1903	42	294	2.69	23-10	127	1904	19	136⅓	3.70	7-11	75
Hank Johnson	1933-1935	69	310⅔	4.72	16-15	145	1925-1932	157	712⅔	4.84	47-36	407
Sam Jones	1916-1921	157	1045	3.39	64-59	307	1922-1926	202	1089⅓	4.06	67-56	363
Jack Kramer	1948-1949	50	316⅔	4.63	24-13	96	1951	19	40⅔	4.64	1-3	15
Louis Leroy	1910	1	4	11.25	0-0	3	1905-1906	14	68⅔	2.75	3-1	36
Duffy Lewis	1910-1917	1	1	18.00	0-0	1	1919-1920	0	0	0.00	0	0
Tim Lollar	1985-1986	48	110	5.48	7-5	72	1980	14	32⅓	3.34	1-0	13
Joe Lucey	1925	7	11	9.00	0-1	2	1920					0
Sparky Lyle	1967-1971	260	331⅓	2.85	22-17	275	1972-1978	420	745⅔	2.41	57-40	454
Danny MacFayden	1926-1932	185	1167	4.23	52-78	344	1932-1934	64	307⅔	4.68	14-10	102
Josias Manzanillo	1991	1	1	18.00	0-0	1	1995	11	17⅓	2.08	0-0	11
Carl Mays	1915-1919	173	1105	2.21	72-51	399	1919-1923	164	1090	3.25	79-39	273
Mickey McDermott	1948-1953	153	773⅔	3.80	48-34	499	1956	23	87	4.24	2-6	38

	Boston Red Sox, 1901-2004						New York Yankees, 1903-2004					
	Years	**G**	**IP**	**ERA**	**W-L**	**K**	**Years**	**G**	**IP**	**ERA**	**W-L**	**K**
Jim McDonald	1950	9	19	3.79	1-0	5	1952-1954	69	270	3.57	16-12	83
Lynn McGlothen	1972-1973	28	168	4.07	9-9	128	1982	4	5	10.80	0-0	2
Bob McGraw	1919	10	26⅔	6.74	0-2	6	1917-1920	24	54⅓	3.48	1-2	17
Marty McHale	1910-1916	8	29	5.90	0-3	18	1913-1915	51	318	3.28	12-27	111
Ramiro Mendoza	2003-2004	64	97⅓	5.73	5-6	49	1996-2002	277	698⅔	4.08	54-34	413
Fred Mitchell	1901-1902	18	112⅔	4.07	6-7	36	1910	0	0	0.00	0	0
Bill Monbouquette	1958-1965	254	1622	3.69	96-91	969	1967-1968	50	222⅔	3.19	11-12	85
Wilcy Moore	1931-1932	90	269⅔	4.30	15-23	65	1927-1933	171	421⅓	3.31	36-21	139
Johnny Murphy	1947	32	54⅔	2.80	0-0	9	1932-1946	383	990⅓	3.54	93-53	369
Rob Murphy	1989-1990	142	162	4.00	5-13	161	1994	3	1⅔	15.88	0-0	0
George Murray	1923-1924	67	258	5.48	9-20	67	1922	22	56⅔	3.97	4-2	14
Bobo Newsom	1937	30	207⅔	4.46	13-10	127	1947	17	115⅔	2.80	7-5	42
Lefty O'Doul	1923-1923	23	53	5.43	1-1	10	1919-1922	11	24⅔	3.64	0-0	9
Bob Ojeda	1980-1985	140	718⅔	4.21	44-39	425	1994	2	3	24.00	0-0	3
Herb Pennock	1915-1934	201	1089⅓	3.67	61-59	358	1923-1933	346	2203⅓	3.54	162-90	700
Bill Piercy	1922-1924	82	429⅔	4.48	16-33	95	1917-1921	15	90⅔	2.98	5-5	39
George Pipgras	1933-1935	29	136⅔	4.54	9-9	58	1923-1933	247	1351⅔	4.04	93-64	656
Bob Porterfield	1956-1958	55	232⅓	4.65	7-16	82	1948-1951	40	158⅓	5.06	8-9	66
Paul Quantrill	1992-1994	93	210⅓	3.47	9-16	105	2004	86	95⅓	4.72	7-3	37
Jack Quinn	1922-1925	145	832⅔	3.65	45-54	226	1909-1921	228	1270	3.15	81-65	478
Jeff Reardon	1990-1992	150	153	3.41	8-9	109	1994	11	9⅔	8.35	1-0	4
Gordon Rhodes	1932-1935	124	676⅔	4.63	27-45	267	1929-1932	41	155⅔	4.57	7-9	65
Red Ruffing	1924-1930	189	1122⅓	4.61	39-96	450	1930-1946	426	3168⅔	3.47	231-124	1526
Allan Russell	1919-1922	110	527⅔	3.74	28-28	210	1915-1919	114	534⅓	3.05	26-36	284
Babe Ruth	1914-1919	158	1190⅓	2.19	89-46	483	1920-1934	5	31	5.52	5-0	5
Ray Scarborough	1951-1952	65	260⅔	5.01	13-14	100	1952-1953	34	88⅔	3.15	7-3	33
Johnny Schmitz	1956	2	4⅓	0.00	0-0	0	1952-1953	8	19⅓	3.26	1-1	0
Rollie Sheldon	1966	23	79⅔	4.97	1-6	38	1961-1965	91	389⅓	4.14	23-15	202
Ben Shields	1930	3	10	9.00	0-0	1	1924-1925	6	26	6.58	3-0	8
Ernie Shore	1914-1917	125	839	2.12	58-33	272	1919-1920	34	139⅓	4.39	7-10	36
Bill Short	1966	8	8⅓	4.34	0-0	2	1960	10	47	4.79	3-5	14
Lee Smith	1988-1990	139	168⅔	3.04	12-7	209	1993	8	8	0.00	0-0	11
Mike Stanton	1995-1996	81	77⅓	3.61	5-3	56	1997-2002	428	434⅓	3.67	30-12	395
Tom Sturdivant	1960	40	101⅓	4.98	3-3	67	1955-1959	115	524⅓	3.19	36-25	333
Frank Tanana	1981	24	141⅓	4.01	4-10	78	1993	3	19⅔	3.20	0-2	12
Jesse Tannehill	1904-1908	116	885⅔	2.50	62-38	342	1903	32	239⅔	3.27	15-15	106
Hank Thormahlen	1921	23	96⅓	4.49	1-7	17	1917-1920	76	452⅔	3.06	28-20	124
Luis Tiant	1971-1978	274	1774⅔	3.36	122-81	1075	1979-1980	55	332	4.31	21-17	188
Mike Torrez	1978-1982	161	1012⅔	4.51	60-54	480	1977	31	217	3.82	14-12	90
Bob Turley	1963-1963	11	41⅓	6.10	1-4	35	1955-1962	234	1269	3.62	82-52	909
Jake Wade	1939	20	47⅔	6.23	1-4	21	1946	13	35⅓	2.29	2-1	22
Gary Waslewski	1967-1968	46	147⅓	3.54	6-9	79	1970-1971	50	90⅔	3.18	2-3	44
Bill Wight	1951-1952	44	142⅔	4.73	9-8	43	1946-1947	15	49⅓	3.83	3-2	14
Stan Williams	1972-1972	3	4⅓	6.28	0-0	3	1963-1964	50	228	3.43	10-13	152
Harry Wolter	1909	11	59	3.51	4-4	21	1910-1913	0	0	0.00	0	0
John Wyatt	1966-1968	110	175⅔	2.92	14-13	142	1968-1968	7	8⅓	2.17	0-2	6
Bill Zuber	1946-1947	35	107⅓	3.86	6-1	52	1943-1946	66	357⅔	3.87	18-23	169

Managers Who Served Both Red Sox and Yankees

Frank Chance	NY 1913 (player-manager) and 1914; BOS 1923
Bucky Harris	BOS 1934; NY 1947-48
Ralph Houk	NY 1961-73: BOS 1981-84
Joe McCarthy	NY 1931-46; BOS 1948-50
Don Zimmer	BOS 1976-80; NY 1999

and a special case:

Edward G. Barrow	served as Red Sox manager 1918-20, and then beginning in 1921 as Business Manager and later General Manager for the Yankees.

Coaches Who Served Both Red Sox and Yankees

Jimmy Burke	BOS 1921-23; NY 1931-33
Earle Combs	NY 1936-44; BOS 1948-52
Sammy Ellis	NY 1982, 1983-84, 1986; NY 1996
Paul Schreiber	NY 1942; BOS 1947-58
Johnny Schulte	NY 1934-48; BOS 1949-50
Stan Williams	BOS 1975-76; NY 1980-81, 1987, 1988
Don Zimmer	BOS 1974-76; NY 1983, 1986 BOS 1992 NY 1996-2001

Afterword
by Johnny Pesky

"It's like these two teams were supposed to share the same brain," said Pesky, who has served the Red Sox for 55 years as a player, coach, manager, broadcaster and ambassador. *"When I was playing, it was always, 'What did the Yankees do today? What did the Yankees do this offseason? Who did the Yankees trade for? We gotta keep up! We gotta catch up!' Jeez, that was over 50 years ago. And it's still going on! It's like every time something good happens to them, we're the other guy in the picture."* —Johnny Pesky, New York Post, April 16, 2004

I've been waiting more than sixty years for this.

Winning the World Series atones for a multitude of sins. To do it the way we did it—sweeping the Angels, then coming back from the brink to beat the Yankees, and then sweeping our old nemesis, the Cardinals. I'm in seventh heaven. When we were down 3-0 to the Yankees, I said "Oh, my God." Yogi said it best, though: "It's never over till it's over." Here I am quoting a Yankee after we've finally bested them. Oh well, anything that Yogi says is okay with me.

I saw grown men cry tears of joy. So did I. I'm unashamed of it. I truly think someone must have shone a star on this team. I'm elated, so glad we won, for the fans and for the players. This may never happen for them again.

I thought that in 1946, in '48, '49, and '50, we had as good a team as you could put on the field, but something always seemed to happen. We thought there was a black cat on the squad or something. In 1986, the ball went through poor Buckner's legs. I really felt bad for him. I was sitting with Sam Mele and Frank Malzone. I said, "We got 'em now." I opened my mouth too soon. I had a good feeling again last year, but once again, remember Yogi's words of wisdom.

It was always special against New York. It was the big city and they had the best players. Gene Woodling, DiMaggio, Henrich, Rizzuto, Joe Gordon . . . We had good teams, too. I always thought we should have won a couple of those years. It was a privilege to play in those games. You always wanted to play your best against New York. You thought more about things. You'd give it a little extra. When you played against great competition like that, you wanted to do well. You wanted to be competitive against them, and to beat them. And we did beat the Yankees pretty often in those years, but it always seemed that the game they had to win, they won. They were strong in every position and it was always a battle.

We never saw the Yankees as enemies. It was just a mutual respect, never a feud. I remember reading about when Joe Cronin fought Jake Powell. They said that they ganged up on Cronin underneath the stands and finally some of the Red Sox had to help Joe out. He knew they were a great team and he wanted to beat them. When you're the underdog, you always want to have the upset.

There have been times that it's gotten heated. When Petrocelli was here and Lonborg and those guys, they had their problems with them. The Yankees always gave you the sense that they couldn't be defeated. If you did something on the field that they didn't like, they got back at you. They'd do it with their bats or they'd end up taking you out on a double play. I remember Joe DiMaggio took me out one time, and almost broke my neck. He was out at second but I didn't get the guy at first because I was on my butt. He just looked at me. He didn't say a thing and neither did I. In those years, you accepted those things. That was the way the game was played.

Fisk and Munson had an individual thing. Munson was a tough kid, and so was Fisk. When Bill Lee got whacked by Graig Nettles, I saw Nettles reach over somebody's shoulder and punch Lee. Lee held his ground, but he got knocked down and hurt his shoulder. There were a couple of guys who thought he was popping off. I don't think we did much talking in that vein, not so you'd want to square off. I never saw Ted or DiMaggio or Henrich or Bobby Brown or Rizzuto or Joe Gordon do it.

And Yogi, well, if you didn't like Yogi, you didn't like yourself. He was a fine man. That's the way we looked at it. We looked at them as people. When you see a guy that's a good player, you admire him.

I think it has escalated in recent years. I really believe that. Sometimes, it seemed like if the Yankees wanted to do something to you, they wouldn't try to destroy you, but they would try to put you off-balance. Throw a ball up and in on you. Not trying to hit you—good pitchers don't have to do that—but sometimes good pitchers have to throw inside to get you off the plate. When you're hitting them pretty good, that was taken for granted. That's a compliment to the hitter.

Alex Rodriguez and Varitek? I just go from what I saw. That can happen. To me, when a guy gets hit by the pitch, you just go to first base. You don't make anything of it. Evidently, he thought they were throwing at him, and he said something, and one word led to another. It looked like he was going to go toward Arroyo and Varitek just grabbed him, and one word led to another and they're on the ground, and there's guys coming from every angle jumping in.

A blood feud? No, I don't believe that. That's too strong. They're making a living; you're making a living. It's your strength against his strength. There's an old saying—you know, you better be nice to the guy across the field because you might be rooming with him next week.

They can say what they want about Mr. Steinbrenner, but I admire him. And Torre's a fine man. If I was looking for a job, and he had an opening, I'd ask him to be one of his coaches. That's what I think of him.

There *is* a rivalry, though. You get tired of coming in second. Deep down in your heart, you think you're as good a player as the guy across the way. I don't hate the Yankees. I never did. I respect them. You take a guy like you find him. He's in the same profession you are. You want to just beat him in competition. That's the way I feel about it.

—JOHNNY PESKY
December 2004

Index